EASTERN ORTHODOX MISSION THEOLOGY TODAY

The American Society of Missiology Series, in collaboration with Orbis Books, seeks to publish scholarly works of high merit and wide interest on numerous aspects of missiology—the study of mission. Able presentations on new and creative approaches to the practice and understanding of mission will receive close attention.

American Society of Missiology Series, No. 10

EASTERN ORTHODOX MISSION THEOLOGY TODAY

JAMES J. STAMOOLIS

ORBIS BOOKS

Maryknoll, New York 10545

The Catholic Foreign Mission Society of America (Maryknoll) recruits and trains people for overseas missionary service. Through Orbis Books Maryknoll aims to foster the international dialogue that is essential to mission. The books published, however, reflect the opinions of their authors and are not meant to represent the official position of the society.

© 1986 by James J. Stamoolis
Published by Orbis Books, Maryknoll, NY 10545
All rights reserved
Manufactured in the United States of America

Manuscript editor: Lisa McGaw

Library of Congress Cataloging-in-Publication Data

Stamoolis, James J.
　Eastern Orthodox mission theology today.
　(American Society of Missiology series; no. 10)

　Bibliography: p.
　Includes index.
　1. Orthodox Eastern Church—Missions.　2. Missions—
Theory.　3. Orthodox Eastern Church—Doctrines.
I. Title.　II. Series.
BV2123.S73　1986　　266'.19　　　85-15596
ISBN 0-88344-215-9 (pbk.)

TO EVANGELINE AND GEORGE,
TO JOHN, JOEL, AND JOSHUA,
AND ESPECIALLY
TO EVIE

Contents

Preface to the Series

The purpose of the ASM Series is to publish, without regard for disciplinary, national, or denominational boundaries, scholarly works of high quality and wide interest on missiological themes from the entire spectrum of scholarly pursuits, e.g., theology, history, anthropology, sociology, linguistics, health, education, art, political science, economics, and development, to articulate but a partial list. Always the focus will be on Christian mission.

By "mission" in this context is meant a cross-cultural passage over the boundary between faith in Jesus Christ and its absence. In this understanding of mission, the basic functions of Christian proclamation, dialogue, witness, service, fellowship, worship, and nurture are of special concern. How does the transition from one cultural context to another influence the shape and interaction of these dynamic functions?

Missiologists know that they need the other disciplines. And other disciplines, we dare to suggest, need missiology, perhaps more than they sometimes realize. Neither the insider's nor the outsider's view is complete in itself. The world Christian mission has through two millennia amassed a rich and well-documented body of experience to share with other disciplines.

Interaction will be the hallmark of this Series. It desires to be a channel for talking to one another instead of about one another. Secular scholars and church-related missiologists have too long engaged in a sterile venting of feelings about one another, often lacking in full evidence. Ignorance of and indifference to one another's work has been no less harmful to good scholarship.

The promotion of scholarly dialogue among missiologists may, at times, involve the publication of views and positions that other missiologists cannot accept, and with which members of the Editorial Committee do not agree. The manuscripts published reflect the opinions of their authors and are not meant to represent the position of the American Society of Missiology or the Editorial Committee of the ASM Series.

We express our warm thanks to various mission agencies whose financial contributions enabled leaders of vision in the ASM to launch this new venture. The future of the ASM series will, we feel sure, fully justify their confidence and support.

William J. Danker, Chairperson,
ASM Series Editorial Committee

ix

Foreword

A common perception of Eastern Orthodoxy is that its principle and practice of mission of the distant historical past have been abandoned today in favor of a religion identified with a particular ethnic group and accepting of strict state control. One can only welcome therefore the appearance of this remarkably thorough and comprehensive study by James Stamoolis, which goes a long way in dispelling such a superficial and basically inaccurate judgment.

This does not mean, of course, that the Orthodox would be justified today in indulging in missionary triumphalism. It is true that the most characteristic principle of Christian expansion—the translation of Scriptures and the liturgy into the vernacular language of the various nations adopting the faith of Orthodox Byzantium—has led to the establishment of national, administratively autonomous churches which at times have lost a sense of the Gospel's universal message. Such a narrowing of the Church's proclamation, however, is actually a modern phenomenon which resulted from the emergence of secularized nationalism in the nineteenth century. The recent resurgence of Orthodox missionary interest and activity in Greece, Africa, and North America indicates that the tradition, which extends back to Byzantine times and continues through Orthodox Russia during the centuries of Muslim occupation of the Balkans and the Middle East, is inherent to the nature of the Church, as the Orthodox understand it, and that unfavorable political and social conditions have never succeeded in suppressing it.

Indeed, in Muslim society, conversion to Christianity was legally impossible, a condition that for centuries reduced Christian Greeks, Arabs, and Balkan Slavs to ghetto existences. Similarly, modern Soviet law forbids both "religious propaganda" and Church sponsorship of normal missionary channels such as schools, publications, and social welfare projects. But perhaps the specifically Orthodox forms of survival in such repressive conditions are the best indicators of missionary consciousness: In its very nature, Christian witness is expressed in the life and faith of the community.

A church can be "witnessing" and therefore preaching through its prayer, through its sense of being "different" from the surrounding society, and through its celebration of the Kingdom of God, present, by anticipation, in the liturgy. The way the Orthodox have succeeded in experiencing their worship as communion with the Risen Body of Christ, and in using it as a powerful educational tool, is probably the most distinctive trait of Eastern Christianity, in contrast to the Western tendency of identifying mission with activism and organization. This does not mean, of course, that missionary planning and the active involvement in the life of the world that Western Christians have practiced so effectively, particularly in the nineteenth and the twentieth centuries, would be of no use to the Orthodox. The very professional missionary enterprise of the Russians in various parts of their Eurasian empire, as well as in Japan and Alaska, indicate the opposite. But fundamental spiritual priorities are always perceived by the Orthodox missionaries—many of them monks—through the spiritual experience available in the liturgy.

It is no surprise, therefore, that in the Orthodox world the disappearance of the missionary spirit regularly coincides with liturgical decadence. The practical reduction of worship to national folklore and of the Christian temple to a museum can be witnessed in many places, and political regimes interested in the disappearance of Christianity are happy to encourage situations where such a reduction prevails. Some ethnic Orthodox parishes in North America are also practicing this reductionism without an understanding of its implications. It is, therefore, symbolically providential that the Orthodox presence in North America started not with the arrival of immigrants on the East coast, but with the advent of missionary monks to Alaska in 1794. Sent to evangelize American natives, these missionaries provided not only the Christian gospel, translated in the tongue of the indigenes, but also some protection against exploitation by greedy and cruel colonialists.

One must hope that as a wider readership finds access to solid information about the history, development, and present theological rationale of Orthodox missions, more scholars following the example of James Stamoolis will be tempted to undertake the study of eminent individuals such as St. Innocent Veniaminov, St. Nicholas Kassatkin, and St. Herman, or of particular situations, such as the survival of missionary consciousness in Christian communities under Islam, the work of orientalists in the pre-revolutionary Russian Theological Academy of Kazan, and the reasons for the contemporary success of Greek Orthodox missionaries in East Africa.

More important still would be further thinking and study of the most crucial fact—which has been discovered by all Christians only in our generation—that true Christian "mission" does not consist only, as was thought in the nineteenth century, in sending missionaries to distant countries considered as "non-Christian," but in a global witness to a secularized world which begins not far away in "missionary lands," but on our very doorsteps. The Orthodox handling of *that* mission, expressed in the words of St. Seraphim of Sarov (1759-1833)—"Save yourself, and thousands will be saved around you"—provides the crucial additional dimension of the problem of Christian mission today.

JOHN MEYENDORFF

Preface

The purpose of this study is to examine the missiological thought of the Eastern Orthodox Church. That the Orthodox Church has any interest in mission work, let alone a developed missiology, may come as a new idea to many. Some of the opposition to the integration of the International Missionary Council and the World Council of Churches revolved around the supposed indifference and hostility of the Orthodox to mission. That the Orthodox have a concern for the advance of the gospel is readily documented. What is needed now is a fuller understanding of the Orthodox Church's contribution. As was expressed in an editorial in the *International Review of Mission* in 1965:

> And now, by God's grace, in the integrated World Council of Churches, Orthodox Churches play their part in the discussion of missionary issues and the planning of missionary strategy. But it is important that this be regarded not merely as the end of a misunderstanding, but as the beginning of a fruitful interpenetration in which there will be much to be received and given on both sides.[1]

This study is an attempt to bring together and systematize Orthodox missiology. It is my conviction that the insight gained from the study of Orthodox theologians will be of benefit to the entire Church.

I have not undertaken the task of writing on this subject because I felt I was the most qualified. That honor no doubt belongs to another. But since the subject is of importance to the Church as a whole and since no one else has undertaken a detailed study, I have reluctantly attempted to provide what was lacking.

The neglect of the missions of the Eastern Orthodox Church has led non-Orthodox into an incorrect view of the Orthodox Church. This neglect has been no less detrimental to the Orthodox themselves. If, by God's grace, some new light is shed on the subject for the Church, then I shall consider the effort to have been worthwhile. Conscious of my own inadequacies, I offer the following quotation from Isaac Walton:

> For these reasons have I undertaken it,
> and if I have prevented any abler person,
> I beg pardon of him, and my reader.

Acknowledgments

It is to the grace of God, especially as revealed in the ministry of several of his servants, that I owe the completion of this work. A sense of divine blessing on me as an individual and on our family has guided our way. Therefore, to God alone is due the honor and glory. *Sola Deo Gloria.*

Numerous Christians have assisted and encouraged us in the years spent in academic study and ministry. It is impossible to mention here all the professors and colleagues in Christian service who have helped me to learn of Christ. They were ministers of God for the upbuilding of the body of Christ.

Of particular assistance in preparing this study were the following:

Professors W. J. van der Merwe and Nico J. Smith, who directed my doctoral work in missiology.

Bishop Anastasios Yannoulatos, who graciously gave of his time during a very busy period to read the first draft and discuss the study with me. Bishop Anastasios also provided many Greek works that I could not have obtained elsewhere.

Professor Demetrios J. Constantelos read the manuscript and offered very helpful suggestions.

To the typists who have struggled with my manuscript, and especially to Ra Lennox and Darlene C. Floss, who are responsible for the final typed format, I owe a debt of gratitude.

My wife, Evelyn C. Stamoolis, in addition to her support and encouragement, wielded a skillful editorial pen which has made the manuscript more readable than it would have been otherwise.

Chapter I

Introducing the Orthodox Church

The Eastern Orthodox Church can be at once described as known and unknown.[1] It is known because the Eastern Orthodox Church is no longer limited to lands traditionally considered to be the province of the Orthodox: eastern Europe, Russia, and the eastern Mediterranean. Greeks and Slavs, driven by economic distress or political persecution, made their way to the West, bringing their Orthodox faith with them. Today there is scarcely an area of the Western world in which a branch of the Eastern Orthodox Church does not exist. One no longer need travel to eastern Europe to find the Eastern Orthodox Church. Orthodoxy is now present in the home territory of the Western Churches.[2]

The extent of the Orthodox Diaspora is generally recognized. What is unknown is the spread of the Orthodox faith by missionary activity. In the West it is generally assumed that the Orthodox never engaged in missionary work.[3] This is not the case, as will be shown in the review of Orthodox missionary activity. Furthermore, the witness of the Orthodox Diaspora has borne fruit in the conversion to Orthodoxy of Westerners of different religious and ethnic backgrounds.[4] As a result of the dispersion of Orthodox Christians to other lands and the concerted efforts of Orthodox missionaries in evangelizing non-Christians, the Orthodox Church is to be found on all six continents.[5] The spread of the Eastern Orthodox faith is such that the adjective "eastern" is a reminder of the place of origin rather than the present location of the Church.

The Orthodox Churches are known for their involvement in the ecumenical movement, symbolized by their participation in the World Council of Churches (WCC).[6] Orthodox prelates have served as WCC presidents since its inception in 1948.[7] At the Fifth Assembly of the WCC, in Nairobi, Nikodim, Metropolitan of Leningrad and Novgorod, was elected president.[8] What is often overlooked is how long the Orthodox have been involved in the ecumenical movement. Orthodox theologians were participants in the early Life and Work and Faith and Order conferences. The patriarchal encyclicals of 1902 and 1920 are important contributions to the cause of Christian unity that are generally ignored by the Western churches.[9]

In the United States the Orthodox Church has finally been recognized as the fourth major American religion.[10] Prior to the official recognition, Orthodox believers serving in the armed forces would have "Protestant" inscribed on their identification tags.[11] A number of books have appeared in recent years in the West on the Orthodox Church, many of them written by Orthodox theologians seeking to explain their faith to their fellow Orthodox as well as to those of other traditions.[12] The Orthodox presence is being heard from in a dynamic way.

Yet in spite of its recognition in Western ecclesiastical circles, the Orthodox Church remains unknown. It is unknown because it is not understood. A German Protestant theologian, Ernst Benz, expresses the problem thus:

> The non-Orthodox western European finds it most difficult to comprehend the Eastern Orthodox Church because he knows little about the life and doctrines of Orthodoxy and even this little is overlaid by many strata of prejudices and misunderstandings, partly religious, partly political in nature. One of the stumbling blocks to our understanding of Orthodoxy has been our natural tendency to confound the ideas and customs of the Orthodox Church with familiar parallels in Roman Catholicism.[13]

A convert to the Orthodox faith succinctly states: "Orthodoxy is not just a kind of Roman Catholicism without the Pope, but something quite distinct from any religious system in the West."[14]

The tendency in both Protestant and Roman Catholic circles is to look upon the Orthodox Church as a type of Roman Catholicism and to categorize it in that manner. Depending on the observer's point of view, it is either a more or a less pure form of Roman Catholicism. This characterization is prompted by the similarities that are observed between the two Churches. Yet appearances are deceiving. The problem lies in the fact that the Orthodox Church is distinctly different from the Western Churches, and the Western Churches' inability to comprehend Orthodoxy stems from the fundamental differences between them. In fact, from an Orthodox viewpoint (as expressed by Alexis Khomiakov), it is the Western Churches, both Protestant and Roman Catholic, that are similar: "All Protestants are Crypto-Papists. . . . To use the concise language of algebra, all the West knows but one datum a; whether it be preceded by the positive sign $+$, as with the Romanists, or with the negative sign $-$, as with the Protestants, the a remains the same."[15]

The Orthodox position sees the basic theological frame of reference as the same for Protestants and Catholics. The Orthodox analysis is not based on polemical considerations but on a theological understanding of the basic themes of the Western Churches.* Therefore, the Orthodox Church sees itself as operating in a different frame of reference.

---

*In this study, the expressions below (unless they appear in a quotation, in which case the meaning of the author is to be observed) are used as follows:

Western Church = the whole of Western Christendom before the Reformation.

Western Churches = Western Christendom regarded as a collection of Churches, which, from an Orthodox perspective, can be considered as having the same frame of reference. This definition does not relate in any way to the union or interrelationship of the Churches so designated. The term "the West" is often used as a short notation for either of the phrases above. The context will provide the referrant if more precision is needed.

The reason for the existence of these two distinct frames of reference is to be found in the past. While sharing in common the Bible and the early patristic heritage, the Eastern Church and the Western Church drifted apart long before they formally separated.[16] This study is not concerned with the causes of the separation, but with the fact and consequences of it. Leading a separate existence, the Orthodox "have known no Middle Ages (in the western sense) and have undergone no Reformations or Counter-Reformations; they have only been affected in an oblique way by the cultural and religious upheaval which transformed Western Europe in the sixteenth and seventeenth centuries."[17] One could say that there are two church histories—that of the West and that of the East. A practical outworking of their different paths of development is seen in the standard church history books, which deal separately with the Eastern Churches and without much integration of their history with that of the Western Churches.

The doctrinal expression of the Orthodox Church, as in the West a function of their historical experiences, is also different from the Western Churches. Without an understanding of the theological frame of reference of the Orthodox Church, it is impossible to interpret correctly and authentically the Orthodox position. The frame of reference of the Orthodox Church will be investigated in the following chapter. However, by way of illustrating the misunderstanding by the Western Church of the Eastern Orthodox stance, one can profitably examine the viewpoint of an Orthodox participant in the ecumenical movement.

Alexander Schmemann, former dean of St. Vladimir's Orthodox Theological Seminary, was a spokesman for Orthodoxy in the ecumenical movement. In an article written in 1963 he issued a warning about a serious problem that "may sooner or later lead to a major ecumenical crisis."[18] Schmemann was referring to what he saw as the "discrepancy between the official Orthodox position in the WCC and the 'real' Orthodoxy."[19] The Orthodox seem to be firmly entrenched in the WCC, and their participation, as measured by reports, declarations, and statistics, is on the increase. As already noted above, the election of Orthodox hierarchs as presidents gives the impression that the Orthodox are providing substantial leadership to the movement.

Yet, in spite of the ecumenical activity of the Orthodox and even in spite of the official statements of the Orthodox leadership, there is strong reservation regarding participation in the WCC on the part of the Orthodox faithful: hierarchy, theologians, and laity. Why? Because the "official" position of the Orthodox Church in the ecumenical movement is divorced from the reality of the Orthodox faith. This situation in which an "official" position is not official can arise because in the Orthodox Church no position can be regarded as official unless it is accepted by the whole Church. For example, the seven ecumenical councils, which were accepted by the whole Church, are regarded as authoritative.[20] However, one is also reminded by history that even ecumenical councils seldom gained immediate universal acceptance. "The first council, that of Nicaea (325), was rejected for more than half a century before it obtained general recognition and came to be regarded as *the* symbol of an ecumenical council par excellence."[21] Thus the process of universal acceptance is not easily defined. That the Orthodox feel the need for some redefinition is evidenced by the desire to convene a Pan-Orthodox Council.[22]

The reason for the difference between the real position of the Orthodox Church and the position it occupies in the WCC is the Western orientation of the WCC. This orientation is foreign to the ethos of Orthodoxy and forces the Orthodox participants in the movement to employ non-Orthodox categories of thought and expression. Schmemann notes: "The tragedy of Orthodoxy is that from the very beginning of its ecumenical participation no such common language, no theological 'continuity' existed between her and her Western partners, within, at least, the organized and institutionally structured Ecumenical Movement. *There was no real encounter.*"[23]

What is necessary for real encounter to take place? Schmemann puts forth three presuppositions that condition the real position of Orthodoxy and need to be understood if the crisis of which he speaks is to be averted. The main problem is the contrasting orientations of the Orthodox Church and the Western Churches. Whereas the West thinks in terms of the Protestant-Roman Catholic division and is concerned with the issues arising out of this polarization, the Orthodox Church goes back past the division of the sixteenth century.

> . . . For the Orthodox Church the fundamental opposition is that between the East and the West, understood as two spiritual and theological "trends" or "worlds" and it is this opposition that, in the Orthodox mind, should determine the initial framework of the ecumenical encounter. We must not forget that the only division or schism which the Orthodox Church remembers to speak of *existentially* as an event of her own past is precisely the alienation from her of the whole West.[24]

If this is the case, then the preliminary inquiry that concerns the Orthodox in the WCC is: How did this split occur and what can be done to remedy the condition that still exists because of it? From the Orthodox point of view, the Western Churches are in error at this point in that they are not making a serious effort to regain the lost unity.

The second and third presuppositions follow the reasoning implicit in the first. If the basic division is between East and West, then the only language that can be used to discuss the problem is the language that was shared by the undivided Church. Thus the second presupposition is that the basic terms of reference for ecumenical discussion must be those supplied by the Orthodox Church, since it represents the tradition of the early and undivided Church. According to Schmemann's analysis, this early tradition is not to be thought of as merely the Orthodox frame of reference but, rather, as the common tradition of the early Church.[25] Within the "common heritage" of all, theological discussion could begin again. This return to the sources is seen as a way out of the maze of Western controversies.

The result of following this methodology would be the rediscovery of the categories of truth and error, concepts of great significance for the Orthodox Church. "Hence, and this is the third presupposition, the only adequate *ecumenical method* from the Orthodox point of view, was that of a total and direct doctrinal confrontation with, as its inescapable and logical conclusion, the acceptance of truth and the rejection of error."[26]

Error, or to give it its theological name, heresy, is not seen as intellectual disagreement, but as a danger that distorts the very concept of salvation and imperils the attaining of salvation. In Orthodox terms, it is a matter of life and death, eternal life or eternal death. "It is, therefore, truth, and not unity, which in the Orthodox opinion and experience had to be the real goal of the Ecumenical Movement; unity in this experience being nothing else but the natural consequence of truth, its fruit and blessing."[27]

These presuppositions that Schmemann sees as conditioning Orthodox involvement in the ecumenical movement are not understood, let alone accepted, by the other participants in the movement. Whether these are legitimate presuppositions must be left for others to debate. What is crucial to the understanding of the Orthodox theological position is the apparent ease with which the real Orthodox position can be misconstrued by outside observers. When Western theological categories are used to interpret the Orthodox position, the result is an incorrect interpretation. Schmemann has warned that it could lead to an ecumenical crisis.[28] But equally important is that it robs the West of the unique insights of the Orthodox Church, insights that could shed light on some problems of the Western Churches.[29]

Chapter II

Eastern Orthodox Theology

THE APPROACH TO THEOLOGY

"The real difference between Eastern and Western Christian theology lies not in particular doctrinal points but in the difference between two ways of approach to the whole subject."[1] To understand the Orthodox Church, one must understand the Orthodox approach to theology. That there can be a different approach to theology may strike the Western Christian as a novel (or perhaps heretical) idea. Because the presuppositions underlying the Western Churches' approach to theology are seldom if ever questioned, they effectively filter the theological analysis of the scriptural data. These presuppositions are the same for all the Western Churches, Roman Catholic and Protestant alike. They are modified by the different confessions, but remain Western in orientation. This is what Alexis Khomiakov meant when he said, ". . . all the West knows but one datum a; whether it be preceded by the positive sign $+$, as with the Romanists, or with the negative $-$, as with the Protestants, the a remains the same."[2]

As has been pointed out above, these presuppositions come from a common heritage that the East does not share. Separate histories arose from the Great Schism, but the difference in thinking can be traced back to a gradual drifting apart. Two mentalities began to emerge. As M. J. Le Guillou writes:

> It was not long before the Fathers of the East and the Fathers of the West, in accordance with their different cultural surroundings began to *think* and to *live* the Christian faith with somewhat different emphases. . . . This was the result of two mentalities which, while being at all times complementary, were too often foreign to one another. To measure the distance between—and the unity of—these two types of mind, one has only to compare St. John Chrysostom and St. Augustine, both interpreters of St. Paul, both deeply engaged in the apostle's conception of the mystical Body, but the one to find therein directions for living, the other to draw out a theology of grace.[3]

6

It is not necessary here to examine at length the reasons for this divergence between East and West. This has already been done by others.[4] All that is needed is a rapid overview of the Western position and then an examination of the different approach adopted by the Orthodox.

What is the datum of the West? Ernst Benz sees it as legalism, the legal relationship between God and humankind.[5] As Benz works out his theory, the pagan Roman concept of the relationship between God and humankind and the precise formulae governing Roman civil religion are in harmony with the Christian position. Thus St. Paul's Epistle to the Romans is seen to underline the concern of the Jewish-Christian congregation with the weighty question of human unrighteousness in view of God's justice: how can the law of God be satisfied and humankind still survive? The answer to this question is found in the doctrine of justification, which increasingly became defined in legalistic terminology. Benz sees the Roman Catholic Church as having continued to develop in this legalistic direction.

> Rome elaborated the specifically Western view of the sacrament of penance which depends completely on the idea of "justification." God has established certain laws for man. By sinful conduct man violates these laws. Justice requires him to make amends to God. The Church supervises this legal relationship. . . . Just as jurisprudence has drawn up scales of crime and punishment, so also the Church has drawn up a scale of sins and the necessary penances.[6]

The practice of indulgences is a further development of this doctrine. A payment of money became an alternative to the act of penance.

The concept of the church in the West similarly was influenced by the legal framework. In Roman Catholicism the church became a "spiritual legal institution," which was occupied with the divine law. This, along with the political conditions in the western half of the Roman empire, led to the rise of the papacy. It is noteworthy that the papacy was not paralleled by a similar development in the East and that the concept is still abhorrent to the Orthodox.[7]

The role of the priest in the Roman Catholic Church developed along similar lines. By virtue of his ordination, he has received the right to dispense the sacraments and absolution. "When a priest says to a sinner after confession, 'Ego te absolvo' (I absolve you), he is exercising this judicial right."[8]

The analysis of the Western Church in terms of its legal framework could be carried on to other areas. The development of canon law would be a case in point. Canon law was never as highly developed in the Eastern Church, whereas in the West it covered almost every area of human existence.

The real issue that unites the West theologically and divides it from the East is the manner in which the theological understanding of the West was shaped by legal concepts. Tertullian is usually given the credit for introducing this juristic terminology into theology.[9] However, the key figure whose theological understanding shaped and continues to shape the Western Churches' theology is Augustine. His work gave definite direction to the legal framework of Western theology. Augustine's thought dominates Western theology in many areas and determines the theology even of those who react against it. The central aspect highlighting the difference between East and West is Augustine's treatment of the doctrine of salvation, in particular the Augustinian concept of justification. From the viewpoint of the Orthodox Church, Augustine's emphasis on individual and personal sin causes him to miss the fuller aspect of salvation, that of making the human being like God. The West today is still "caught in an individual and negative view of salvation."[10] This point cannot be overstated.

> In order to understand many major theological problems which arose between East and West, both before and after the schism, the extraordinary impact upon Western thought of Augustine's polemics against Pelagius and Julian of Eclanum must be fully taken into account. In the Byzantine world, where Augustinian thought exercised practically no influence, the significance of the sin of Adam and of its consequences for mankind was understood along quite different lines.[11]

A third figure who shaped Western theology but whose concept of soteriology was never accepted in the East is Anselm of Canterbury. He maintained that the purpose of Christ's death was to pay satisfaction to the honor of God, which had been injured by human sin. Again the theme is the legal relationship between human beings and God. Humankind is in debt to God, and the debt cannot simply be dismissed; adequate satisfaction must be rendered. Since humankind is unable to provide this required satisfaction, God supplies it in the death of Christ. In the words of Justo González:

> This treatise by Anselm was epoch-making. Although they did not follow it at every time, most later medieval theologians interpreted the work of Christ in the light of this treatise. After them, most Western theologians have followed the same path, although this manner of understanding the work of Christ for mankind is not the most ancient in the writings of the new Fathers, nor does it appear to be the main thrust of the New Testament.[12]

With this judgment the Orthodox Church agrees and charges the West with deviating from the original concept of salvation: " . . . in contrast to the Western Church's legalistic concept of salvation, formulated by Anselm of Canterbury and continued down to the present day, in the Orthodox Church, under the leadership of such men as Irenaeus and Athanasius, the mystical concept of salvation, as held by St. Paul and Apostles, was ever faithfully retained."[13]

If the foregoing analysis of the theological frame of reference of the West is correct, what then is the key to understanding the frame of reference of Orthodox theology? What is the meaning of the words "the mystical concept of salvation"? On the one hand, it is very easy to define the difference negatively. For example, L. A. Zander sets out the following summary:

> The East was not influenced by Augustine; its anthropology is different from that of the West.
> The East was not influenced by Anselm; its soteriology is different from that of the West.
> The East was not influenced by Thomas; its methodology is different from that of the West.[14]

While this is helpful in pointing out areas of disagreement, it does not explain what the Orthodox themselves believe. The key to the correct understanding of Orthodox theology lies in the answer to the question of the purpose of theology. "Christian theology is always in the last resort a means: a unity of knowledge subserving an end which transcends all knowledge. This ultimate end is union with God or deification, the *theosis* of the Greek Fathers."[15]

While this concept of *theosis* may sound strange to Western Christians, smacking of pantheism, the Orthodox understand by it what the West calls "union with Christ." However, it is union with Christ understood from the point of its eschatological realization.[16] While participation with Christ is realized in the present, *theosis* in its fullness is not yet known.

Since the West also has a doctrine of the believer's union with Christ, the question arises as to the difference between them. There is little difference between the doctrines; there is a great deal of difference in the emphasis on the doctrine in each respective system. By abstracting the idea of redemption from the totality of Christian truth, the West is unable to focus properly on the idea of union with Christ. Vladimir Lossky points out:

> The thought of union with God is forgotten because of our preoccupation solely with our own salvation; or, rather, union with God is seen only negatively, in contrast with our own present wretchedness. . . . The final goal of our union with God is, if not excluded altogether, at least shut out from our sight by the stern vault of a theological conception built on the ideas of original guilt and its reparation.[17]

Union with God in the East is seen, then, as a more comprehensive event than redemption. Perhaps another comparison with the West that might illuminate the difference is the concept that in the West redemption is primarily concerned with justification. Sanctification is viewed as another stage, somewhat less important. The Orthodox East views redemption in a more comprehensive manner, with justification (though the term is rarely used as such) and sanctification both being considered necessary elements.[18]

However, they are not merely necessary elements for the concept of salvation; they are necessary elements for the central theme of the whole of Christian theology. The favorite patristic statement to express the Orthodox position is, "God made Himself man, that man might become God."[19] Here is in essence the Eastern understanding of the purpose of the incarnation and the ultimate end of humankind.

Consistent with the emphasis on *theosis,* the basic motif of Orthodox theology is love, God's love rather than his justice. Because God loved humankind he wrought his plans of redemption. God does execute his vengeance and wrath, but God's love is primarily what is the experience of the human being. God is the seeking God, looking for the lost sheep; the loving Father, awaiting the Prodigal's return.

Much has been made of the mysticism of Eastern Orthodox theology. Benz finds it a prime characteristic.[20] Vladimir Lossky uses the term "mystical theology" to denote a spirituality that expresses a doctrinal position.[21] "Mystical" is an apt adjective for the theology that approaches the divine mystery of why God should care for people and why he should become "Man" for the sake of human salvation. It at once gives the clue for both the proper reverence for the subject and the methodology for approaching the subject.

In the Orthodox tradition, theology is related to life. There is no division between the "personal experience of the divine mysteries and the dogma affirmed by the church."[22] Divine truth is lived as well as expressed in creedal formulae. The necessity for the internalization of the divine mysteries is repeatedly stressed. ". . . We must live the dogma expressing a revealed truth, which appears to us as an unfathomable mystery, in such a fashion that instead of assimilating the mystery to our mode of understanding, we should, on the contrary, look for a profound change, an inner transformation of spirit, enabling us to experience it mystically," writes Benz.[23]

In the experience of Christian truth the personal application comes to the fore. Theology is something in which all believers can and must participate. It is no wonder that Orthodox theology is seen as "practical" theology and some have commented that it is expressed more in liturgy and prayer than in dogmatic confession.[24]

Thus the discussion of the Orthodox approach to theology leads one to notice the place of Orthodox worship. In a later chapter the study will return to Orthodox worship, and in particular the place the liturgy has in the missionary outreach of the Church. It is sufficient for the purpose of introducing the subject to note the centrality of worship to the Orthodox experience of Christian truth. For the Orthodox, all theology is worship; all worship is theology. Bearing this out is the large proportion of the liturgy that is taken from the Bible.[25] The examination of Orthodox theology then must include an examination of the liturgy.

The question arises, How much of this theological framework is accepted and understood by the Orthodox believer? Again one must beware of answering in a Western manner. The content of the faith is, of course, important and is stressed by the Orthodox in catechetical manuals.[26] But what needs to be understood is the Orthodox ethos, an ethos nurtured by worship and expressed in the theological context of *theosis*. Whether or not these concepts could be consciously articulated by a practicing Orthodox is by and large a matter of conjecture. However, Orthodox believers would point to their participation in the corporate worship of the church as a vital element in their religion.

In the history of Orthodoxy there has been the close identification of nation and church, so much so that in certain areas the church is thought of primarily as an ethnic unit rather than a religious organization. This has led to movements of religious revitalization, such as the Zoe brotherhood in Greece.[27] The lack of real piety and Christian theological understanding among the Orthodox constituency has not gone unnoticed by Orthodox clergy and theologians.[28] Yet in spite of the problems faced by the Orthodox churches in the course of their history, the spark and real practice of the Orthodox faith was kept alive and still offers another Christian alternative to the theological approach of the West.

AREAS OF THEOLOGICAL DISCUSSION AMONG THE ORTHODOX

It is doubtful today if any church possesses complete dogmatic uniformity among its theologians. In all churches one can find differences of opinion and conviction among those sworn to uphold and promulgate the faith. This being the case, it is not surprising to see some areas of discussion and possible disagreement among the Orthodox. Not all areas of discussion are relevant to the topic of mission theology. Comments will be made here on the areas that impinge on the main topic.

Pseudomorphosis and Westernization

What is really Orthodox and what is foreign to the true ethos and character of Orthodoxy? This question is being asked by Orthodox theologians in an attempt to sift through Orthodox theology from the seventeenth century to the present day in order to reject Western influence.

How did these Western concepts come into Orthodoxy? After the fall of Constantinople in 1453 and the ensuing capture by the Ottoman Turks of the other Greek areas, Greek students were deprived of the opportunity for advanced study in their homeland. There were a few theological schools, but these were not on a par with the university centers found in the West. "Promising Greek students, then, who wished to continue their early studies, had no choice but to go to the universities of western Europe."[29] Padua, Pisa, Florence, Halle, Paris, and even Oxford had Greek students. In Rome, Pope Gregory XIII founded in 1576 the College of Saint Athanasius, a college especially intended for Greeks. Timothy Ware says:

This western training, given under non-Orthodox auspices, inevitably influenced the way in which Greek theologians of the seventeenth and eighteenth centuries approached and interpreted their faith. However great their desire to remain loyal Orthodox, most of them looked at theology to a greater or lesser extent through western spectacles. Naturally this tendency towards westernization was not limited to those who had actually studied in the West, but also affected many who themselves had never left the Orthodox world. Consciously or unconsciously, most Greek writers of the time adopted theological categories, terminology, and forms of argument foreign to the tradition of their own Church; Orthodox religious thinking underwent what a contemporary Russian theologian, Father George Florovsky, has appropriately termed a *pseudo-morphosis*.[30]

It needs to be clearly understood that the theologians who were influenced by Western thought remained Orthodox. There were a few defections to Roman Catholicism and fewer still to Protestantism in the sense of those who formally renounced their Orthodoxy. What concerns contemporary Orthodox theologians are those who remained Orthodox in name but incorporated Western elements into their theology.

To illustrate the type of influence that is meant by Westernization, one can examine an example of a "Protestantizer" and a "Latinizer." The best-known Protestantizer of the Orthodox Church is Cyril Lucaris, Patriarch of Constantinople.[31] Lucaris sets forth his position in a brief confession of faith that has strong Calvinistic overtones. A Latin edition was published in Geneva in 1629; the Greek edition was published in the same city in 1633.[32] It has been called "a Calvinist symbolical book written under Orthodox influence, rather than an Orthodox book written under Protestant influence."[33] Karmiris considers only three of the eighteen chapters to be fully Orthodox in doctrine. So blatant is the Western element in the confession that later councils have denied that Lucaris was the author, in an effort to save the honor and prestige of a man who had been ecumenical patriarch.[34]

That Lucaris did write the confession of faith seems to be generally accepted today. At the very least he approved of it, as the Greek copy written and signed by him testifies.[35] From his letters to Protestant friends, it would appear that Lucaris had hoped to effect the reformation of the Orthodox Church.[36] There is also no doubt that he was confessing his personal faith. In a letter to Antoine Léger, a Swiss Calvinist, he wrote:

> If I die, I wish you to be able to testify that I die an Orthodox Catholic, in the faith of Our Lord Jesus Christ, in the teaching of the Gospel as contained in the *Confessio Belgica,* in my own *Confession,* and in all the Confessions of the Evangelical Churches, which are all alike. I hold in abomination the errors of the Papists and the superstitions of the Greeks; I approve and embrace the doctrine of the most excellent teacher John Calvin and of all who agree with him.[37]

Here one finds the reasons for Cyril Lucaris's actions. His purposes were to enlighten his fellow Orthodox who were in a state of ignorance and to combat the propaganda of the Roman Catholics.[38] He had been sent as an exarch of the Patriarch of Alexandria to Poland and had seen the effects of Roman Catholic activity there, including the infamous Brest-Litovsk Union of 1596. Indeed he narrowly escaped with his life; his companion, Nicephorus Cantacuzenus, was put to death by the Polish authorities.[39] During his five years in Poland, Lucaris labored to raise the educational standard of the Orthodox community. To this end he established schools and set up a printing press to publish Orthodox books.

As was shown above, the theological framework of the Orthodox East was different from that of the Latin West. Apart from any consideration of Lucaris's personal conviction, there was nowhere else to turn other than to the Reformers in his battle with the Roman Catholics. In so doing he consciously adopted the Western formulations that make his confession seem to be non-Orthodox and alien to the tradition of the Eastern Church. However, Cyril Lucaris did not consider himself to be in opposition to the Orthodox Church, only in opposition to the ignorance that he found within the Church.[40]

It is understandable in light of the Turkish domination of the Greek Church that a theological problem as was just described could have arisen. It would be a natural assumption that the Russian theology developed more along Orthodox lines. However, there was considerable Western influence in the history of Russian theological development. Dependent on Constantinople from the introduction of Christianity until 1453, Kievan Russia did not progress much beyond the assimilation of the Byzantine heritage. Specifically, Russian emphases at this stage of " 'Russian Byzantinism' . . . belong to the general area of piety rather than theological reflection."[41] The situation was complicated by the Mongol conquest and the subsequent transfer of political and ecclesiastical centers to Moscow. These factors, combined with the growing national unity around Moscow, led to the development of the messianic claim that Moscow was the center of Orthodoxy.[42] Yet there were no theological schools in Moscow until late in the seventeenth century. Without "any stable tradition of theological learning"[43] and increasingly dependent on the state, the Church became open to Western thought-forms and categories. Schmemann writes:

It is therefore, an ironic fact that the establishment of theological education on solid and permanent foundations was the work of Tsar Peter the Great, whose administrative and ecclesiastical reforms marked at the beginning of the eighteenth century a radical "westernization" of the whole Russian life. . . .

The new theological school was no exception within the deeply "westernized" culture of the new Russian society. . . . [It was] created and staffed almost exclusively by the imported "alumni" of the Theological Academy of Kiev which . . . soon became the main centre of a Latin and

Scholastic "transposition" of Orthodox theology, the very expression of the latter's "western captivity." . . . Not only did Latin remain for more than a century its language, it remained itself for a long time a "western" theology reflecting nearly every stage of the western—Catholic and Protestant—theological development and existing as a theological "superstructure" deeply alienated from the living experience and continuity of the Church.[44]

It is the founder of the Kievan academy, Peter Moghila, who serves as an example of a "Latinizer."[45] Like Cyril Lucaris, his contemporary, Moghila was interested in raising the level of education of the Orthodox community. However, unlike Lucaris, who sought to combat the Roman Catholic position by using Protestant arguments, Moghila combated the Protestant position by use of Catholic methodology. He was successful in checking the Protestant tendency among the Orthodox in the Ukraine.[46] He was not so successful in presenting the authentic Orthodox teaching. His work resembles closely the current Roman Catholic theological works in approach and tone. Furthermore, on certain theological points where Roman Catholicism and Orthodoxy differ, Moghila opted for the Catholic position. For example, contrary to Orthodox teaching he maintained a third abode for the departed, in almost all respects identical to the Catholic concept of purgatory. He accepted affusion as an acceptable alternative to immersion and he adopted the Roman Catholic understanding of the manner and time of consecration of the eucharistic elements.[47]

Moghila's "Confession" was modified by a Greek, Meletios Syrigos, before it was approved by the Council of Jassy in 1642. Syrigos expunged some of the Roman tendencies, including the three mentioned above: purgatory, affusion, and the consecration of the Eucharist at the Words of Institution rather than the Epiclesis as held by the Orthodox.[48] Syrigos, though, was a Westernizer himself and retained in Moghila's "Confession" many Western elements. The "Confession" still stands as a "high-water mark of Latin influence upon Orthodox theology."[49]

It is not the purpose here to comment on these "Western" additions to Orthodox theology. Rather, their presence needs to be noted so that Western theologians can be prepared to recognize non-Orthodox elements in Orthodox tradition, as indeed, the Orthodox do themselves.[50]

That Orthodox theology has been influenced by Western categories in the past needs hardly to be argued.[51] However, there are some who believe that Orthodox theological education is still in Western captivity. One such writer is Christos Yannaras, who holds that theology in Greece is still academic and therefore alien to the Orthodox ethos. This academic theology entered Greece with the establishment of the faculty of theology of the University of Athens in 1837. The university is modeled after the German universities; the faculty of theology "is a faithful copy of the theological faculties of Germany."[52] The question was not raised if this pattern "was appropriate for the special character and different sources of Orthodox theology."[53] Nor was the question asked a hundred years later when the faculty of theology of the University of Salonica was commenced on the same lines (1941–42). Yannaras's point is simply that Western rationalistic methodology is not appropriate to the Orthodox theological task and that this methodology is doing harm to the Orthodox Church. The trend toward Westernization is dangerous because it cuts the Orthodox off from their past. "But," writes Yannaras,

> one cannot reject one's roots with impunity. The result has been immediate and tragic. . . . In the area of ecclesiastical life as a whole, our primacy among the Orthodox Churches—a primacy founded on theology and tradition and not on nationalism—is seriously in doubt and it seems that it may even be lost. This loss will have tragic consequences for Orthodoxy as a whole, for ecumenical Orthodoxy, and the responsibility of Greek academic theology for this turn of events is very great.[54]

The issue of Western influence can thus be seen to be a serious problem for the Orthodox. There is an ongoing inter-Orthodox debate on this subject. One should take heed of this caveat sounded by the Orthodox themselves, to the effect that not all "Orthodox" theological statements have the same weight.[55]

The Fathers in Dogmatic Theology

There exists in Orthodox theology a tension between two theological approaches to the task facing Orthodox theologians today. In the midst of general agreement that the inroads of Westernization must be checked, the question arises: What should be the determinative philosophical framework of Orthodox theology? The alternatives usually posed are either a return to the Hellenistic mind or an acceptance of the Western philosophic tradition. These two orientations are more evident in Russian theology than in Greek theology, though as was shown above, the charge has been made that Greek academic theology remains Western in orientation.

The reason for the prominence given to the new philosophic orientation in Russian thought is that Western philosophy was the "source and mother of the Russian 'religious philosophy' of the nineteenth and twentieth centuries."[56] For those who favor the "conceptual" framework of Western philosophy, the Orthodox critique of the past theological traditions must include a reexamination of the Patristic period itself. While this examination and analysis would be on a different level from that of a seventeenth-century confession like Moghila's, nevertheless it would not necessarily accept all previous patristic tradition as binding. As an example of an extreme representation of this view, Panagiotis Bratsiotis refers to Stephen Zankow.

> According to Zankow, Orthodox Church dogma can be reduced to the Trinity and the Incarnation as expounded by the ecumenical councils.

Dogma is genuine doctrine proposed by an ecumenical council and accepted by the whole Church, and only a proposition laid down in this way can have the mandatory force of dogma. . . .

This liberal view, which finds no firm support either in primitive theology or in that of the Byzantine Church, has been rejected almost unanimously by Greek theologians who follow ancient theological tradition.[57]

The label "liberal" is thought by Schmemann not to be a totally correct designation of this orientation. He would rather stress the intent of those who hold to this methodology of attempting to go "beyond" the fathers. Their efforts are directed at a "new synthesis or reconstruction," a transposition of theology into a new "key." Those who have this view—and the best representative of this position in Schmemann's opinion is Sergius Bulgakov—believe that it is "the specific task and vocation of Russian theology to accomplish this transition."[58]

The other orientation is that of a return to the spirit of the Fathers and precisely to the philosophical framework of the Hellenistic age.

The tragedy of Orthodox theological development is viewed here precisely as a drifting away of the theological mind from the very spirit and method of the Fathers, and no reconstruction or new synthesis are [sic] thought possible outside a creative recovery of that spirit. "The style of the Patristic age cannot be abandoned. This is the only solution for contemporary theology. There is no one modern idiom which can unite the Church."[59]

Hellenism is thus seen to be of both permanent and practical value to the Christian Church. The Hellenistic categories are integral to the very existence of the Church. There can be no going beyond that which is seen to be foundational. A major proponent of this view, George Florovsky, writes: "Russian theological thought must go through a strict school of Christian Hellenism. . . . Hellenism in the Church was made eternal, was integrated into its very texture as an eternal category of Christian existence."[60] Florovsky's viewpoint is in agreement with that of the Greek theologians who view the heritage of the past as still binding today.[61] For the purposes of this study it is sufficient to note these trends and to understand that both orientations desire to make Orthodox theology relevant to today's world.

Theologoumena

"The dogmatic teaching of the Orthodox Catholic Church is identical with the teaching of the one, ancient and undivided Church, this teaching having been preserved integrally and without change over the centuries in Orthodoxy," Karmiris writes.[62] The doctrinal continuity of the Orthodox Church from the earliest time is a cardinal tenet of the Orthodox Church. Thus without equivocation the Orthodox can state that "Orthodoxy is the Church of Christ on earth."[63] As such, Orthodox dogma contains all the truths necessary for salvation. Furthermore, because Orthodox dogma is the sum total of all the truths of Scripture and Tradition, all Orthodox doctrine is "equally obligatory for all believers, as absolutely necessary for salvation."[64]

It is important to understand what is meant by this statement. First of all, it is not denied that Orthodox dogmatic formulations exist that arose in response to external theological challenges. At the points of Western pressure, Orthodox reactions, such as the confessions of the seventeenth century, came into being. These formulations are granted a place in the Orthodox tradition, though they are generally recognized as having been written in a particular historical setting and as expressing the spirit of their own age. For this reason they are not employed "as the main and primary sources of Orthodox dogmatic teaching, but simply as relative, auxiliary, and completely secondary sources, and only if and when they are in agreement with Holy Scripture, and ancient, authentic Orthodox Tradition. Their heterodox influence must, above all, be completely avoided."[65]

However, one must not assume that because there are secondary sources there are secondary dogmas. It is the entire deposit of truth that is binding on all believers. There is no option as to what is necessary and what is secondary. "There can be only one Church founded by our Lord, and in that Church there can be but one single Faith. This one Church is the Orthodox Church; the one Faith is the whole of Orthodox doctrine."[66]

Having established the wholeness of Tradition,[67] it is necessary to caution against the confusion of Tradition, that which is accepted by the whole Church, with traditions or local customs. Local custom is not to be held in contempt; in the course of time some local customs have become universally recognized. But at the same time, local customs are not universally binding.[68]

Closely related to this concept of tradition as distinct from the Tradition is the category of *theologoumena*. Ware states: "Many beliefs held by Orthodox are not a part of the one Tradition, but are simply *theologoumena,* theological opinions; and there can be no question of imposing mere matters of opinion on other Christians. Men can possess full unity in the faith, and yet hold divergent theological opinions in certain fields."[69]

This divergence of theological opinion can be clearly seen in the area of missions. For example, in regard to the possibility of external mission for the Orthodox Church, one Orthodox prelate has categorically stated that mission is impossible in the present situation.[70] On the other hand, another prelate presses for the establishment of a missionary society to carry out the missionary mandate.[71] The Orthodox are aware of the past missionary efforts of their Church. However, the divergence of opinion springs from the lack of a definite theology of mission in the Tradition. Mission is a part of the Tradition[72] (those who advocate current missionary work base their position on the missionary awareness of the fathers), but a formal definition as such is lacking.

While one might lament the lack of a definition of mission, there is no need to despair as if nothing could be said. As George Florovsky pointed out in a discussion of the doctrine of the Church: "It is impossible to start with a formal definition of the Church. . . . There is none which could claim any doctrinal authority. . . . This lack of formal definition does not mean, however, a confusion of ideas or any obscurity of view. . . . One does not define what is self-evident."[73]

For the greater part of the history of the Orthodox Church, mission was self-evident. What was self-evident is now being given definition. To record and understand this definition reached by Orthodox theologians is the task of this study.

Chapter III

The Historical Background: Byzantine Missions

There is no comprehensive history of Eastern Orthodox missionary work. Were such a history written, it would encompass several volumes. There does not even exist a suitable survey of Eastern Orthodox missions from Byzantine times through to the Russian Revolution of 1917, let alone to the present day. As will be shown below, surveys and studies do exist for periods of Orthodox missions. However, while Byzantine missions before the split between Rome and Constantinople show definite characteristics distinct from those conducted by the Western Church,[1] all mission work of that period is often labeled "patristic." Furthermore, since most of the Russian Orthodox mission work took place within what are now the boundaries of the USSR, it was not well known outside Orthodox circles. When these two facts are combined with the realization that the histories of Orthodox missions are not well known,[2] one begins to understand why it is often thought that the Orthodox Church is not interested in mission.[3]

The opinion that the Orthodox Church is uninterested in mission is now being challenged.[4] Several studies have been influential in affecting scholarly consensus in this area. For an overview of Orthodox missions, the most readily available and, to a large extent, serviceable in learning the basic points of Orthodox missiology are Kenneth Scott Latourette's *History of the Expansion of Christianity*[5] and *Christianity in a Revolutionary Age*.[6] The best worldwide survey of the Orthodox Church is found in the volume edited by the Zoe Brotherhood of Theologians, entitled *A Sign of God, Orthodoxy 1964: A Pan-Orthodox Symposium*.[7] While not strictly a history of missions, it provides sketches of the planting of the Orthodox Church in mission countries. It has the advantage that most of the articles are written by nationals of the Orthodox community in the country concerned. This diverse authorship, however, causes some unevenness in the book's style and content.

It is not the purpose of this chapter and the following three to give a historical survey of Orthodox missions. While these chapters are indeed a

19

survey, the purpose in them is not to discover missionary history but, rather, missionary theology. An attempt will be made to identify and extract the basic missiological method of Orthodoxy. For this reason, the treatment given to certain missionaries will be disproportionate to that accorded to others. The aim of these chapters is to focus on individuals who have contributed most to the Orthodox understanding of missionary work.

There are two further reasons why this overview is necessary. In light of the small amount of missionary work presently being done by Orthodox missionaries,[8] the most fruitful area for Orthodox missiologists to research is the past. Furthermore, in a church where Tradition is the operative concept, current practice must conform to the principles of Orthodox missions as done in the past. Therefore, for both precept and example, one must look at Orthodox mission history.

With the fall of Constantinople in 1453 and the subsequent collapse of the remainder of the eastern half of the Roman empire, a dark night settled on the Orthodox Church. It is true that the Church was permitted to exist and function, but there were many restrictions placed on the Christians.[9] Conversion was a one-way street. Conversion to Islam was encouraged while conversion to Christianity was punished by death.[10] Because of the long period of oppression and the suffering of the Greek Church in recent years,[11] the rich heritage of the past tended to be forgotten.

Missiologists are indebted to modern scholars who have pointed out the nature of the Byzantine enterprise. Francis Dvornik in his *Byzantine Missions among the Slavs* laboriously documents the missionary concern and activity of the Eastern Church.[12] Demetrios J. Constantelos has demonstrated the tenor of the enterprise, which exceeded the ancient world in caring for the less fortunate and needy among them.[13] As Constantelos points out, this included the barbarians whose physical as well as spiritual needs had to be met.

The most famous of all Byzantine missionaries are the brothers Saint Cyril (826–869)[14] and Saint Methodius (c. 815–885). Both had served the imperial government prior to undertaking their missionary work to the Slavs of Moravia in 862. Their suitability for the mission lay in part with their knowledge of the Slavic language, gained while growing up in Thessalonika, an area with a large Slavic population. Beyond that, they were clearly gifted men. Both had been able administrators and Cyril had served as a professor of philosophy in the Imperial Academy. Both had served on other imperial missions in which part of the task was a defense of the Christian faith. It was only natural that these brothers were chosen to teach and establish the faith in Moravia. Before they had even departed on their mission, Cyril constructed a Slavonic script[15] and commenced the translation of the Bible into Slavonic. Their work in Moravia was thus grounded in the language of the people, a key point in Orthodox mission policy.

The emphasis on the local language did not go down well with the Frankish missionaries, who were competing for the religious loyalty of the people. The Western clergy maintained that only three languages, Hebrew, Greek, and

Latin, were suitable for expressing Christian truth.[16] However, the Byzantine missionaries had little difficulty in refuting the Frankish position and "everywhere that political circumstances allowed," Orthodoxy, that is, Eastern Christianity, flourished.[17]

To strengthen their position, the brothers undertook a journey to Rome. There they were well received, no doubt in part because they had brought with them the remains of St. Clement, which they had discovered while on an earlier imperial mission in the Crimea.[18] The real reason for their journey seems to have been to gain papal approval for their Slavonic liturgy and thus to resolve the problem created by the intervention of the Germans. The method of approach was to place the work in Moravia directly under the pope.[19] While initially successful in their appeal for permission to use their vernacular liturgy (the Slavonic liturgy even being celebrated in Rome[20]), the brothers faced opposition in Rome that would eventually lead to papal proscription against the use of the vernacular.

From the missiological point of view, it can be argued that the Western Church missed an opportunity to gain the allegiance of the Slavic peoples. This allegiance was later gained by the creation of Uniate Churches, which are Eastern Churches that are in communion with Rome, but have papal permission to retain their own language, rites, and common law.[21] Even more important was the loss of a significant input to the mission practice of the Roman Church. It is only in the mid-twentieth century that Roman Catholicism is experimenting with an idea presented to the papal court in the ninth century, that of liturgy and Scripture in the vernacular.

Cyril died while at Rome and Methodius was consecrated a bishop to provide the nascent Slavic Church with a hierarchy, several of their disciples having been previously ordained. On his return to Moravia, Methodius was captured by his ecclesiastical opponents and detained for two and one-half years. Through Pope John VIII's intervention Methodius was released and able to occupy his see. But he was at first forbidden by Pope John VIII to use Slavonic,[22] though later, and for the duration of Methodius's life, permission was again granted. After Methodius's death, the situation again changed and Pope Stephen V forbade use of Slavonic. Methodius's disciples were driven out and Byzantine Christianity ceased in Moravia.

Moravia's loss, however, was the rest of the Slavic world's gain as followers of Methodius carried on their work of evangelism and translation in Bulgaria. The body of literature in Slavonic, including the Bible and the liturgy, played an important role in the Christianization of Russia. The influence of Sts. Cyril and Methodius far outlasted their own efforts. It is no wonder that they are commemorated in the liturgy as "Equals to the Apostles, evangelizers of the Slavonians."[23]

At this point the distinctive features of the Slavic mission should be noted. These features are regularly cited as the key elements in authentic Eastern Orthodox missions. The first element is the use of the vernacular for worship. The gospel is to be preached and the converts instructed to offer praise to God in their own language. Along with this goes the emphasis on Bible translation. It was regarded as the natural right of a person to use one's own language to worship the God of all the earth.

The reason for this belief was the Orthodox view of the event of Pentecost. Just as God had confused the languages of people at the Tower of Babel as punishment, so the miracle of tongues at Pentecost is a sign of God's blessing and of his desire to see the redemption of all nations. The two acts of God not only offset each other, but the second baptizes the vernacular languages, so that language becomes a means of blessing and praising God.[24]

Meyendorff concedes that this practice was not without problems. "By facilitating direct access to the Scriptures and the liturgy for the young Slavic Churches, it could cause a certain fragmentation of the Universal Church into national Churches, especially since the Byzantine conception of relations between Church and State had been exported into all the Slavic countries."[25] Another aspect of the ready access to the Bible is the multiplicity of sects in Russia, many of which sprang up because of the people's ability to read the Scriptures for themselves. This complicated scene is well laid out by Serge Bolshakoff.[26]

The second distinctive element of the Slavic mission is the use of indigenous clergy. The usual procedure was to have the most promising converts ordained as soon as possible. In the more remote areas, ordination was delayed simply because there was no bishop to perform this service. Often ordination of the first clergy had to wait until the missionary returned to the homeland where he was consecrated as a bishop. This step came when the church officials felt the new church had grown to where it needed the oversight of its own bishop or archbishop. In the matter of theological education of the clergy, great importance was placed not on formal study but on a proper grasp of the essentials of the faith and, most of all, the liturgy. In recent times in Greece, ordinary villagers have been ordained to the priesthood.[27]

The emphasis on indigenization leads to the third element, that of responsible selfhood of the church. Canon law permits the establishment of local churches, and to this end the noblest Orthodox missionary efforts aspired.[28] As in other matters, there has not always been agreement between the mother church and the mission church over when self-government is required. Also, politics often played a role in keeping the local church from independence. Sadly, in church history one can see instances where independence was declared by the local church rather than granted by the church under whose jurisdiction the work originally fell. The process of becoming self-governing, or autocephalous, continues today, as exemplified in the formation of the Orthodox Church in America.[29]

It is significant for the study of Orthodox mission theology that these three elements are found in the work of Sts. Cyril and Methodius. In part because of the long period of oppression under Turkish rule and the pseudomorphosis of Orthodox theology referred to in the preceding chapter, there is a tendency to regard anything in contemporary Orthodox theology that resembles Western theological thought as a borrowed item. Indeed, often the Orthodox position is stated in such a way as to seem to be a mediating stance between Catholic and Protestant conceptions.[30]

However, this does not necessarily produce the authentic Orthodox position. Orthodox theology should not be forced into an artificially created third view, no matter how attractive the concept of an Orthodox *via media* may seem.[31] Orthodox theology needs to be taken in its own framework. Likewise, Orthodox mission theology and practice must be seen in its own right and not as a copy of Western methods. One has in Sts. Cyril and Methodius a pattern for Orthodox missionary work that the Orthodox are justified in citing as an example of the true Orthodox approach to the problem. One should be clear on what this means and what it does not mean.

It does not necessarily mean that this methodology was enshrined in all Orthodox practice. The truth is that it was often not followed. But it does show the approach that the Orthodox Church approved and allowed. This would be all the more significant when one considers the objections that the Cyril-Methodian mission met from the Western Church. Rome did not encourage the use of the vernacular in worship, and only reluctantly and for a limited duration permitted it.

By no means should one regard the practice of Cyril and Methodius as a unique departure for the Orthodox Church. As Benz points out, missionary work was undertaken among the East Gothic tribes who came under the influence of Byzantine priests and monks.[32] The best known of the missionaries to the Goths is Ulfilas (Gothic, Wulfila), who translated the Bible into Gothic. Benz sees the translation as the reason for Ulfilas's success. "This alone made it possible for the Gothic tribes to assimilate Christianity."[33] Latourette comments that with Ulfilas we probably have the first instance of a missionary reducing a language to writing and creating an alphabet.[34] What has become standard procedure for certain missions in the twentieth century[35] was first begun by a missionary with a connection to Constantinople.[36]

The principle of using vernacular languages was also found beyond the eastern boundaries of Byzantium. Approximately a century after the mass conversion of Armenia, the Bible was translated into Armenian and slowly a body of religious literature became available. Armenia, caught between the Roman and Persian empires, suffered because both sought to control it. When Persia gained dominance, the Church suffered. Interference from Constantinople led to a break with the "majority Church of the Empire."[37] Yet the Armenian Church in spite of the break was able to stay alive. High among the reasons for its survival would appear to be the existence of a religious literature in the vernacular.

Chapter IV

The Historical Background: Russian Missions

Post-Byzantine Orthodox mission history is mainly the history of Russian Orthodox missions, owing to the above-mentioned disability of the Greek Church under Islam. Until quite recently there were no books available on the subject. At the turn of the century, Eugene Smirnoff, chaplain of the Imperial Russian embassy in London, could produce as his *apologia* for writing a book on Russian Orthodox mission the fact that no other book existed.[1] Smirnoff had originally intended to write only an article to appear in a periodical. When the account soon exceeded magazine-article length, he decided to publish it as a separate book. Smirnoff's account lacks scholarly apparatus; he states in the preface that this was done so as not to burden the reader with references to the Russian originals (unverifiable to the majority of his readers). The book is still a useful introduction. The main emphasis is on missions within the boundaries of Russia, and in this the work is of most value. Missionary work outside Russia (China, North America, and Japan) is covered in only nine pages.

The Russian Revolution drastically changed the picture of Russian missions. The next book written on the subject lays the emphasis on missionary work outside Russia. Thus Bolshakoff, writing forty years after Smirnoff, can cover a field virtually untouched in his predecessor's book. No one in the intervening years had produced a book on Orthodox missions. Bolshakoff could himself say, "There is not a single scholarly book in English, German or French, so far as I know, which deals with Russian Foreign Missions. Even in Russian one cannot find such a book—at least brought up to date."[2]

This demonstrates why, in part, Russian Orthodox missions are so unknown. The only significant addition to the history of Orthodox missions comes from the pen of a Roman Catholic scholar, Josef Glazik.[3] However, not even Glazik's books cover the entire sweep of Russian Orthodox mission history.

This study will not attempt a general survey of Russian Orthodox missions because that is readily obtainable in the above-mentioned books. But it will

24

look at the broad sweep of that history to see if the principles observed in Byzantine missions were carried through in the Russian Church's work and if any new principles were added. This historical background will serve to set the stage for a review of contemporary Orthodox missionary theology, since most Orthodox theologians see themselves as heirs, not only of their particular national Orthodox history, but of the whole Orthodox experience.[4]

MISSIONS INSIDE "RUSSIA"

As was shown already, the pioneer work of Sts. Cyril and Methodius in translating the Bible and the liturgy into the vernacular was a major factor in the eventual conversion of the Slavs. Driven out from Moravia, the disciples were received with honor in Bulgaria. Clement, head of Methodius's disciples, labored with great success.[5] Significant was the interest and support of the Bulgarian king, Boris. Forced to accept baptism as a condition of peace after being defeated by the Byzantines, he later became increasingly religious, and the reality of Christianity marked his life.[6] The subsequent history of the Bulgarian national Church is darkened by the struggles of the Byzantine Greeks for domination both of the government and of the church.[7]

Whether the Orthodox faith came to Russia from Bulgaria or Constantinople is not a concern here. An unsuccessful delegation was sent by Photius in 864.[8] Yet Christian influence was still present and Ware speaks of "a steady Christian infiltration."[9] The translation of the Bible and the liturgical books had already been completed. "The Russians therefore had but to avail themselves of this precious heritage."[10]

Avail themselves they did. While there were Christians in the royal household before his time,[11] it was Vladimir who deserves the title "baptizer of Russia."[12] Timothy Ware writes: "Vladimir set to in earnest to Christianize his realm: priests, relics, sacred vessels, and icons were imported; mass baptisms were held in rivers; Church courts were set up, and ecclesiastical tithes instituted. The great idol of the god Perun, with its silver head and gold moustaches, was rolled ignominiously down from the hill-top above Kiev."[13] Thus Orthodoxy became the established religion of Russia, a position it occupied until 1917.

The conversion of the Slavonic tribes appears to have been completed in the time of Vladimir. There was little serious opposition in the south and what pagan opposition appeared in the north was overcome.[14]

The Finnish tribes were not so quick to receive the gospel. The work of evangelization among these people was the work of monks, or "colonist-monks" as they are called by Smirnoff.[15] These men, in search of solitude for their hermitages, penetrated the northern forests. One could think of them as akin to the desert fathers, which in motivation they certainly were. However, there was one significant difference; the northern forests were inhabited. Through their devotion and the labor of their hands, as well as their words, they bore a witness to the primitive nomads around them.

The colonist-monks' role was that of bearers of civilization as well as the gospel. Their hermitages grew into monasteries, and around the monasteries grew settled towns. They taught not only the gospel but also what it meant to be a citizen of the Russian state. "The colonist-monks, by converting the Finnish tribes to Christianity, ingrafted Russian culture into them by peaceful means, and gradually transformed them into the flesh and blood of the Russian people."[16]

But one need not only see the ministry of these forest dwellers as incorporating the pagan into society. For while their social role was undeniable, they themselves did not plan particularly for this. Their departure, as Meyendorff points out, was theologically motivated.

> Christian monasticism is an eschatological phenomenon. Leaving the towns, where a minimalist "Christian society" was established, they went and founded new communities in conformity with the law of the Kingdom. . . . Their ministry was thus a prophetic ministry, whose role was to announce the imminence of the Parousia, and the presence "within you" of the Kingdom. In this respect, the ministry of the monks is in its very nature very close to that of the apostles: both witness to the sovereignty of Christ over history and over the world.[17]

Note carefully this interpretation of monasticism. In it there is a demonstration of the holistic approach to life that came to characterize the best of the Orthodox Church. Paradoxically, those who rejected the world were often in the best position to proclaim to the world the total sovereignty of Christ. It is this self-denial, later to be spoken of as Russian kenoticism,[18] that marks the lives of many of the Russian missionary heroes. An example of withdrawal in order to return to proclaim Christ's word to the world is seen in the monk St. Seraphim (1759–1833). He lived alone in the forest for ten years (1794–1804), then spent another twenty years in solitary devotions, after which time he opened the door of his cell to the people who flocked to him in great numbers for spiritual counsel.[19]

The gospel spread in Russia and with it Russian identity. However, the Russification did not always endure, as evidenced by the reaction against the Russian language and the substitution of Finnish in the Orthodox Church of Finland.[20] Not all monks felt they needed to forge Russians out of pagans. Willing to work with the vernacular languages and within the culture, they labored to bring Christ to those who did not know him. And as Meyendorff points out, "The long tradition of Byzantine missions showed them the right way," that of bringing the gospel in the language of the people.[21]

The most outstanding example of an Orthodox missionary in the Middle Ages is St. Stephen of Perm (1340–96). Well educated, he left the quiet of the monastery to bring the gospel to the savage Zyrians of the northern forest. To be free from a connection with colonization and to facilitate the reception of the Christian message, he created a Zyrian alphabet and translated the liturgy and the gospel.[22] He taught his adult converts as well as the children to read. From the most promising of his students, he chose the leadership of the church.

Thus one sees in Stephen's work two of the characteristics that were pointed out as essential traits of Orthodox missionary work, the use of the vernacular and the selection of indigenous clergy. The third characteristic, that of a national Zyrian Church, the goal to which Stephen was working, never materialized. Shortly after Stephen's death, the Zyrian language was replaced by Russian, an expected occurrence considering the power structures of the time.[23] But this in no way detracts from Stephen's accomplishment and the example he was to later Russian missionaries in his use of the vernacular and indigenous clergy.[24]

Monks and clergy were not the only missionaries. Tryphon, a layman from Novgorod, undertook to bring the gospel to the Lapps living in the remote northern regions. While it is permissible in the case of an emergency for a layperson to administer baptism, it is not the normal procedure.[25] So after Tryphon had "converted several hundreds of the inhabitants," he patiently waited for a priest to baptize them.[26] He subsequently took monastic vows (Tryphon is his monastic name) and founded (1532) the Monastery of the Holy and Undivided Trinity on the shores of the Pechenga River on the Kola peninsula. It remained for a long time an important Orthodox missionary outpost. Tryphon was as good an engineer as he was missionary. One of the monasteries he fortified, the Solovetzki Monastery, resisted numerous assaults (by the Swedes and then the English) over a 200-year period without being taken.[27]

The history of Russian missions, unfortunately, is not all exemplary. Some missionaries did not take the trouble to learn the language of those among whom they were to labor. Others were content to use the power of the state to aid in the "conversion" of unbelievers.[28] One such worker was Bishop Misail of Ryazan (d. 1656), who did not hesitate to use the sword to win allegiance to the gospel. Fulfilling the words of Jesus as recorded in Matthew 26:52, the bishop himself was slain. That his actions were not held in high esteem by the Church is evidenced by its refusal to canonize him in spite of his "martyrdom."[29]

The internal disputes that beset the Russian Church also had an influence on missionary activity. Not only was energy dissipated that could have been employed in missionary causes, the dissension resulted in a greater subjugation of the Church to the state. For example, there was the sixteenth-century dispute between the Possessors, or Josephites (after their leader, St. Joseph of Volokalamsk), and the Nonpossessors over the ownership of land by the monasteries. At that time approximately one-third of the land in Russia was owned by monasteries. The debate between the two groups spread to other issues, such as the treatment of heretics and the relationship between Church and state. As their name suggests, the Nonpossessors were opposed to monastic estates and held in general to a more spiritual view of the monk's vocation. Thus they opposed the use of civil punishments to deal with heretics (a very enlightened view considering that their contemporaries in Western Europe were employing the civil authority to deal with heretics) and drew a distinct line between the realm of the state and the realm of the Church. The Possessors carried the contest (though the Church has canonized St. Nilus, the leader of the Nonpossessors, as well as St. Joseph), and the Church suffered in the next century because of their victory.[30]

The reforms of Peter the Great (reigned 1682–1725) further hindered the Church's mission. Monasticism was put under strict imperial control. The changes wrought under his administration are still an issue in Russian Orthodoxy.[31] While to some observers Peter appears as an "ardent enthusiast of the Church's evangelical mission to the south and east"[32] because of his encouragement of Chinese and Siberian missions, others feel his interest was politically rather than religiously motivated.[33]

Peter's successors, Elizabeth (reigned 1741–62) and Catherine II (reigned 1762–96), further weakened the potential forces for mission. The former confiscated most of the monastic properties, while the latter closed half the monasteries and severely limited the number of monks permitted to remain in the functioning monasteries. These moves affected missionary work in the distant provinces of Russia where the monastery was the only cultural and charitable center:[34]

> If in some cases the state was indirectly favourable to missions, there were occasions when the effect was the opposite and serious obstacles were put in their path. In the eighteenth century it was forbidden to preach the gospel to the Kirgiz nomads; in the nineteenth the Lamaist hierarchy was officially recognized and upheld by the government; the Peking mission was continually receiving formal requests not to convert the inhabitants lest they incur the wrath of the Chinese authorities. Missionaries who evangelized too assiduously were often recalled, the government preferring to support those who were content to dispense baptism as though it were a mere legal formality. . . . [35]

THE RUSSIAN ORTHODOX MISSIONARY REVIVAL

Despite continued dependence on, and control by, the imperial government, the nineteenth century saw some advances in the areas of Russian missions. While not comparable to the work of Protestant and Roman Catholic missions of the same period, for the Orthodox it can also be called "the Great Century" in that it saw the beginning of new and innovative missions.

Macarius Gloukharev (1792–1847) and the Altai Mission

Macarius was the son of a parish priest. He excelled in his studies and won admittance to the Ecclesiastical Academy in St. Petersburg. His abilities secured for him a professorship at the Ekaterinoslav Seminary (1817), and at the age of twenty-nine (1821) he was made rector of the Kostroma Seminary.[36] Since he had taken monastic vows, it seemed certain he was headed for the episcopate. However, his involvement at Ekaterinoslav with some disciples of Paissy Velitchkovsky, the man who reintroduced hesychasm* to Russia,[37] led Macarius deeper into the contemplative life. He abandoned his ecclesiastical career and withdrew into monastic seclusion. He progressively sought more and more remote hermitages, finally settling in the Glinsk desert. Here he devoted his time to the translation of the fathers and the mystics, both Eastern and Western.

In 1828 the Holy Synod issued a call for missionaries in an attempt to reverse the trend of apostasy among the eastern Russians. It was mentioned above how the government used Christianization to produce Russification, and it was in these areas where the converts were reverting to paganism. Macarius, though "small, frail, even sickly—the typical intellectual ascetic," volunteered for missionary service.[38]

Choosing a particularly difficult region, the Altai mountain ranges of central Asia, he went out with two companions to preach the gospel to the warlike nomads inhabiting the area. As part of their total witness to the people, the three missionaries agreed to hold all things in common. This was not simply a monastic vow of poverty, but was regarded as "a means of achieving complete unanimity." This unanimity was seen as an integral part of the evangelistic mission. "Mission must first and foremost be a witness to unity."[39]

Macarius, in the tradition of earlier Orthodox missionaries, began by studying the languages of the different tribes. Visiting the various nomad encampments to gather data about the languages, he used every opportunity to proclaim the gospel. But his efforts were unrewarded. The people remained unresponsive to his message. Should he abandon his mission, concluding that these tribes were not as yet ready for the Christian message? Not willing, in his own words, "to judge a people's unreadiness to receive the universal faith in Jesus Christ," he firmly believed that among those with whom he worked the Lord had his own people. " 'No people exist,' he affirmed with vigor, 'among whom God does not recognize His own; there are no depths of ignorance or darkness which the Lord cannot penetrate.' "[40]

Therefore, instead of abandoning his missionary work he changed his method of approach. Realizing the inadequacy of verbal proclamation, he undertook to be a servant among them. By living out the implications of his faith, he sought to be an example to those around him in two areas: medicine and hygiene. In the former he introduced preventive medicine as well as curative practices. In the field of hygiene he was not content with teaching what was correct; "small, frail, even sickly" though he was, he actually went into

---

*Struve defines hesychasm in the following manner: "This doctrine, which we generally associate with Gregory Palamas, but which in fact goes back to early Christian monasticism is one of the most authentic and most complete expressions of Christianity. The immediate aim of hesychasm is fellowship with Christ and the Holy Spirit, through silence and continual prayer (the prayer of Jesus), meditation on Scripture and the regular observance of the sacraments. Its final aim is the mystical penetration of the whole being by the Holy Spirit." ("Macaire Gloukharev," p. 309).

homes and did the cleaning himself. "This symbolic action sums up the theology of mission that Marcarius lived out in practice. To sweep the floor as a humble servant is to identify oneself with Christ, to bear witness to Him in a way which is more authentic than speeches."[41]

It becomes clear how Macarius's theology is related to missionary practice. In the charter for their common life, Macarius and his companions not only set an example, they stated a theological concept of the type of life that should characterize the Christian community. In his ministry to the physical aspects of human existence, Macarius was not merely trying to win a hearing but was demonstrating that the total human condition is of interest to God. This reminds one of the colonist-monks who brought the gospel to northern Russia and who, in Meyendorff's words, proclaimed "the sovereignty of Christ over history and the world."[42]

Macarius differed from other Orthodox missionaries of his time. Rather than hurry the converts through baptism, as was typical,[43] Macarius insisted on a long period of instruction for his converts. During the fourteen years of his service in the area he performed only 675 adult baptisms. One would think that with such long-term prebaptismal instruction, baptism would be the climax of the educational process. However, this was not the case, since Macarius viewed baptism as the commencement of a Christian lifestyle.[44] He settled his converts as far as possible into newly established villages, composed entirely of Christians and governed by missionaries.[45] This was both for the protection of the converts from reprisals from their pagan neighbors and to enable them to witness through their lifestyle to the truths of the gospel. This was in line with Macarius's concept of total Christian witness.

It was this concept that led Macarius to emphasize the founding of schools and hospitals. Struve sees the founding of more schools and hospitals than churches by Macarius as evidence of the spirit of service that marked the man.[46] While it is true that Macarius certainly believed in service, he also realized that the efforts of previous missionaries had been dissipated because their converts were not well enough grounded in the faith. To Macarius, service was not an end but a means to further his real goal: the spread of the true Christian gospel among the people with whom he labored.

Evidence of this belief can be deduced from his efforts later in life to instill among the entire Russian people an interest in missions. In this way missions would not be confined to a small group within the church, but would become the interest and work of the entire church. Being no mere armchair theorist, Macarius sent a report on the subject to the tsar, which only seems to have succeeded in annoying the tsar. Further, he laid practical plans. If the Russian people were to be involved in mission, they must have a greater knowledge of Christ than was presently manifested. Since Bible translation worked well as a missionary tactic, it was only logical to apply the same principle to the home church. Therefore, Macarius embarked on a modern Russian translation of the Old Testament.

In order to carry out his grand scheme, he needed to be free of his missionary responsibilities. Having found a suitable successor, Macarius petitioned the Holy Synod for permission to travel to the grotto of St. Jerome in Bethlehem. However, permission was not granted and eventually he became abbot of a monastery (1843). It was here that he became "painfully aware that the Russian masses were only superficially Christian, and therefore inadequate for the great apostolic task God had in store for them. Putting aside his other work, he devoted himself to mission at home and opened the monastery doors to all who wished for instruction."[47] Finally having been granted permission to travel to the Holy Land, the missionary never undertook his journey, dying on the very day he had proposed to set out.

That there was a certain romanticism and visionary aspect to Macarius is indisputable. But when one looks at what he was able to accomplish, one finds that his romanticism produced solid fruit. When he left the mission in 1843, there were five Orthodox settlements and two churches, three schools, and one orphanage. He attracted capable followers and successors, two of whom later became archbishops. At the close of the century there were 25,000 converts, 188 Christian villages, 67 churches with services entirely in the vernacular languages, and 48 schools with instruction in the vernacular.[48]

Macarius also left a legacy of missionary practice. In preparation for his work, he took a university course of natural science, anatomy, and botany. During his course of study a young woman offered to go out as a missionary. Macarius encouraged her by passing along the notes from the lectures, since at that time women were not permitted to attend university. He encouraged her to study mid-wifery and to develop her natural talent in the painting of icons. His employment of women on his missionary staff was innovative for his time. His interest in missionary training led him to propose the creation of a missionary study center where instruction would include medicine, nursing, and agriculture.[49]

It is undeniable that Macarius Gloukharev was a missionary theorist of the first rank. Struve calls him "the first to work out an Orthodox theory of missions."[50] That circumstances did not permit the further development of his ideas does not detract from the stature of the man. Was he influenced by the Western ideas pouring into Russia?[51] Certainly he was aware of the other Christian traditions. He translated Western writers, had defied Orthodox Church authorities by praying with Quakers, and had even "dreamed" about constructing an ecumenical worship center in Moscow with separate chapels for the main Christian denominations.[52] But whatever influence this exposure had upon him, the crucial experience for Macarius was his confrontation with the hesychist tradition. Orthodox spirituality transformed his life. Therefore, the Orthodox Church can claim one of its own sons, nourished in authentic Orthodox tradition, as a missionary strategist.

Ilminski (1821-91) and Linguistic Principles

Another gifted missionary strategist was a man who in the traditional sense was never a missionary. Nicholas Ilminski remained all his life a lay academician, but his influence on the course of Russian missions was far greater than that of many ordained men. A brilliant linguist, he was selected to be part of a translation committee that was to translate the Bible and liturgical books into the Tartar language. The committee proceeded on the basis of using the best form of the Tartar language, that of the Qur'an and of the mosques. Ilminski himself spent two years in Cairo perfecting his knowledge of the Arabic language. Yet for all their efforts, the falling away of the Tartars from the Christian faith continued. Bolshakoff says: "The root causes of the mass apostasy were the same as in many other Christian missions: mass baptisms without any serious preparation of the converts, and subsequent neglect to instruct them properly. The Russian Government, in order to attract the Tartars into the Orthodox Church, showered every kind of privilege upon the converts: distribution of lands, exemption from military service, even monetary rewards."[53]

The services were in Slavonic and there were no native Tartar clergy. The entire enterprise was ripe for Muslim counterpropaganda. The problem was compounded by the translation committee's use of the literary language of the Qur'an and the Arabic script, since the Tartars possessed no script of their own. Thereby the Tartars' link with Islam, instead of being severed by the work of the translation committee, was actually being strengthened.

It was Ilminski who proposed breaking this link by using the colloquial dialect of the Tartars, such as they used in everyday speech, and substituting Russian characters for the Arabic script. Without a doubt, this was a stroke of genius. The language of the Qur'an was considered by the Tartars themselves to be the learned language of books, a thing completely apart from their popular language. By using this popular language, the principle of addressing the gospel to the people in their own language was finally being followed.

Ilminski verified his hypothesis by testing out his translations made into the popular language. "The Tartar boys understood his translation of the Gospel narrative of the Pool of Bethesda, and even corrected some of his expressions. A white-haired old man amongst the baptized Tartars, hearing the prayers in his native tongue, fell on his knees before the icon, and with tears in his eyes thanked God for having vouchsafed to him at least once in his life to pray as he should."[54]

Ilminski recognized that the strength of Islam lay in the employment of a system of schools attached to the mosques in which Tartar boys were instructed in the learned language of the Qur'an. In fact, Islamic propaganda used the learned language. Ilminski established his own system of schools using the popular language. Thus Ilminski found an outlet for his translations and as the case turned out, young missionaries to spread his work around.[55]

What gave Ilminski's work wider influence were his principles of translation. The translator needed a sound theological education and a knowledge of Greek and Hebrew in order to have a correct understanding of the Slavonic texts. Furthermore, since there was a difference of construction between Slavonic and the native language, great effort had to be taken to make an accurate translation in the idiom of the vernacular.[56] Ilminski's principles compare favorably with modern missionary practice. All the more so when one remembers that most missionaries presently engaged in translation work are working from their own languages to the vernacular, perhaps with less of a background in Greek and Hebrew than that specified by Ilminski, though with the benefit of more reference tools.

Ilminski's familiarity with the languages of Russia and Siberia led him to the conclusion that if a careful translation were done for one of the languages, then it would be a simple matter to use that translation as the basis for translations into other languages. The great benefit would be the shorter time required to translate the liturgical and biblical literature into other languages. A subsidiary benefit that Ilminski pointed out was the high degree of uniformity of the ecclesiastical literature among the people of a given area. This is no doubt of considerable importance in a liturgical church such as the Orthodox Church. However, its importance should not be overlooked in less liturgical churches, where it is desirable to have relatively uniform translations of the Bible in the various vernaculars of a region. Needless confusion caused by different approaches in translation could be avoided by Ilminski's method.

Throughout, Ilminski's goal was that the people among whom he labored would become truly Christian. He saw the use of their language as the means by which this end could be accomplished. He said: "We believe that the evangelical word of our Saviour Jesus Christ, having become incarnate, so to speak, in the living tongue of the Tartars, and through it having associated itself most sincerely with their deepest thought and religious consciousness, would produce the Christian revival of this tribe."[57] Ilminski's vision came true.[58]

Bishop Innocent (1797–1879) and Alaska

One of the most successful and possibly the greatest[59] Russian missionary was John Veniaminov.[60] Though of humble birth, Veniaminov rose to the highest office of the Russian Church, that of metropolitan of Moscow. His intellectual gifts were combined with mechanical skills that enabled him to work well with his hands, excellent qualities for the task that lay ahead of him. Showing no special missionary inclination, he refused when first asked to undertake missionary work in the Aleutian Islands, giving as a reason his family responsibilities. Apparently the plight of the baptized but shepherdless Aleuts, as described by a passing traveler, touched Veniaminov, for he changed his mind and volunteered to go out. It took fourteen months of travel for him and his family to reach their field of service. When they arrived, they found no church building, and not even a house to provide them shelter. The missionary's first task was to build them himself.

Studying the Aleut language, he not only mastered the spoken language with its gutteral sounds but composed an alphabet for it. One of the books he later wrote in Aleut, *Indication of the Way into the Kingdom of God,* was translated into Russian, and between 1839 and 1885 was published in forty-six editions.[61]

Smirnoff reports it was circulated in the tens of thousands among the common people.[62] This is a good example of the often repeated argument that external mission aids the internal church situation.[63]

John Veniaminov appears to have been an extraordinary missionary. In addition to building a church and furnishing the inside, he built a school and taught the children, using manuals he himself had written. To be able to visit and evangelize the other islands in the Aleutian chain, he learned how to manipulate and navigate a kayak. Completing his work in the Aleutians, he moved on to the mainland of Alaska where he had amazing success with tribes who previously would have no contact with Europeans.

On his return to St. Petersburg after fifteen years, Veniaminov's abilities were recognized by the Orthodox hierarchy. He had returned to present a plan of missionary strategy to the Holy Synod. While in St. Petersburg, news reached him of his wife's death in Irkutsk. It was then that he took monastic vows and changed his name from John to Innocent. In 1840 he was consecrated bishop of Kamchatka, the Kurilian and the Aleutian Islands. Years later Yakutsk province was placed under him and still later the Russian provinces of Siberia were added to his diocese. Not content to sit in his episcopal residence and direct the work from there, as did most of the other bishops, Innocent logged thousands of miles visiting his far-flung diocese. He changed his episcopal see three times to keep in better touch with his areas of responsibility and places where he desired to plant new missions.[64]

There are many similarities between Innocent, who went to the Aleutians in 1823, and his contemporary, Macarius Gloukharev, who went to the Altai Mountains in 1828. A zeal for real conversion marked both men; Innocent also baptized converts only after a long period of preparation. Both favored the use of the vernacular languages, Innocent being more prodigious in his output of material. Both were concerned to make mission the work of the whole Church. But where Macarius was unable to see his vision become reality, Innocent did. In 1870 Innocent was able to found the Orthodox Missionary Society. The society collected funds for the support of missionaries and the construction and maintenance of charitable and educational institutions. It did not carry on administrative functions as do mission societies in the Western Churches. Bishop Innocent died in 1879 after a life of service to Christ and the Church.[65]

Chapter V

The Historical Background: The East Asian Missions

THE MISSION TO JAPAN

Up to this point, the survey of Russian missions has only considered mission-ary work on Russian territory.[1] Modern Russian foreign missions could well be considered as commencing with the arrival in 1861 of Nicholas Kassatkin (1836–1912) in Hakodate as chaplain to the Russian consulate in Japan. Kassatkin was a devout man who even as a child had shown an interest in undertaking missionary work.[2] His desire to preach the gospel to the yet unevangelized was strengthened by a contact with Bishop Innocent, who advised him to concentrate on learning the Japanese language.[3] While Nicholas was not sent out to Japan to function as a missionary, his duties at the consulate were light enough to provide adequate time for language study. In this manner he spent his first years in Japan.

The stimulus and opportunity for the beginning of Nicholas's missionary work came when he was confronted by an extremely nationalistic Japanese by the name of Sawabe. Sawabe, a samurai, was associated with a group of military men who wanted to drive out all foreigners from the country. Sawabe regarded Nicholas as an agent of political aggression and therefore as his sworn enemy. Since the priest's religion was what Sawabe thought would damage his country the most, he determined to engage Nicholas in a discussion, resolving to slay him if unable to best him by argument.

Taken aback by the priest's calm response to his angry threats, Sawabe agreed to listen to an explanation of Christian doctrine. As Nicholas explained about the Creator of the universe, the samurai gave the exposition his whole-hearted attention.[4] Greatly impressed and desirous of learning more, Sawabe arranged to return to speak with Nicholas. Thus commenced the process that resulted in the conversion of Sawabe. Making no effort to conceal his new conviction, Sawabe spoke to his friends about Christianity. Some reviled him for coming under the influence of a foreigner, but one, a physician named

Sakai, earnestly inquired about the new religion, often asking questions Sawabe could not answer. Sawabe in turn asked Nicholas, who was able to impart to Sawabe sufficient knowledge so that Sakai finally decided to meet the priest himself. Another Japanese, a man called Urano, also sought out Father Nicholas for instruction.

At the time it was illegal for Japanese people even to study Christianity, let alone become converts. The laws had not been rigorously enforced in the past, but the appointment of a new official in Hakodate led to rumors of a persecution. The casually interested dropped away and the three earnest inquirers thought it advisable to leave the area. Before departing they desired to be baptized and unobtrusively made their way to Nicholas's house one night in April 1868. There everything had been made ready and, with a Russian guarding the door, Nicholas baptized his first converts in Japan. Following the Orthodox custom, the candidates received Christian names at their baptism, thus becoming Paul Sawabe, John Sakai, and Jacob Urano. Going out after the ceremony, they made their way to a waiting junk. The weather prevented their immediate departure and increased the chances of their being detected, though they were soon able to escape. Sawabe shortly returned to Hakodate as he was not able to find a place to hide where his presence would not endanger those concealing him. Providentially, the disturbed state of the country prevented the authorities from having the time to enforce the laws prohibiting Christianity.

Nicholas, from the conversations he had with Japanese officials,[5] whom he was teaching the Russian language, realized that a change in attitude was taking place in Japan and that the time was ripe to commence a regular Orthodox mission. He therefore applied for a furlough to enable him to put his plans before the Holy Synod and to enlist the support of friends. The plan he presented demonstrates his conviction that the new converts must be active in evangelism. It is this principle, as much as Nicholas's own character, that accounts for the success of the work in Japan, for it enabled the gospel to be spread by the learners themselves without relying on extensive missionary support. There were never more than four foreigners in the work during the entire history of the Orthodox Church in Japan. The mission's organization is seen in the rules drawn up by Nicholas.[6]

The evangelists shall be organized as a deliberative body.

These evangelists shall teach Christian truth to other people while still continuing to study it for themselves.

There shall be two kinds of meetings. In the first, the evangelists, together with others who know the essential doctrines but desire further study, shall meet to read and explain the New Testament. Such meetings shall be held twice a week, the evangelists taking turns in conducting them. None of the number should fail to attend; if any person is unavoidably prevented from coming, he ought before the next meeting, to learn from some one else what was said. The second meeting is for the benefit of those—whether men, women or children—who are commencing to study Christian doctrines. The evangelists shall explain to them the Creed, the Lord's Prayer, and the Ten Commandments. This meeting shall be held twice a week. The evangelists shall divide the people into classes for instruction. If for any reason a person is not present at a meeting, the evangelist shall ask some one of the absentee's family to inform him of what was said or shall go himself to the person's house for that purpose.

In neither kind of meeting shall there be discussion until after the explanation is finished, although the meaning may be asked of anything that has not been understood.

Besides conducting the two kinds of meetings already mentioned, the evangelists shall go about the city every day trying to win new enquirers. If among those interested are persons unable to attend the meetings, the evangelists shall go to their houses in order to explain the Creed, the Lord's Prayer, and the Ten Commandments. This is to be regarded as of prime importance and should be done even if, for lack of time, the evangelist is obliged to omit the meeting for reading the New Testament.

When persons have thoroughly learned the Creed, the Lord's Prayer, and the Ten Commandments, and are established in the faith, they shall be presented to the priest for baptism.

Whenever any point of doctrine is not understood, it shall be brought to the priest for explanation, and, if it is a matter of importance, the explanation shall be written down in a notebook.

On Sundays the Association of Evangelists shall meet at the house of the priest to report what has been done during the previous week, as well as to consult together and decide on what shall be done in the week to come. These decisions shall be recorded by the evangelists in their notebooks.

A record shall be kept of baptisms, births, marriages and deaths.

A book for recording receipts and expenditures shall be prepared and put in the care of a person to be chosen by the Association.

The money first collected shall be used for the propagation of Christianity.

When sufficient money has been gathered, a young man shall be taught the Russian language and sent to a theological school in Russia. On the completion of his education, he shall return to Japan and there establish a school for teaching Christian doctrine and the sciences. He shall also translate religious books. Another young man shall be sent to a medical school in Russia and on completing his studies shall return to found a hospital and a medical school.

When the number of baptized believers reaches five hundred, one of the evangelists shall be chosen for sending to Russia that he may be ordained to the priesthood. Afterwards, one person shall be ordained for every additional five hundred converts. When there are five thousand believers, a request shall be made for the appointment of a bishop.

The evangelists who go to teach Christianity in the different provinces shall strictly observe the above rules.

The evangelists were full-time Christian workers. It was primarily to seek funds for their support, in addition to the necessary authorization from the church leaders in Russia, that obliged Nicholas to return to Russia. The great strength of these rules lay in the use of indigenous workers and the method of having them teach others while they were yet learning.

Paul Sawabe was doing what he could in Nicholas's absence. Several inquirers were living with him and studying together Christian doctrine. At first many of the inquirers thought that the new religion would be an aid to the political renovation of Japan, but they gradually came to be convinced of the truth of Christianity. Even before Nicholas's return, these men had returned to their homes in other parts of Japan and were engaged in telling others what they had learned.

Meanwhile, Nicholas's mission in Russia was prospering. Refusing the offer of a bishopric in Peking, he expressed his earnest desire to return to Japan. The Holy Synod agreed and approved of his strategy for carrying out the work of the mission. He also received financial support from many individuals, one merchant giving him 10,000 rubles. When asked by Father Nicholas for his name, the generous benefactor refused to divulge it, merely replying, "God knows."[7]

The origin of the work in Japan has been described in great detail because it illustrates the preparation and type of operation that was laid down before an official Orthodox mission to Japan was formed. Until Nicholas returned to Japan in February 1871, there was no Orthodox mission in the official sense. Whatever funds that had previously been expended came either from Nicholas's salary as a chaplain or from the resources of the believers themselves. Paul Sawabe had even gone so far as to sell his sword, a tremendous sacrifice on the part of a samurai, in order to provide for the needs of the inquirers living with him. Furthermore, the work was promoted by the eagerness of the inquirers and converts themselves who, though in possession of only a part of Christian truth, showed no reluctance in sharing with others what they themselves had learned. It would also seem that, in the providence of God, the unsettled times contributed to an openness and responsiveness to new ideas on the part of the people. The work of evangelization had commenced with a solid foundation in the lives of the Japanese people themselves. The indigenous nature of the initial stage of the Japanese Orthodox Church was to continue throughout its history.

Soon after Nicholas returned, a group gathered under him for instruction in Christian doctrine. Some of these were the inquirers who had previously studied with Sawabe. After a number of them had received baptism, three went back to their home area of Sendai as evangelists. It is characteristic of the zeal and faith of the converts that they went without arrangements having been made for their financial support. The evangelists, unwilling to burden others, anticipated providing for themselves by their own labor.

Early in 1872 Nicholas moved to Tokyo, primarily on the advice of Sawabe, who regarded Hakodate as being too far away to influence the entire nation. This was a decisive move for the mission. In the city Nicholas eventually succeeded in purchasing a piece of land on a hillside overlooking Tokyo proper. On the land, originally registered in the name of the Russian legation, Nicholas established a school and continued the work he had begun in Hakodate. On this same site he later built a cathedral, which, while officially called the Cathedral of the Resurrection, was called by the Japanese "Nicolai-Do" ("House of Nicholas").[8]

The work did not progress without tribulations. Several converts were imprisoned for a while, among them Sawabe and Sakai.[9] This first imprisonment was for about two months. Later Sakai was arrested again, ostensibly on another charge, but in reality because he was a Christian. However, the authorities found it necessary to release him because of his Christian witness among the inmates of the prison. "To keep him in prison was nearly equivalent to placing a Christian chaplain there."[10] The official persecution ended with a decree issued on February 10, 1873, that ordered the removal of the anti-Christian edict from the public notice boards.

With the work of the mission developing so rapidly there were not sufficient priests to govern the work of the church. Nicholas turned to the tradition of the Orthodox Church, which provided for lay representation at church councils.[11] Every two years the Great Synod met, with lay delegates present from every congregation. The Great Synod decided on the business of the individual congregations and the Japanese Church as a whole.

The first Japanese to be ordained to the priesthood was Sawabe, with Sakai being ordained as deacon. These were performed by a Russian bishop who was visiting Japan in 1875. Five more evangelists were ordained in 1878, traveling to Vladivostok for the service. The number of Japanese priests rose steadily. In 1883 there were eleven, in 1890 eighteen.

At the outbreak of the Russo-Japanese War, Nicholas, who by that time was a bishop, faced the difficult decision of whether to stay in Japan or return to Russia. Two priests, who were part of the Russian diplomatic mission and who assisted him in the mission work, returned home. Nicholas called a council of workers and Christian leaders to ask their opinion. It was their unanimous feeling that he should remain. Accepting this decision, Nicholas stayed in Japan during the course of the war, though he withdrew from the public prayers, since in the Orthodox liturgy these include prayers for the nation and its armed forces,[12] and he as a Russian subject should not pray for the defeat of his country.[13]

The Church's progress was slowed by the war. However, the Japanese priests had an unusual opportunity to minister to their fellow Orthodox believers in the form of Russian prisoners of war. There were 73,000 Russian prisoners in Japan and the Japanese Orthodox Church attempted to meet their spiritual needs. Out of gratitude the Russians constructed several chapels for the Church.

During the war years, Nicholas kept working on the translation of religious literature into Japanese.[14] In 1906 Nicholas was raised to the rank of archbishop. He had the privilege in 1911 of celebrating fifty years of missionary service. When he died on February 16, 1912, the Japanese Orthodox Church had a membership of 33,017 organized in 266 congregations and served by 35 Japanese priests, 22 deacons, and 106 catechists.

Recognition of Nicholas's accomplishments has not been limited to Orthodox authors. Bishop Tucker of the Episcopal Church called him "the outstanding missionary of the nineteenth century."[15] Richard Drummond adeptly sums up the measure of the man thus:

> The life and life-fruits of Nicholas compel us to recognize him as one of the greatest missionaries of the modern era. In accordance with Orthodox tradition he respected highly the language and cultural traditions of the people among whom he served. He respected the people and loved them as persons. He went beyond the common traditions of Orthodoxy in freeing his work to an extraordinary extent from the political aims and interests of his homeland. His apostleship was remarkably nonpolemical for the day; he was in singular fashion an apostle of peace among men. His method of evangelization was concentrated upon the family, and he stressed above all the raising up of national workers and the indigenization of the Church, even as he urged it to remember its distinctive association with the kingdom of God.[16]

The example set by Nicholas and followed by the clergy was one of evangelical poverty. This affected the social classes they were able to reach with the result that most of the converts were drawn from the poorer classes. As long as the work could be supported from Russia, this did not have any effect on the Church. Perhaps it even contributed to its growth.[17] However, when the Russian Revolution cut off mission funds, the effect of not having an adequate local support base was felt. Without the supply of outside funds, the seminary and other educational institutions had to be closed and the number of clergy reduced.

The Japanese Orthodox Church has continued to bear witness to the Orthodox faith. The Cathedral of the Resurrection was destroyed by the earthquake of 1923. Through the sacrificial giving of the Japanese the cathedral was rebuilt. In addition to the problems arising from the destruction caused by the earthquake, the political situation in Japan contributed to ever increasing pressures on the Church to break its ties with Moscow. Compelled by the Japanese government to prepare a new constitution, the Church was forced to declare its independence in 1940. After World War II the Church submitted to the jurisdiction of the North American Metropolitanate rather than return to Moscow's jurisdiction.[18] However, with the granting of autocephalous status to the North American Metropolitanate (which then became with several other groups the Orthodox Church of America),[19] the Japanese Orthodox Church retained its autonomous status under the Patriarchate of Moscow.[20]

THE MISSION TO CHINA

The Orthodox Church in China had a strange beginning.[21] In 1683 the members of a Russian exploration party were captured in the border area of Siberia claimed by both Russia and China. Taken to Peking as prisoners, they were eventually enrolled in the military establishment of the emperor and given a section of the city wall to defend. Accompanying the exploration party had been Maxim Leontiev, parish priest of the fortress of Albazin. The Russians were allowed to practice their religion and the emperor gave them an old Buddhist temple to use as a church. Their number was added to in 1686 when the fortress of Albazin fell to the Chinese and some of its Cossack defenders were given the option of serving the Chinese emperor. The Cossacks took Chinese wives and soon became "denationalized" but nevertheless remained Orthodox. At the very beginning the removal of the Russians to China was seen as an opportunity to work for the conversion of the Chinese.[22] In 1692 some Chinese were baptized, including one of Mandarin rank.[23]

Peter the Great was quite interested in Orthodox work in China and proposed sending an entire delegation. The Chinese were not as ready to receive the Russians as Peter was to send them. Whether Peter's motives were purely evangelistic or controlled by political aspirations remains a moot point.[24] The members of the Russian mission were considered by the Chinese to be Chinese civil servants, since they acted in the capacity of chaplains to the Orthodox-descended guardsmen. This arrangement of having all the missionaries considered to be Chinese civil servants continued until 1737. However, the mission was still supported by the Chinese government until 1858.[25]

The religious work of the Russians was primarily confined to preserving the faith of the Albazin descendants. Members of the mission were also engaged in the study of Oriental languages. "In the practical field we find no real missionary activity. . . . For two centuries the contribution of the Orthodox missionaries of Peking was limited to scientific research and production."[26]

A revival of missionary activity occurred after 1858 when the diplomatic legation was separated from the mission. The monk Isaias Polikin was able to establish a Christian community at Dun-Dinan. He worked at creating an indigenous clergy but efforts along this front proceeded slowly. It was not until 1884 that a native Chinese was ordained to the priesthood. On the whole the mission was better known for the Orientalists it produced and for its scientific research. The lesson is not lost on modern Orthodox missiologists. Anastasios Yannoulatos observes that "All these facts serve to illustrate the point that a sound theoretical basis, together with education and good will, are not enough for a substantial and sustained growth of missionary work. . . . The Orthodox did not try to exploit the favorable circumstances which prevailed for the spread of the faith."[27]

The mission took a new turn with the arrival of Innocent Figourovsky. He had four aims: first, to deepen the knowledge of the Chinese Christians by upgrading preaching and catechism; second, to pay special attention to the youth—in particular, he strengthened the school system; third, publishing—he set up a printing press on which he published a Russian-Chinese dictionary; fourth, to enlarge the social work and to build new mission stations, both of which he accomplished. Innocent's work, however, was almost totally destroyed in the Boxer Rebellion. All churches but one were burned; the press and library also were lost. The Orthodox had a greater loss *in proportion* to their numerical strength than did either the Roman Catholics or the Protestants.[28]

Innocent, now a bishop, returned to China after the rebellion and started to rebuild. The money paid in compensation for the losses incurred enabled a building program to commence. He was an innovative missionary. To minister to the spiritual needs of the 80,000 Orthodox in Manchuria, many of whom were working on the railroad line, he turned some railway cars into chapels and schools. Of his thirty-four workers, fifteen were artisans and technicians.[29] The approaches used bore results. "It is clear that the Russian Church had had a striking growth in the opening years of the twentieth century. However, when compared with the Roman Catholics and Protestants it remained distinctly a minority enterprise."[30]

The Russian Revolution carried in its wake mixed blessings for the Orthodox mission in China. On the one hand, funds were cut off, forcing the closure of many missionary stations. On the other hand, the immigration of White Russians added appreciably to the Orthodox element in China. Most of the Russians settled in Manchuria, and the Diocese of Harbin became a center of Orthodoxy even under the Japanese occupation.[31] An Orthodox university and a theological seminary were both founded in Harbin. However, in spite of this activity, it would seem that the emigration from Russia slowed rather than speeded up the work of the Orthodox mission. Yannoulatos suggests some possible reasons: (1) a hesitancy to engage in proselytizing in a host country; (2) absorption of clergy into ministering to the needs of refugees; (3) a lack of missionary vision, leading to a ghetto mentality.[32]

The Orthodox Church continued in China, despite the problems associated with World War II and the Communist takeover of the mainland. This led to the Orthodox Church of China having a Chinese bishop in 1950 and becoming autonomous in 1957. According to figures published in 1961, there were an estimated 20,000 Orthodox believers.[33] However, since the activities of the Red Guards in the autumn of 1966 in closing all places of worship then still open, it is not clear what the position of the Orthodox Church is now. The Orthodox Church, in spite of its Russian connection, fared no better than other Christian Churches.[34]

THE MISSION TO KOREA

The Orthodox Church's missionary work in Korea was established later than the other missions discussed above. Late in the nineteenth century some

Korean emigrants in Russia had become Orthodox.[35] In order to provide for the spiritual nurture of these Orthodox Koreans who returned to their country, and to further the progress of Orthodoxy among the Korean nation, a mission was established in July of 1897.[36] The Korean government would not grant the missionaries sent out by the Holy Synod permission to enter Korea.[37] For two years they waited at the border town of Novokievsk before finally returning to St. Petersburg.[38] The visas were at last granted after long negotiations and the first missionaries arrived in Korea in 1900.

The head of the mission, Archimandrite Chrysanthe Scetkovskij, diligently worked at strengthening the Orthodox Koreans, who for a long time had been bereft of the sacraments. In this work, as well as in his efforts at evangelism, he saw the necessity for the translation into Korean of the liturgy, catechism, and the ordinary prayers. He applied to the head of the China Mission, Innocent Figourovsky, for assistance in this task, as the mission was well known for its work in this area. However, the outbreak of the Boxer Rebellion with the martyrdom of the Chinese Christians and the destruction of the library put an end to any assistance from that quarter. The translation work was abandoned, and the efforts of the missionaries were devoted to furthering the other aspects of mission, such as the establishment of a school.[39]

The Russo-Japanese War halted all work of the mission. Korea was unable to remain neutral and the Russian nationals, including the missionaries, were forced to leave. After the war, the mission returned under a new head, Archimandrite Paul Ivanovsky. The six years under his leadership proved to be the most successful for the mission. Many works were translated, including the entire collection of liturgical books. Under his administration the first Korean was ordained to the priesthood. The missionary work continued under other leaders until the Russian Revolution when, as in the case of other Orthodox missions already surveyed, the work suffered a severe setback and its further development was arrested.

Subsequently the Korean Church came under the supervision of the Diocese of Japan. The Orthodox Church has suffered because of the vicissitudes of Korean history. During the Korean War, the Church was without pastoral oversight owing to the capture and exile of the Korean priest, Alexios Kim. This action nearly caused the extinction of the Church. However, help in the form of chaplains accompanying the Greek Expeditionary Force, "sent by Divine Providence at the most critical and difficult moment," enabled the Church to continue.[40] This is another demonstration of the assistance given by Orthodox to their fellow Orthodox of a different nationality. At present there is a small Orthodox community in Korea. Some young Koreans were trained in Athens. The priest of the Seoul congregation as of this writing is Father Daniel Na, a graduate of Holy Cross School of Theology in Massachusetts.[41]

Chapter VI

Orthodox Missions Today

THE ORTHODOX DIASPORA

From the time of the Russian Revolution until the early 1960's, no organized Orthodox missionary work existed.[1] This is not to say that during this period there was no spread of the Orthodox Church. Indeed, in geographical terms the twentieth century has witnessed the greatest territorial expansion in the Church's history. But the spread of Orthodox believers and the subsequent planting of Orthodox Churches was not a missionary venture. The Orthodox Churches followed the Orthodox faithful and ministered to the needs of the immigrant communities. The language of worship was the language of the immigrants' homeland: Greek, Russian, Serbian, and so forth.[2] There was no organized effort to spread the Orthodox faith. The Church was seen as a social and cultural home as well as a place of spiritual sustenance.[3]

It is not surprising that linguistic and cultural distinctives kept the Orthodox Church in the Diaspora a church of immigrants and their descendants. In addition to the ethnocentricity of the immigrants' churches, their financial position did not enable them to carry out missionary work and their social standing kept non-Orthodox from wanting to emulate them.[4] While both the social status and the financial resources of the Orthodox have improved, the ethnic consciousness of the Orthodox Diaspora is still a force to be reckoned with. The problem of creating a nonethnic Orthodoxy that is able to adapt to living in the Diaspora will not be easily solved.[5]

This ethnocentricity that has characterized Orthodoxy, especially in the Diaspora where opportunities existed for evangelistic witness,[6] has given rise to the notion that the Orthodox Church takes no interest in missions. Orthodox theologians generally admit that the impression given by the Orthodox is one of noninvolvement in missionary concerns.[7]

Therefore, when there does appear to be some renewal of missionary interest in the Orthodox Church, questions are raised both within and without the Orthodox Church. The work toward external mission, as advocated, for example, by the Inter-Orthodox Centre of Athens, was met with doubting

44

opposition.[8] Mission to the non-Orthodox in the lands of the Diaspora seemed difficult enough, but foreign mission was regarded as practically impossible.

THE AFRICAN ORTHODOX CHURCH

The renewal of missionary interest and the establishment of a mission program in the Church of Greece and the Greek Orthodox Archdiocese of North and South America came about by the phenomenon of an African Independent Church. The history of the African Orthodox Church is available from several sources.[9] It was *not,* as Walbert Bühlmann claims,[10] a product of Greek Orthodox missionary work. Rather, three separate groups formed around charismatic leadership.[11] These groups later joined together and petitioned the patriarch of Alexandria and All Africa for official recognition. Though this was granted in 1945, no action toward establishment of episcopal authority was taken until 1958, when a metropolitan was appointed by the patriarch of Alexandria.[12] Even this was not a resident metropolitan for the area, but one who resided in Egypt.[13] D. E. Wentink, writing on the Orthodox Church in East Africa says:

> Since 1959 the Patriarchate of Alexandria has assumed direct responsibility for the African Greek Orthodox Church. It seems, however, inadequate to speak of a Greek Orthodox mission in East Africa. The origin of this Christian community lies within Africa itself. Some African priests have been ordained by the Metropolitan and in several places Orthodox Churches are built with the aid of the Greek Orthodox Church . . . but on the whole the African Orthodox Churches rely very much on themselves.[14]

The preceding comment was made in 1968. Subsequently, more aid has been provided to the churches in East Africa. As one might assume, the situation has not always been tension-free. When other churches begun by missionary ventures were becoming free from external control, a church that had been founded on the principle of the African believers having complete control was coming under the jurisdiction of a Greek patriarch.[15] David Barrett speaks of conflicts with Greek missionaries who came to assist the Church.[16] There was also disagreement concerning the question of establishing an African episcopate. Furthermore, while the Church needed educated priests and teachers, those sent overseas for training often clashed with the older priests when they returned.[17]

In spite of the origin, problems, and internal conflicts, the Orthodox Churches of East Africa[18] have been responsible in large measure for the missionary renewal of the Church of Greece. To quote Wentink again:

> Spartas' visit to Greece in 1959 [Spartas (Ruben Mukasa) was the founder of Orthodoxy in Uganda] started a chain-reaction of activity in

the Greek Orthodox Church. The Greek Church was confronted with the strong request to send Greek Christians to Africa. Spartas appealed to the Orthodox to start a mission, and since his visit the search for a missionary emphasis in Orthodoxy has received more impetus. The results have been the organization of several groups pledging themselves to prayer and financial help, mainly youth groups, and a renewed orientation to the missionary situation in the Christian Church in general.[19]

Not only the Church of Greece, but also the Greek Orthodox Archdiocese of North and South America has received stimulation from the work in East Africa. In 1965 Theodore Nankyamas toured seventy-five Greek parishes in the United States to raise support for the work in Uganda.[20] Besides the visits of Africans to Greece and the United States, tours of the work in East Africa have been undertaken by Greeks. The reports of these expeditions have done much to raise the missionary consciousness of the established Orthodox Churches.[21]

Missionaries have gone out from Greece and the United States to help the African Orthodox.[22] However, for the most part, assistance has come in the form of financial aid and scholarships for overseas study. There is no doubt that the connection with world Orthodoxy has been beneficial to the African Orthodox.[23]

One could perhaps characterize this episode of Orthodox mission history as the case of a mission looking for a church. From the inception of the African Orthodox Church, Spartas was looking for recognition and help from other Orthodox Churches.[24] This was never seen as being intrinsically opposed to independence. The basic selfhood of the Church is evidenced by the constitution of the Church in Kenya: "The African Greek Orthodox Church shall be controlled by the Africans under the supervision and guidance of the Holy Ghost, through the spiritual, physical and fraternal help of the Holy Patriarchal See of Alexandria, Egypt. It shall be an absolutely independent Church in all internal administration."[25]

The exact status and size of the African Orthodox Church in the 1980s is somewhat difficult to determine. The latest published material (1980) on the Orthodox Church in Uganda gives no statistics.[26] Norman Horner in 1975 reported that African Orthodox in Kenya were estimated to be between 70,000 and 250,000, although he reported that observers favored the higher figure.[27] He gives the Ugandan Orthodox community at 30,000 and the number of believers in Tanzania at less than 100.[28]

As of 1984 there was no priest in Tanzania. The Orthodox Church in Kenya has gone through a difficult period, which was marked by conflict between the African auxiliary bishop, Arthur Gathuna, and the Greek archbishop appointed to the East Africa Diocese by the patriarch of Alexandria. One source of tension was the Kenyans' perception of increasing Greek control over their Church.

The future looks more promising with the appointment in 1982 of Anastasios Yannoulatos as metropolitan for the East Africa Diocese. As the architect of the Orthodox missionary movement, Yannoulatos has the sensitivity to bring healing and restoration to the Kenyan Church. Since his appointment, he has been able to open the seminary in Nairobi. Funds for this seminary had been provided by Archbishop Makarios from his visit in 1971 and the actual physical structure had been completed, but unoccupied, for several years. Under the direction of Professor Andrew Tillyrides, the seminary accepted its first class of twelve students in 1983.[29]

The problems faced by the African Orthodox Churches reflect the background from which those problems arose and the realities—political, social, and economic—that confront modern Africa. Perhaps the most encouraging feature for the worldwide Orthodox Church is the tenacity that the African Churches show in remaining Orthodox.

In light of its origins and in view of the present structure of the Church, with its own African hierarchy,[30] it is not possible to consider this Church a product of mission in the sense of the Orthodox Churches considered above in this chapter. Nevertheless, the relationship with the Orthodox Church affords Orthodox missiologists with both a practical situation in which to work[31] and a testing ground for patristic missiology. The needs of African Orthodoxy are a cogent reminder to the Orthodox faithful that mission is a present reality as well as a historical fact. It is perhaps no exaggeration to say that the Orthodox Churches that contribute to the work in Africa have received more than they have given in terms of a renewed spiritual vision.

Chapter VII

The Aim of Mission

From the inception of the Christian community to the present time, "Mission has always been the activity of the Church."[1] But serious theological reflection as to the nature and character of the missionary task of the Church did not arise in the earliest history of the Church. As J. H. Bavinck points out, it is not unusual to undertake an activity that is the obvious course of action.[2] So it was also with the missionary expansion of the Church. Reflection did not take place until obstacles were encountered.

Bavinck's observations apply as well to the Orthodox Church and its apparent lack of a scientific approach to mission theology. From the outset the task of bringing the gospel to the nonbelievers needed little or no theological justification. As has been shown above, the Orthodox Church has a long history of missionary activity. Serious theological reflection on the missionary mandate was formulated in the Patristic period.[3] John Chrysostom is but one example of an Eastern Father who actively supported in word and deed missions to nonbelievers.[4] Important Russian missionary strategists have been discussed above, demonstrating that creative thought on the missionary mandate was not absent in the Orthodox Church.

All of this theological reflection belongs to the fullness of the Orthodox Tradition. Contemporary Orthodox theologians are aware of their heritage and make free use of it in formulating the beginnings of an Orthodox theology of mission. Therefore, while a profitable study could be made of either Patristic missions or Russian missionary thought and practice, the purpose of this study is to examine the approach to the science of missions taken by contemporary Orthodox theologians. The study will naturally delve into the historical aspects of Orthodox missions, but the goal will be the description of mission theology from the contemporary Orthodox perspective.

THE ORTHODOX PERSPECTIVE

It has been pointed out above (see chap. 1) that Orthodoxy is not understood in the West. The Orthodox are generally thought either to be like the Roman

Catholics or to occupy a theological position between Protestantism and Roman Catholicism. The expectations of the Western Churches frequently force Orthodox leaders to construct an Orthodox position on a subject in opposition to the Protestant and Roman Catholic positions. As Schmemann has pointed out, this is a false position for Orthodoxy to occupy.[5] The different history of the Orthodox Church has led to a different theological development.

In certain areas, among them missiology, Orthodox theology has not been systematically developed. The lack of systemization is conceded by the Orthodox theologian of missions, Anastasios Yannoulatos, who believes that the solution is "to start from the general presuppositions and principles of Orthodox theology and to meditate upon Orthodox soteriology, ecclesiology and eschatology in the perspective of mission."[6] This task has not been undertaken as yet by an Orthodox theologian. What has been produced are articles or short studies that point to the eventual development of Orthodox mission theology. However, simply because there is no complete systematic development of mission theology is not to imply that nothing can be said on the subject. A great deal has been written by contemporary Orthodox theologians that indicates the basic structure of the Orthodox theological understanding of mission.

This contemporary missiological writing is a primary focus of this study. These Orthodox authors draw heavily from the historical work of Orthodox missions as surveyed in chapters 3 through 5. Therefore, their work reflects the historical understanding of the Church. Because these Orthodox missiologists stand in the tradition of Orthodoxy, encompassing both its history and its theology, they serve as guides for the construction of an Orthodox theology of mission. Certain limitations become apparent in the plan. First, not all areas of the subject can be covered as adequately as would be desirable. This is due largely to the lack of material written on those areas. Second—and this is not in a real sense a limitation—because of the different theological frame of reference between East and West, certain subjects are handled in slightly different ways. However, it should be clear to the reader what the corresponding subjects are in the Western theological framework. Third, following the same line of thought just given, certain subjects are not dealt with at all, as they would need to be were this a study of Western mission theology. Other subjects, which are appropriate to the Orthodox understanding of mission, are dealt with instead.

For the sake of comparing the approaches East and West, chapters 7 through 10 will consider an analysis of mission theology in terms of aims, methods, and motives. The succeeding chapters will deal with the liturgy as a method of mission and the church as the agent of mission.

THE ULTIMATE AIM: THE GLORY OF GOD

In discussing the Orthodox understanding of the aim or goal of missionary work, one is immediately thrust into one of the primary emphases of Orthodox theology, the glory of God. Yannoulatos writes: "A key to the Orthodox understanding of the process of history is, I think, 'the glory of the most holy God,' viewed in the perspective of His infinite love. . . . The process of human history, of which the Bible speaks, begins and ends with the glory of God.'"[7]

The theme of glory does not begin with human history, but was a precondition to creation. The Lord Jesus Christ points to this glory when he prays to the Father, asking to be glorified "with the glory which I had with thee before the world was made" (Jn. 17:5). Nor does the theme end here on earth, but carries on into eternity. The new city of God where the redeemed will dwell together with him has itself the glory of God (Rev. 21:11). Viewed from the perspective of eternity past, that is, before the creation, and eternity future, that is, after the new creation, the glory of God is a continuous manifestation. And this is how it should be, as God is unchangeable.

Viewed from the perspective of human history, the revelation of God's glory to humankind, and the reflection and increase (by praise) of God's glory by humans is seen in a different light. Yannoulatos writes: "Man rejected the absolute glory of God and, in seeking to create his own glory and in worshiping himself, he separated himself fom the living God and provoked a cosmic catastrophe—the appearance of a new condition, death, in which the glory of the living God is overshadowed. The sin of men is a continual hindrance to the diffusion and manifestation of the glory.'"[8] God does not give human beings up entirely. There are still revelations of God's glory to humans. Examples of these revelations can be found in the Old Testament (e.g.. Exod. 3:2; Isa. 6). Furthermore, God repeatedly sends his servants to warn people. Finally in the fullness of time, he sends his Son, the revelation of the Father (Jn. 14:9).

As Yannoulatos points out, the Lord's whole life was characterized by glory. At the birth of Jesus, the angels sing of God's glory. By his miracles, his glory was manifested. On the Mount of Transfiguration the disciples saw a demonstration of the glory that was to come.[9] This glory is in God's plan for redeemed individuals to share.[10] It is, however, the cross and the resurrection that most fully reveal the glory of God.

> In Orthodox worship the cross is presented mainly as *the* symbol of victory and glory, and always closely connected with the Resurrection. The distinction between "the agony of the cross" and "the glory of the Resurrection" which is so common in the West is unusual in the Orthodox Church. Both are revelations and manifestations of the glory of God. In general, the Incarnation, the Passion, the Resurrection—the whole movement of the divine philanthropy in *kenosis*—are not only expressions of the divine love, but at the same time new manifestations of the glory of God. One could say that *agape* and glory are two aspects of the same thing: the life of God.[11]

The bringing together of these aspects, agape and glory, emphasizes again the central themes of Orthodox theology. Around these themes the Orthodox theological framework is constructed. These are the characteristics of Orthodox theology that form the focal point for Orthodox worship. It is not at all strange, then, that they also form the focal point of Orthodox missiology. For the love of God and the glory of God come together in the redemption of individuals. God, who is the God of love, loves people and works toward their redemption. The redeemed in turn praise God for his purpose in redemption and thus spread further abroad the glory of God.

The redeeming work of God does not end in the redemption of humankind, but extends to the redemption of the cosmos. The creation of God will reach the purpose and place for which it was created. The restoration of the universe supplies an added dimension to God's mission. God's mission is an overall plan that redeems human beings and renews and restores the physical creation to what God had intended it to be before he created it. In all this, the glory of God is revealed.

If the ultimate purpose of God's mission is the revelation of his glory, then God's purpose in calling humankind is for humans to be partakers of the divine glory. The created order is to be a reflection of God's glory. This is clear from the biblical teaching on the subject. Furthermore, God has given a share of his mission to the Church so that the two are (or should be) the same mission. Therefore, as to the ultimate goal of Christian mission, Yannoulatos can write: "Since the Christian mission is incorporated into God's mission, the final goal of our mission surely cannot be different from His. And this purpose, as the Bible (especially *Ephesians* and *Colossians*) makes clear, is the "recapitulation" (*anakephalaiosis*) of the universe in Christ and our participation in the divine glory, the eternal, final glory of God."[12]

Jesus Christ after the ascension becomes the focal point of the new humanity. Yannoulatos quotes Roels, showing how Christ is "the rallying point of the restored unity, the reintegrating center of human and cosmic life."[13] Christ calls the nations to himself; the Church as an imitator of Christ also calls human beings to their new center, the Lord Jesus Christ. "We could say," writes Yannoulatos, "that the centripetal tendency of the Old Testament . . . is replaced not so much by the centrifugal movement of the disciples towards the nations as by a new centripetal movement, whose center is Christ."[14]

It is not merely to rally around him that Christ calls human beings. He calls them to be disciples, to carry out his commands and to discharge his mission. But he also calls them to himself so that they might share in his glory (1 Pet. 5:1). "Our participation in this glory has already begun with our incorporation into Christ."[15] While Christian believers partake of the divine glory now, the ultimate consummation and full complement of that glory is reached only in the return of Christ. "When Christ who is our life appears, then you also will appear with Him in glory" (Col. 3:4, RSV).

The process of glorification is thus seen as not yet having been completed. Believers partake now in the divine, but the full realization of that glory is yet to come. God is presently at work changing them, as it were, by degrees of glory (2 Cor. 3:18). Likewise, while all things are potentially reconciled by Christ, there remains the fulfillment and eschatological revelation of this reconciliation.

When all things are subjected to Christ, that is, when Christians are fully incorporated into Christ and the reconciliation of creation is complete, the end (*telos*) has not yet been reached. "When all things are subject to Him, then the Son Himself will also be subjected to Him who put all things under Him, that God may be all in all" (1 Cor. 15:28, RSV). The ultimate goal of mission is that the glory of God fill the universe.

Thus the purpose of mission is linked with God's cosmic plan from eternity for all eternity. From this perspective there can be only one ultimate aim, or goal, of mission, the furtherance of God's glory, which fits in fully with the framework in which Orthodox theology operates. The Church's mission, the mission of every Christian, is to acknowledge, promote, and participate in the glory of God.

THE IMMEDIATE AIMS OF MISSION

Having discussed the ultimate aim of mission, it remains now to discuss the immediate aims. This is not to imply that these aims are secondary to the true goal of mission; instead the reference here is to the stages, or steps, by which the ultimate goal is approached. They cannot be out of harmony and spirit with the ultimate goal. "The immediate goals of mission must surely follow the same line and direction as the ultimate goal; they must be the starting point and preparation for that goal. In the march of the Christian mission, our eyes must constantly be fixed on the objective, on the end, the *telos*, if mission is not to lose its ultimate direction," Yannoulatos writes.[16]

The extent to which this principle has been consistently maintained is certainly open to debate. The immediate aims of Orthodox missions have frequently been in harmony with the ultimate aim, as stated so forcefully by Yannoulatos. It is also true that one can find examples where the intermediate aims of mission conducted by the Orthodox Church seem to be unconnected with the ultimate aim. Though the concern of this study is the theology of mission as understood by contemporary Orthodox theologians, yet the historical precedents of mission are worthy of examination, both to reveal the correct Orthodox approach to missiology as well as to ascertain the errors of past approaches.[17]

It is apparent from the discussion of the ultimate aim of mission, the glory of God, that Orthodox and Western concepts of the aim of mission are similar, if not identical.[18] This impression will be further strengthened by the discussion of the secondary, or immediate, aims of missions. In fact, the differences between East and West are "not so much in the definition of the common aims of missionary activity as in our choice of the means of realizing them."[19]

The Planting of the Church

The word "planting" is a better word to use than "extension." In the Orthodox tradition and the best of Orthodox mission practice, the goal is a national church that embodies the particular characteristics of that people. This should not be confused with the concept of a *volks kirche* in which the entire nation is considered Christian, although there have been tendencies toward this in predominantly Orthodox countries.[20] Rather, the goal is the establishment of a local church in which the people can worship God in the light of their own natural gifts and characteristics, giving to the Church universal their distinctive contribution to the praise of God. Again we quote Yannoulatos:

> The establishment of the local Church which, through the mysteries and through her whole life, will participate in the praise and the life of the one holy, catholic and apostolic Church, whose head is Christ (Eph. 1:22, 4:15, 5:23, Col. 1:18), is surely the basic goal of mission, according to Orthodox tradition and theology. In speaking of the establishment of the local Church, we do not mean a spiritual colony or appendix of another local Church. In each country, the Church is called to glorify God with her own voice. That means that in missionary work there must be a sincere respect for the identity of every nation; an investigation into the way in which God gave His witness in the past of each particular people (Acts 14:16–17: *ouk amarturon apheken heauton*), an endeavor not only to adapt, but also to incarnate the Logos of God into the language and customs of the country; and the sanctification of the people's characteristics, so that they may become truly themselves, develop their own voice and add their own contribution to the common doxological hymn— always in harmony with the praise of the whole Church.[21]

Whether the goal not to produce spiritual colonies has always been met would need to be settled by an exhaustive historical survey. The Byzantine practice of appointing Greeks to the episcopal sees of "mission" churches was certainly detrimental to the development of local control. The Bulgarian Orthodox Church is an example of this type of control from Constantinople. Converted in the ninth century by Byzantine missionaries, the Bulgarians were granted ecclesiastical independence in 918, only to lose it in the eleventh century after Bulgaria was defeated in 1018 by Basil II. The Church's independence was reestablished in the thirteenth century, but again abolished when the Turks gained control of Bulgaria. "The question of independence was long a sore point in the nineteenth and twentieth centuries, for the Bulgarians were governed by Greek bishops who, especially in the towns, sought to suppress the Slavonic liturgy and generally Hellenize the Church."[22] Such abuses of Orthodox mission theory often had political motives behind them. (The political element in missionary work is dealt with below.)

In the best examples of Orthodox missions, the goal was the establishment of local churches. The repeated emphasis on the use of the vernacular and the establishment of an indigenous clergy bears witness to the desire, if not the outcome, to have the church become incarnate in the life of the people.

What are the necessary prerequisites for the establishment of a local church? Before people can believe, the gospel must be preached. "The preaching of the Gospel is a basic condition for this fulfillment, and is consequently the immediate objective and goal of mission."[23] The fulfillment spoken of here is the eschatological fulfillment, the goal of glorifying God. To reach this ultimate goal, men and women must be incorporated in the body of Christ. There are two classes of people, those joined to Christ and those apart from Christ. Preaching the gospel is at the very heart of mission. Furthermore, the preaching has as its aim the transformation of human beings. "So mission is not a question of proclaiming some ethical truths or principles, but the beginning of the transfiguration inaugurated by the 'light of the gospel of the glory of Christ. . . .' "[24] N. A. Nissiotis says: "It is a great mistake when we think that by discussing social questions, or by analysing the secular environment, or by helping in educational and material needs we are performing mission. . . . There is one immediate need for those outside the Church: to be converted and become members of this community in a visible, concrete form."[25]

The main task of mission is the conversion of those outside the Church. Those who do not share in the divine life offered by Christ are in need of this one thing. Service, even service done in the name of Christ, "is not absolutely necessary as a sign of the authenticity of the Christian mission."[26] People do not believe because of service; "they are called to believe because they are converted by the power of the saving grace which is to be announced to them by word and shared by them through the sacraments in the Church."[27]

Thus preaching is preaching with a purpose, that people might believe and be converted. "Conversion" is the proper word to use, since those who are outside the Church need to be introduced to the grace of God in Christ. Yet mission is not just to the outsider, but is also "the way in which Church people . . . try to arouse the sleeping faith of the nominal Christian."[28] It is therefore evident that the aim of mission is not merely the gaining of converts, but the active incorporation of the believers, all believers, into the life of the Church.

There are two missiological reasons for this emphasis on incorporation. The first is that only in the Christian community can people participate in the life of Christ given by God. To be truly what they were meant to be, they must experience the grace of God. In the Orthodox tradition this grace is transmitted to people by the work of the Holy Spirit in the sacraments. In the Holy Eucharist, in particular, people partake of the spiritual nourishment needed to share in the life of Christ (cf. Jn. 6:53–58).[29] "The sacraments constitute the Church. Only in the sacraments does the Christian Community pass beyond the purely human measure and become the Church."[30] Therefore, only as a participant in the life of the community through the sacraments can one really fulfill the goal of Christ's mission for oneself.

The second aim, or reason, for incorporating the convert into the Church is so that the Church itself in its doxological and liturgical service may be a witness to mission.

A worshiping liturgical community is not only the image of the realized communion between God and man and of the union of the human race in one Body in front of God without any exception or distinction of individuals; it is not only the bulwark where the principalities of this world are weak and find no place. It is, basically, the missionary outcry of the Church triumphant to the whole world and the doxological announcement of His Kingdom which is present and which is to come.[31]

In addition to the preaching of the gospel, the liturgical display of the gospel forms the Orthodox witness to the world. Rather than being a self-centered and self-satisfied community in worship, the Church reaches out in mission to the world. Alexander Schmemann sees two aspects of the Church's response to the gift of God. "The first one is *God-centered*: it is sanctification, the growth in holiness, of both the Christian individual and the Christian community, the 'acquisition by them of the Holy Spirit'. . . ."[32] The second aspect in the Church's response is "*man or world-centered*."[33] Therefore, in responding to God's gift in worship, the Church not only fulfills the conditions leading to its own members' sanctification, but also witnesses to the world. The liturgy is offered on behalf of the world that the world might be reconciled to God. Seen in this way, liturgy is service, missionary service to the world. "Although the sacrament of the Eucharist since the very origin of the Church, was a celebration closed to the outsiders, and full participation in the Eucharist remains reserved for the members of the Church, liturgical worship as a whole is an obvious form of witness and mission."[34]

Without anticipating the fuller discussion of the meaning of liturgy for mission in Orthodoxy, it can be stated that this liturgical witness is not as paradoxical as it might first appear to those of Western tradition.[35] For in the very least, the worshiping community gives witness to a higher authority to which it owes its ultimate allegiance. Worship points to the transcendent reality, Orthodox liturgical worship all the more because of its repeated praise to the Triune God. But more can be said of the powerful witness of the Orthodox liturgy.

The traditional story of the conversion of Prince Vladimir, and through him the Russian people, is based on the positive impression the Russians had of Orthodox worship. The account relates how Vladimir, dissatisfied with the religion of his fathers, examined in turn the four main options open to him: Islam, Judaism, Latin Christianity, and Orthodox Christianity. After examining representatives of each position, he sent a high commission to observe the practices of each religion in its own territory. Unimpressed by the other rites they observed, Vladimir's nobles returned with glowing accounts of what they had seen in Saint Sophia in Constantinople: "When we stood in the temple we did not know where we were, for there is nothing else like it upon earth: there in truth God has his dwelling with men; and we can never forget the beauty we saw there. No one who has once tasted sweets will afterward take that which is bitter; nor can we now any longer abide in heathenism."[36]

Whatever weight is attached to this story, the fact remains that at that time Saint Sophia was a glorious sight. It "was probably the finest building in the world and certainly the richest product of Byzantine art."[37] Furthermore, the services held there were awe-inspiring and majestic, and would have been all the more so to the Russians, unaccustomed to such things.[38] Thus in the case of the beginning of Christianity in Russia, the liturgical witness of the Orthodox Church plays an important, if not decisive, role.

To conclude this section on the planting of the church, the following observations can be recorded.

1. The immediate aim of mission is the establishment of local churches. Included in this aim are the following goals: (a) the preaching of the gospel; (b) the conversion of pagans and the awakening of nominal Christians; (c) the incorporation of converts into the active life of the church; (d) the mobilization of the church, in its fullness and in all its manifestations, including the liturgical witness in the mission of God.

2. These aims are all in accord with the ultimate aim of mission, the glory of God.

As has been pointed out above, these aims are not peculiar or unique to Orthodoxy, but are in line with the missionary aims of other Christian Churches. The features that have been developed to a greater degree by the Orthodox—the place of the liturgy in missions and the concept of the church in missions—will be dealt with in succeeding chapters.

Political Aims in Mission

Although contemporary Orthodox mission work in the few places where it does exist is devoid of political aim, it will be useful to at least touch upon the subject because of its importance in the historical tradition of Orthodoxy. Before doing so, it is in order to examine possible objections to the subject's inclusion in this section. In the first place, the Church itself can have no political aims; therefore, to discuss the political aims of mission would appear to confound the role of the civil government with that of the Church. In the second place, is this not a confusion of missionary motivation with missionary aim? For if it is granted that some sort of political compromise is in view, does it not speak of the motivation for mission rather than its aim?

To answer these objections, one must look at the particular history of the Orthodox Church. From the time of Constantine, the Church has been closely allied with the state. Therefore, the aims of the state have become the aims of the Church.[39] The pattern continued in the Russian Church. This is not to say that every churchperson thought himself or herself to be subservient to the desires of the secular ruler; there are sufficient examples of those who were not to make such a claim ludicrous. It does, however, call attention to the close relationship that existed between the political aims of the secular ruler and the activity of the Church. At the same time, this close relationship does not preclude the aims of mission, as envisioned by the civil structure, being diametrically opposed to those championed by the ecclesiastical authorities. The aims could be, and very often were, complementary. It is further proper to speak of the "political aims" of mission instead of "motivation" because the concept in view is the purpose that is hoped to be gained rather than the impetus behind the missionary activity. The subject of the political, or civil, motivation of some missionaries will be dealt with later.

Political Aims in Byzantine Missions: The Mission to the Khazars

The Khazars were a Turko-Tartar nation occupying the lands between the Don and Volga rivers. They controlled the Crimea and were sufficiently powerful to be sought as an ally by the emperors of Constantinople.[40] When the suburbs of Constantinople were attacked on June 18, 860, by Russians intent on plunder,[41] the Byzantines recognized the need for a reaffirmation of an alliance between themselves and the Khazar empire. This was not the first time political necessity had brought the Byzantines and the Khazars together. They had joined forces in the past to war against the Persians and again to defend themselves against the Arabs.[42] While the Byzantine form of Christianity had entered Khazaria, the religious climate was also subject to Islamic and Jewish missions. The Jewish faith had the greatest degree of success, since one of the khazans, or rulers, accepted Judaism. Jewish sources date this conversion at about 730. By the first half of the ninth century, the Khazar upper classes had converted to Judaism.

Among those chosen to travel to the Khazar capital on the imperial embassy were the brothers Constantine and Methodius, who in later days were to gain a place in history as "the Apostles to the Slavs." The author of *The Life of Constantine*, which was written shortly after Constantine's death, would lead his readers to believe that the main purpose of the Byzantine embassy was to convert the Khazars to the Christian faith.[43] *The Life of Constantine* contains detailed accounts of the religious discussions held at the court. Among the questions discussed were the Trinity, the law of Moses, and Christian morality. The facts of the case appear somewhat differently, as the emperor sought the assurance that the Khazars would remain the allies of the Byzantines against the Russian threat. This seems to be confirmed by the message from the khazan to the emperor and recorded by Constantine's biographer. "We are friends of the Empire and we are ready to be at your service whenever you may wish it."[44]

If the mission was political in nature, why was Constantine chosen to take part? The answer may be that whereas the nobility had accepted Judaism, the majority of the Khazars were still pagans. As a result of the theological discussions in which Constantine participated, some 200 of them requested baptism, a request that their ruler allowed to be fulfilled.[45] The success achieved by the religious dimension of the mission could certainly aid its political aims. To have Christians in the court of the khazan would be a definite advantage. In presenting an able defense of the Christian faith, Constantine won the admiration of the Khazars. It is not to be supposed that the entire purpose of the embassy was religious; this is clearly the invention of Constantine's biographer. But that the embassy actually was sent out and that theological discussions took place in the khazan's court would seem to be well founded. Thus the "missionary work" undertaken among the Khazars bore fruit. While the evangelists themselves need not, and indeed should not, be considered tools of the emperor to accomplish a secular purpose, yet the close unity of church and state produced a situation that would seem strange in this age. The truth seems to be that apart from the necessity for a political mission, the religious mission would not have been undertaken.

Political Aims in Russian Missions: The Mission to the Chinese

The clearest example of the establishment of a religious mission for a political aim can be found in the story of the Russian mission to China. The history of the Orthodox Church in China dates back to the capture of some Russians by the Manchus in 1683. The priest Maxim Leontiev (Maksim Leont'ev is a variant of the name) was taken with them to Peking. Though "prisoners of war" in an undeclared war, they were treated relatively kindly and allowed to keep their Orthodox faith, being given an old Buddhist temple for their use as a church. The ecclesiastical authorities in Russia did not learn of the existence of this Orthodox Church in Peking for some ten years, when news of it was carried to Tobolsk by a returning trade caravan.[46] Maxim Leontiev had sent along with the caravan a request for some liturgical items. The request did not go unheeded and the next trade caravan departing for Peking carried with it the items and two priests who were to consecrate the church of Leontiev. The metropolitan of Siberia, who made all these arrangements, also wrote to the priest to encourage him in his mission. "And your imprisonment is not without advantage for the Chinese people since the light of Christ's Orthodox faith is being revealed to them by you."[47] It is noteworthy that the first communication from the religious authorities to the deported priest sees his plight as an opportunity for the advancement of the gospel.

The news of the Orthodox presence in Peking did not reach the tsar for still another three years. Peter the Great was himself in western Europe at the time, and the government minister who communicated this news to Peter also wrote to the tsar's host in Holland. The disclosure caused no small stir, as the nations of Europe were already anxious to exploit the land routes across Siberia to China. However, Peter was in no mind to allow unrestricted travel across his lands to China, so that the hopes held by men such as the philosopher Leibniz were dashed. Peter pressed his ministers for more information and was rewarded by hearing two or three years later of the true impoverished state of the Orthodox community in Peking. However, Peter had not waited for this information, but upon first hearing of the Orthodox presence ordered that his subjects (one can assume he meant those in China as well) "act carefully and not rashly" so as not to arouse the anger of the Chinese leadership.[48]

In 1700 Peter issued a ukase, which was mainly concerned with trade in Siberia and with China but also included a section on the propagation of the Orthodox faith in these areas. He called for study by some learned monks in the areas of language and culture to better refute these unbelievers and turn them soundly to Orthodoxy.[49] The missionary work in Siberia was already well under way when Peter issued his edict; however, the appointment of a new metropolitan gave added impetus to the work. One of the main benefits of this Christianizing was that the converted were now also considered to be Russianized as well. However successful the missionary work was in Siberia, there was not the accompanying success in fulfilling the portion of the edict that spoke of the conversion of the Chinese.

There appear to be two reasons for this lack of success. First, the Chinese gave no indication that they wanted to be evangelized. To be sure, they invited the Russians to send a replacement for Maxim Leontiev, but this was so he could minister to "their Russians," meaning those in the service of the Chinese. Furthermore, the Chinese desired to contact a Mongolian tribe, the direct access to whom was cut off by a hostile tribe. Therefore a lengthy detour through Russian territory was necessary. The plan evolved that the Chinese contingent on their return from their Mongolian embassy would collect the priests from Tobolsk. Thereby the permission for the priests to come to Peking could be seen as the reward for allowing the Chinese to cross Russian territory.[50]

It is clear from the correspondence that passed between the two empires that the Chinese regarded the clerical party that was coming to Peking to have religious duties with regard to the Albazinians only. The Manchus were working out their Inner Asian policy.

> Peking alone had to become the temporal capital of Inner Asia. . . . The symbolic force of a visit by the Dalai Lama or the Urga Khutughtu to Peking was worth more than all the cannon the Society of Jesus could cast and in the long run, if not immediately, cost much less. Manchu policy in Inner Asia was always intent on this kind of showmanship. . . . The same held true for the Russian "lamas." They traveled the road from Urga to Kalgan to Peking and prayed not in a Christian Church but in what was known in Peking as the *lo-ch'a miao* or Albazinian temple. And their journeys showed that Russian as well as Mongol clerics found it necessary to make regular peregrinations to a city that bustled with the business of looking after the peoples of the steppe. Inner Asia required this kind of consistent ideological control. . . . The Russian mission, despite itself, became part of the picture.[51]

Further evidence of the political usage of the Russian mission by the Manchus is to be found in their refusal to grant permission for an Orthodox bishop to reside in Peking. Bishop Innocent, the first to be appointed to the See of Peking, waited in vain for three years on the border before the Russians gave up and reassigned him.[52] Apparently the presence of a prelate who could ordain priests in Peking and thus eliminate the need to seek entry visas for Russian priests was too great a threat to the ideological control the Manchus sought to maintain. A few years after the Bishop Innocent affair, the treaty of Kiakhta (June 14, 1728) set a limit on the number (ten) and composition (four clerics and six students) that the Chinese would accept. The Russians were finally able to understand that the Manchus would not accept anything or anyone they were prepared to send. The students were there ostensibly to learn Chinese so that they could serve as interpreters in Russia. The clerics were there to minister to the Albazinians and their descendants. All in all, the Russian mission fitted into the Chinese model.

The second reason for the lack of success in evangelization is that the Russian government was not interested in converts as much as it was interested in obtaining information on China. Their main agents in this respect were the members of the Orthodox mission. "Ever since Peter's first comment on the matter, in 1698, Russian missionaries had been advised not to press their advantage by being too zealous in the pursuit of their professions."[53] The students were also key sources of information. Various students demonstrated their ingenuity by obtaining maps of China, books on Chinese history and political policy, and on at least one occasion "several important secrets useful to the Russian empire."[54] In this regard the Chinese mission differed from the other missions sent out in the eighteenth century. In the others, the evangelization of the natives led to their eventual Russification and thus satisfied both the ecclesiastical and the imperial authorities. The Chinese mission could have accomplished the former without any hope of attaining the latter. Indeed, the Orthodox clergy's purpose in Peking was to save the Albazinians from being swallowed up in the vast morass of paganism. But what did it mean to Russify Chinese subjects? It would be almost as difficult to work with the descendants of the original Albazinians as it would have been to convert the native Chinese. In any case, this did not appear to be the Russian government's understanding of their position. The China mission should be seen as having primarily a political aim.[55]

Chapter VIII

The Method of Mission

The discussion of missionary method properly follows the discussion of missionary aim, since in so many instances the aim of mission determined the method of mission. When the aim was the planting of an indigenous national church, a certain methodology was pursued.[1] When a political aim such as Russification was the goal, then a different methodology emerged.[2] In the contemporary mission of the Orthodox Diaspora yet another method comes to the fore.[3]

Common to all these is the aim of numerical increase to the Church, although between the first two examples given, the value of the quantity of increase, irrespective of quality, was keenly debated. Therefore it is appropriate to consider all the methods used historically in Orthodox missions, even if some are not considered to be worthy because of the tactics employed or the permanence of the results achieved.

What were the methods by which Orthodox missionaries added to the Church? For purposes of examination they can be classified in the following manner: (1) the use of the vernacular and the employment of indigenous clergy: the incarnational approach; (2) the reliance on governmental privileges and assistance: the political approach; (3) the attempt to live alongside non-Orthodox and influence them by example: the Orthodox presence approach (this third approach will be the subject of the following chapter).

THE INCARNATIONAL APPROACH

It is no exaggeration to say that the most carefully considered method of mission has at the same time been the most successful, especially if success is measured in terms of lasting numerical growth and not merely the number of baptisms recorded. The incarnational approach, the translation into the vernacular yet more than the translation, the very embodiment of God's truth in the language and culture of a people, has been the hallmark of the best of Orthodox mission work.

The historical survey given above provides the background for the employment of this methodology. In this section the focus is on the theological rationale underlying it.

A central theme in Orthodox theology is the incarnation. "God made Himself man, that man might become God."[4] From the fathers to the present, Orthodox theologians have emphasized the necessity of the incarnation for the salvation of humankind.[5] In the same manner in which it was necessary for the Second Person of the Trinity to assume human flesh to communicate the message of salvation, the truth of God must assume a form in which the message of salvation can be communicated. The Living Word became Incarnate; thus the written word must also become incarnate. Christ comes to humankind in a form it can perceive and understand; thus the word of Christ must also come in a form that can be perceived and understood. God, who speaks through his revealed and recorded word, must speak in a language the hearer can understand. Thus it is the role of the missionary to be an imitator of Christ.[6] As Christ translated God's thoughts to humankind, the missionary in turn translates them into another language to fulfill the gospel commission (Mt. 24:14, 28:19).

It is therefore convenient to refer to the missionary method that stresses the translation of the Bible, liturgical texts, and other religious literature into the vernacular of the target people as the incarnational approach.[7] The translation of the Bible and the employment of the vernacular in Christian mission has long been a hallmark of the Orthodox Church. Missionaries from Byzantium consistently employed this method in their efforts to bring the message of salvation to the heathen tribes. Whereas the Roman Catholic Church insisted on the universal use of Latin as the language of worship, Orthodox theology dictated the use of the living language of the people.

> In its services the Orthodox Church uses the language of the people: Arabic at Antioch, Finnish at Helsinki, Japanese at Tokyo, English (when required) at New York. One of the first tasks of Orthodox missionaries—from Cyril and Methodius in the ninth century, to Innocent Veniaminov and Nicholas Kassatkin in the nineteenth—has always been to translate the service books into native tongues.[8]

In the incarnational approach the prime consideration is the entry of the truth of God into the life and thought of the people. The bare minimum is the translation of the texts. Yet the incarnation involves more than literary skills. To be an effective communicator of Christ to the people, the missionary must live in a manner that communicates Christ's life. The incarnation does not take place in a sterile environment, but in close contact with the real world. The missionary lives with the people, "he will become one of them, he will become 'flesh from their flesh.' A new 'incarnation' will take place."[9] And thus it was with the notable Orthodox missionaries of the past. St. Stephen of Perm, Macarius Gloukharev, and Nicholas Kassatkin are but three examples.

What were the distinguishing features of this approach? One can observe the following common points: (1) an understanding of, and at times a respect for, the culture of the people with whom the missionary worked;[10] (2) an emphasis on the missionary's learning the vernacular and, if need be, creating a written language and translating the sacred texts;[11] (3) the incorporation of the indigenous people into the ministry, especially into holy orders.[12]

The logical fourth element of this methodology would be the responsible self-government of the new church. However, there has been the tendency for the mother church to continue its control over the mission church. This control was manifested in the bishops who continued to be nationals from the sending church. This trend continued long after the majority, if not the entire remainder, of the clergy were indigenous. Since in the Orthodox tradition the bishop can be effectively said to be head of the church,[13] the elevation of indigenous clergy to the episcopate is a convenient reference point for determining the selfhood of the local church. The close relationship between Church and state in most Orthodox countries (especially during the period of missionary expansion) has meant that the granting of selfhood often had political overtones.

Cultural Understanding

"It is time that we all become conscious of the fact that only a policy of sincere respect for the personality of individuals and nations, of selfless love and humble service, a 'policy' which is based exclusively upon the spirit and laws of the kingdom of God, can form the basis of Orthodox Mission."[14] What Anastasios Yannoulatos here sees as the key element in the commencement of the renewed Orthodox missionary impetus has been present in Orthodox missions since the earliest times. While not necessarily articulately formulated and often concealed under the second element of the incarnational approach (the use of the vernacular), the respect for the personality of a people can be documented by numerous examples. For what else is the preservation of the vernacular—even to the extent of the creation of an alphabet—if not this respect? Language is one of the most important marks of a people, if not *the* most important.[15] The work of Cyril in devising an alphabet for the Slavs, or that of Stephen for the Zyrians, was not only an attempt to evangelize the people, but at the same time an attempt to preserve their cultural heritage, to preserve their identity as a people.

A further element of Orthodox missionary practice that facilitated the adoption by and incarnation of Orthodoxy into the various local cultures was the example of many missionaries who employed the incarnational approach. Following the pattern of a certain type of Orthodox spirituality and in conscious or subconscious imitation of the Lord who "became poor" (2 Cor. 8:9), these missionaries lived in "evangelical poverty."[16] In addition to the spiritual benefits of this lifestyle (which was practiced by Macarius Gloukharev and Nicholas Kassatkin, to name only two), the disruption to the local culture is minimized. The missionary has no big financial base to affect radical change. Even if missionaries have adequate resources with which to operate, they choose to use them in such a way that the host culture is disturbed as little as possible. As overseas aid is still an issue in many countries of mission where Western missions have worked, it can be readily understood how a life of evangelical poverty lessens any harmful impact on the receiving culture. Cultural awareness and understanding form a foundational emphasis in the best of Orthodox missions.

Before passing on to the second element in the incarnational approach, it is appropriate to consider here the role of the Orthodox Church as a preserver of culture. Two examples stand out, that of the Greek Church under Turkish domination and of the Russian Church under Mongol oppression and later under Soviet repression. The Greek Orthodox Church played a decisive role in the 400 years of Turkish rule. This is the type of faith that was planted in the countries of mission. It is reasonable to say that no church has undergone similar oppression for as long a time. The spiritual vitality and fortitude of the Orthodox Church needs to be recognized. "Throughout all its vicissitudes the Church was determined to keep its flock conscious of the Greek heritage. . . . It was Orthodoxy that preserved Hellenism through the dark centuries. . . ."[17] The Orthodoxy that survived was a popular religion, a religion of the people, as much a part of their life as their cultural heritage. So it is today in Greece, especially in the rural areas.[18]

The vitality and resilience shown by the Orthodox Church even today in Communist Russia should not escape the notice of anyone interested in missions.[19] Orthodoxy's close cultural identification, even though at times creating difficulties,[20] has been more of an asset than a liability. It is important to note this cultural interpenetration, as Steven Runciman so clearly states when speaking of the survival of Orthodoxy under the Ottoman empire: "The story also has an international interest; for it shows what can happen to men and women who are forced to become second-class citizens. In these days, when there are still countries in which large sections of the population are second-class citizens, it is perhaps, not without relevance."[21]

The cultural awareness demonstrated by certain Orthodox missionaries with the subsequent beneficial effects on the developing church can provide a valuable example to current missionary thinking. The proposition that the Orthodox have pioneered the indigenization of the mission churches needs to be given serious consideration.[22] The distinct elements of the Orthodox Church's understanding of mission that contribute to indigenization and which offer new directives for Western missions are considered more fully below.

A further note is needed here concerning the Hellenization of Orthodoxy. There are examples of attempts at the Hellenization of their Balkan neighbors by the Byzantines.[23] The issue is deeper than that of the use of language or Byzantine customs. It revolves around the question of the normative position of the Hellenistic categories. "Hellenism," writes George Florovsky, ". . . assumed a perpetual character in the Church. . . . Of course what is meant here is not that ethical Hellenism of modern Hellas or of the Levant, nor Greek phyletism, which is obsolete and without justification. We are dealing with Christian antiquity, with the Hellenism of dogma, of the liturgy, of the icon.''[24]

Confusion arises when local expressions of Hellenism become merged with the universal and normative Hellenism described by Florovsky. The reaction to this mixture then obscures the essential basis of Orthodoxy in its Hellenistic expression. Criticism leveled against Orthodoxy without an understanding of this distinction is off the mark. The Russian theologians draw attention to this, primarily because they strive to formulate a Hellenistic Russian Orthodoxy rather than a Greek Russian Orthodoxy.[25] Thus it would be appropriate to speak of a Hellenistic Japanese Orthodoxy in which the Hellenistic categories find expression in the cultural setting of Japan. The distinction pointed out in Orthodoxy might be of use in defining Christian doctrine in a non-Western cultural setting for the missionary work of the Western Churches.

Language and Mission

The use of the vernacular is a cardinal principle in the Orthodox Church.[26] Therefore, it was only logical that in the missionary work of the Church a great emphasis was placed on translation of the Bible and the liturgy into the vernacular. This has been documented at length in the preceding historical section. It merely remains for the purposes of this methodological analysis to record the observations of some contemporary Orthodox writers.

An invaluable introduction is provided by Elias Voulgarakis in a short but powerful article on "Language and Mission" in *Porefthendes*.[27] He points out that "one of the basic reasons of the failure of many of the Russian missions, . . . as the missionaries themselves confessed, was the ignorance of the language and the use of interpreters."[28] Voulgarakis recognizes the universal acceptance of the use of the vernacular, but poses the question: Which language should the missionary learn? If it is the tribal language of the people rather than their trade language or national language, then the missionary is tied to a small area and perhaps a small group whose language, at least in its literary form, may be disappearing. Furthermore, Voulgarakis links the renewal of mission with the rotation of missionary personnel. Therefore, if the missionary is not flexible enough in his linguistic skills, that is, if he is tied to one particular language, then his transfer to another station is "nearly impossible." What is clearly reflected in this conception of missionary placement and rotation is the limited resources available to contemporary Orthodox missions. This arises both from the lack of candidates and from the lack of funds with which to support them. In Orthodox circles the missionary force is generally regarded as a small elite group.[29]

Balancing Voulgarakis's concern for economy in the placement and replacement of missionary personnel is his recognition of the duty of the missionary to fulfill the Lord's commission by taking the gospel to the whole world, even the smallest tribes. He resolves the conflict between the dominical command and the practical realities by suggesting that the missionaries use that which would be considered a second language in a wider area than the tribe. This relieves the problem of missionary transfer and produces two side benefits: "First, it creates a uniform, super-national, and well-formed (from the point of view of Christian terminology) means of communication among Christians; second, it coincides with the recent tendency, observed in most nations, of promoting and spreading the usage of these second languages."[30]

Voulgarakis adduces the example of Paul's sermon at Lystra, which he maintains was given in Greek and not in Lycaonian, as "the first instance of the use of this method."[31] That Paul spoke in Greek is not stated in the text but is a reasonable assumption, since the apostles did not immediately grasp the significance of the Anatolian's actions and acclamations (Acts 14:11ff).

While there are other aspects of Voulgarakis's methodology to be considered, it is convenient to examine his initial propositions. The first observation is that his view clearly acknowledges the realities of the modern situation. Faced with limited funds and personnel and charged with a worldwide mission, it is imperative that the wisest possible allocation of resources be made.

Does this practical accommodation correspond to the historic Orthodox position? To answer, one must decide what historical precedent in missionary history to choose. Certainly, as Voulgarakis has pointed out, many Russian missionaries failed because they did not learn the language of the people. However, there exists a strong tradition, exemplified today in the diversity of languages in which the Orthodox liturgy is celebrated, that insists on translation into the common tongue of the people. The distinction is beautifully illustrated by the labor of Nicholas Ilminski, who discovered that the Tartar language was actually composed of two independent languages, the literary language and the conversational language. Only when the conversational language became the language of the Church did the real breakthrough occur in the Christianizing of the Tartars.[32] Furthermore, a review of the preceding historical section will demonstrate the concern of Orthodox missionaries for small tribal groups and their efforts to translate the gospel into these lesser languages. Therefore, from the point of view of Orthodox mission history it is difficult to agree with Voulgarakis's propositions. Communication in a second language is always a compromise solution, never the ideal solution. It could be further argued that Orthodoxy qua Orthodoxy would not and could not be communicated except in the mother tongue of the hearer. To use a secondary language is to betray the very incarnation of the Truth that distinguishes Orthodoxy from the other Christian sects.

In the light of the missiological principles long held to be valid in the Orthodox Church itself, the proposed compromise falls short of both the ideal and the goal of conversion. Would not an adherence to the incarnation principle demand an approach with more limited worldwide objectives, concentrating on depth instead of wide coverage? In point of fact, this is exactly what has occurred, since Orthodox missionary activity in the developing countries is limited to the church in East Africa and some aid to the Korean Orthodox Church.[33] Perhaps the most useful aspect of Voulgarakis's proposal to use a secondary language is to reveal the tension that exists between the resources available and the task as perceived, a tension that can contribute to the creative involvement of the whole Church in mission.

Voulgarakis makes several important observations in his "Language and Mission" article. He points out the need for the missionary "to penetrate the intellectual environment of the natives" in order to understand their way of thinking.[34] The missionary must then adapt his pattern of thought and expression to that of the nationals so that his preaching will be fruitful.

The necessity for a correct translation of the Bible and other religious literature demands that some, if not all, the missionary force have a "complete knowledge of the language."[35] This is needed not only for full understanding on the part of the new church, but also to avoid the danger of heresy. With reference to the cultivation of language, Voulgarakis points out the effect of cultural preservation on behalf of the indigenous peoples, a point noted above: "The various glossological works which have been elaborated by missionaries, prove in a convincing way that the interest of these people was not limited to the mere fishing of souls but was extended to the promotion of the cultural causes of the people among whom they worked."[36]

One of the most interesting sections of Voulgarakis's article, and in some ways the most important, is his discussion of the glossological problem involved in the transmission of the gospel. As he comments, the language of a people is shaped by their history, but when the Christian faith is introduced, it brings with it new notions unlike those in the local environment. How should these new concepts be expressed? At this point the necessity for understanding the nationals' intellectual sphere becomes clear. A misunderstanding in this area can lead to needless theological controversy. "A different interpretation of the terms 'nature' and 'person' between the Alexandrian and the Antiochean Schools in the fourth century was the main cause of the well known theological disputes."[37] If the thought patterns of the indigenous people are not taken into account, heresy or some form of syncretism could easily result.

The preceding remarks highlight the glossological problems common to all missionary work. The Orthodox Church faces two additional dilemmas. The first, called "the pedagogic" by Voulgarakis, is to what extent the Orthodox mission should use homogeneous terminology, namely, that of other denominations or even non-Christian religions. "Is this identity not giving rise to the risk of a confusion among the various denominations and of the creation of a climate of confessional indifference, so harmful during the initial stages of the development of a Church? Is it not possible that the differentiation of terminology constitutes the best pedagogic means of making people aware of the differences between the various Confessions?"[38] The question needs only to be posed before other questions immediately arise: Where should the differentiation stop? Do new terms for God and the Trinity need to be invented or can the existing terms be used? Should differentiation only be made where doctrinal differences exist between Orthodoxy and other denominations? Should there be an Orthodox translation of the Bible? It should be kept in mind that these questions do not come out of a confessional prejudice, but from a sincere effort to proclaim the truth as the Orthodox see it. A glance at the difficulty that the Orthodox and the Western Churches have in understanding each other should convince one of the seriousness of this problem. Voulgarakis offers no answers, but raises the questions in an effort to examine the practical obstacles facing Orthodox mission.

The second dilemma facing Orthodox missions in this area is the linguistic problem, "the expression of the new terms according to the spirit of the native language."[39] The example of Western missions in this area has at times not been enlightening. Terms, often chosen without sufficient knowledge of the language, are now found to be inadequate to express the full range of Christian truth. The reevaluation of these terms and their replacement is hindered by the adoption of the inferior terms by the Christian congregation. "This emphasizes the hard task of the Orthodox for a conscientious and careful work of translation."[40]

Voulgarakis's article is helpful in outlining the problems of translation in missionary work. But it is also a good indication of the type of thinking going on in Orthodox circles with regard to the missionary enterprise of the Church and how, in particular, they see their own role in it.

Other voices are also raised in the context of contemporary Orthodox mission thinking. In a report describing the visit of a delegation from the Theological Faculty of the University of Thessaloniki to the Orthodox Church in Uganda, one reads the following:

> Our liturgical books, at least the most essential ones, should be translated into the local language. . . . This most valuable and important work requires a whole team of experts, who would work on nothing but that for several years. First of all a selection should be made of what is to be translated; then, translators having command of both languages would share the actual translating job; finally the translated texts should be printed and distributed. This means employment of many people and a need for correspondingly ample funds.[41]

The report emphasizes what the Church in Greece could and should do to aid the Orthodox in Uganda. There still remains scope for the reinstitution of translation, the incarnation of the written word, in Orthodox mission.

Indigenous Clergy

Closely related to the principle of translation in the vernacular, and at times growing out of it, is the employment of nationals as clergy.[42] The emphasis on the indigenization of the ministry is precisely what would be expected in the incarnational approach. The rapid growth of Orthodoxy in several countries of mission seems to be directly attributable to the employment of indigenous workers.

In current practice the same emphasis is being placed on the role of the national clergy. Those writing from the perspective of a "sending" country, such as Greece or the United States, speak of missionaries filling the posts of teachers and technicians.[43] The aim is not to supplant the indigenous clergy but to assist them and the developing church. This does not preclude an evangelistic task for the missionary. "Missionaries will be a living witness of faith and love, a witness of Christian life among their brothers. . . . The only qualifications required are a burning vocation and a special education in mission."[44] The emphasis on service obviously applies to countries where an Orthodox Christian nucleus is already established. Should the opportunity and means arise for pioneer mission work, the evangelistic burden would initially fall on the missionary. The methodology proposed for such an occasion is clearly and ably laid out by Efthimios Stylios in his "The Missionary as an Imitator of Christ."[45]

In the case of the Orthodox work in East Africa, the Africans themselves echo the same theme. Theodoros Nankyamas, a Ugandan, sees the whites in the role of servants whose labors done in love will elicit an interest in Orthodoxy. Thus in both a pioneer enterprise and in the development of the church, service becomes a witness to Orthodoxy, while the evangelist is one of their own. "In Kenya, people prefer missionaries of the same color as they, to the white ones."[46]

The advisability of having ministers of the same tribe, nation, or race as the congregation is neither new nor unique to Orthodoxy. It is sufficient to state that the use of indigenous clergy has been the traditional methodology and that it is still seen as the present practical method of approach. In historical perspective the continuance of the foreign presence in the episcopal ranks was an area where the indigenization of the church was not carried through completely. This could possibly have led to the inhibition of growth in the younger churches, though the data are far too diverse and complex to allow sweeping generalizations to be made. Certainly the level of theological education that was present in a missionary bishop could not be easily produced on all mission fields. Furthermore, the fact that Orthodox bishops are chosen solely from the monastic ranks of clergy forms another potential barrier to the selection of bishops from new converts. At this stage in the development of worldwide Orthodoxy, the younger churches are now able to supply candidates for the episcopal office from their own number, as witnessed by the elevation of three priests of the African Orthodox to episcopal rank in the 1970s.[47]

Practical steps are being undertaken to make the principle of indigenous clergy a reality. Orthodox students from the developing countries are being trained in Greece and the United States. This course is strewn with difficulty for the Church, since many who go overseas never return to their homelands. Those who do return often find that their new education and viewpoints put them in conflict with those who have not gone abroad.[48] Nevertheless, in view of the resources available, the advanced training of the clergy is best accomplished in this manner.[49]

In light of this emphasis on indigenous clergy, the question naturally arises as to whether the day of the foreign missionary is ended. The withdrawal of missionary personnel is a goal, but only as it relates to the primary and immediate goal of mission, the planting of the church (see above, pp. 52–56). John Papavassiliou writes: "The purpose of mission is not to maintain permanently missionaries in the country of mission. A mission attains its purpose when a flourishing local Church joins the respective patriarchate. When several native priests are ordained in the country of evangelization, the missionary work is finished."[50] This judgment, however, does not signify that the appointment of national clergy means the end of all foreign aid. On the contrary, the author of the preceding quotation writes in the same article that certain types of development aid might still be needed. "The Greek Orthodox mission is already invited by the Orthodox Church of Uganda. Native clergymen seeded and irrigated the soil, we are only invited to help them for consolidation and cultivation."[51]

Two things are immediately clear. The work with established churches is by invitation. The call is raised, "Come over and help us."[52] This working by invitation is a good indication of the locus of authority. It is the young church that has the responsibility for the work. One of the benefits to the missionary enterprise of the Orthodox Church is the clear line of authority and responsibility. Because of the preservation of this line, needless conflicts between missionary and national are avoided. The further implications of the church-centered structure of missions is treated in a succeeding chapter.

The second point that is obvious from the statement is that the missionaries working with an established church are not seen primarily as evangelists. That is not to say that the missionaries are not active witnesses to their faith, for they certainly should be. But the emphasis falls on the special assistance they can render the church. The strengthening of the church is a necessary step in the further spread of Orthodoxy. The vision for Africa involves a strong base that would enable the Orthodox faith to penetrate far into that continent. "The African Orthodox missionaries will preach Christ and His Gospel and they will be the leaven that will raise all the dough of Africa."[53] The African Orthodox will carry the gospel to black Africa, and the Orthodox missionaries from other countries will equip and strengthen them for this task.

NONINCARNATIONAL APPROACHES

Not all Orthodox missionaries adopted the incarnational method. Just as there were political aims in Orthodox missions, so also there were political methodologies. The conclusion that political aims always mandate political means is erroneous. The aims of the government (and in most of the cases it is the Russian government that is in view) did not necessarily coincide with those of the missionary. Therefore it is possible to observe many cases where the missionary used the incarnational method even though the mission had been established for political reasons. One indeed wonders if the Russification of the

Siberian peoples was not the real motive behind government sponsorship of missionary work. As has been demonstrated above, government interference in missions could also lead to the disruption of evangelistic work when it was perceived to be in the best interest of the government that the people in question should not convert.[54] In spite of the problems with the government, Russian Orthodox missions still preserved the light of the ancient incarnational tradition, which blazed with new glory in the nineteenth century.

Historical accuracy demands the chronicling of the methods used by some missionaries, which, for lack of a better term, can be called political and social evangelism. By this is meant a method that presents to the potential convert benefits of a political or material nature that would induce the person to become a Christian. As can be expected, these Christians did not have a long religious life-span, since most reverted to their non-Christian religions at the first opportunity, assuming that they had ever given them up to begin with.[55] That missionaries would actually resort to these practices may seem strange to someone who is unaware that the missionaries themselves were accorded political, social, and material benefits for their labors. Nor were the most spiritual clergy in Russia averse to accepting such honors. The example of Father John of Kronstadt who "would give away the very shoes from his feet, but, as his photographs bear witness, he did not refuse to wear the rich cassocks which admirers pressed on him, nor the decorations which his sovereigns bestowed upon him."[56] Here was an acknowledged spiritual teacher and pastor, whose Christian influence spread all over Russia and beyond.[57] This example should serve as a reminder not to judge a previous age by the standards of the present age. If decorations and awards seem strange trophies for spiritual victories, they apparently were not so conceived in the past in Imperial Russia.

The rewards and inducements offered to the potential converts ranged from a drink of vodka to the remission of the military-service requirement.[58] It is little wonder, as Orthodox writers themselves have noted, that the "converts" lapsed. Compounding the error of offering material inducements, the church failed to provide adequate instruction to the newly baptized. They were left on their own, either because the missionary had little or no knowledge of their language and thus could not instruct them, or simply because he moved on to the next area to baptize. Yet—and this is the fact that justifies the inclusion of this section under the topic of missionary methods—these converts were considered members of the Orthodox Church. The importance of this cannot be overstated.

Some of the numerical growth of the church can be attributed to what has been called political and social evangelism. Critics of Orthodoxy have often maintained that political and social evangelism was the only way known to Russian Orthodoxy.[59] As it has been demonstrated above, this accusation is inaccurate. There is, however, a tradition of *cuius regio, eius religio*. Starting with Vladimir himself, remembered in the Slavic liturgy as "the Saint equal to the Apostles, the great Prince Vladimir,"[60] one can see a history of political evangelism. Arthur Stanley has written:

Another prominent feature of the conversion is the fact that . . . Russia was Christianized without the agency of missionaries, and chiefly by the direct example, influence, or command (whichever we choose to call it) of its Prince. . . . There is no Apostle of Russia except Vladimir, who bears the same title as that of Constantine, "Isapostolos"; *"Vladimir equal to an Apostle."*[61]

In the light of the apostolic standing accorded to Vladimir for his evangelistic work, one can only reach the conclusion that such methodology is legitimate in the carrying out of the Orthodox missionary mandate. Would then the same type of national conversion be acceptable today? From the point of view of tradition it is difficult to see why it would not be. From the point of view of the present realities, it is difficult to see how such a thing could happen.

In Russia itself, long before the Revolution of 1917 that ended foreign missions, the identity between the fact of citizenship and adherence to the Orthodox Church had been broken. Religious uniformity was no longer required, whether in the case of the Buddhists in eastern Russia or the Old Believers in western Russia.[62] While there are doubtless places on earth where a national religious conversion could be obtained, such tactics seem to be eschewed by Orthodox theologians. Using the examples of missionaries of the past, current Orthodox thinking runs along the lines of the incarnational method. Furthermore, it is recognized that the days when belief could be imposed are over. Outside pressures are resisted in the name of freedom. Spiritual colonialism and political colonialism are both unacceptable. In the words of Chrysostomos Constantinides:

People are tired of seeing the so-called historical Churches appearing as protecting Churches of the people with the spirit of the ecclesiastical colonialism having in mind to conquer or impose their bulky ecclesiastical and theological dictatorship. Today, the flags of freedom and independence, of equality and justice are hoisted up all over the Globe. The Theology of the Church must be a Theology of freedom, saving and making every man equal. . . .[63]

The use of force or threats (Vladimir said that anyone refusing baptism would henceforth be regarded as his enemy) is no longer considered a worthy method. Leonidas Philippides, a professor at the University of Athens, lays down as the cardinal principle "the non-violent presentation of Christian truth. . . . No action is permissible against the unwilling, apart from an effort to make the light of knowledge shine upon them."[64]

These quotations could be multiplied several times over. The age of Vladimir is over. His honor may remain, but his tactics are no longer suitable. Orthodoxy faces its missionary challenges in a new way, or in the new version of the old way, and breaks with one stream of tradition.

Not only is political evangelism passé, the social emphasis in evangelism also draws some fire. Metropolitan Chrysostomos of Myra calls for: "The complete disavowal of all the methods of contact with others, that have been tried and failed. Schools, alms-giving, bribing, social work, and eventually enslavement of consciences and buying of souls, proselytism, recruitment of orphans and destitutes and so on and so forth, are actions and systems that have been complete failures."[65]

The severity of the attack and the comprehensiveness of his anathema forcibly bring out this point. All enterprises which, in spite of good intentions, exploit the indigenous people are to be abandoned. The metropolitan pictures a national as shrinking back in terror at the thought of dying in a hospital, preferring his own familiar surroundings. The approach that puts these establishments between the person and Christ needs to be radically restructured. It does not serve to bring the lost to Christ, but only to confuse and enslave them to the system of the missionary. What is needed is a clear and nonexploitative approach that will draw people to Christ, drawn not because of the system or the technology but because of the intrinsic worth of the Christian message.

A similar thought is expressed by Papavassiliou, at one time a professor at the University of Athens and later an archimandrite in East Africa:

> I suspect however that sooner or later the missionaries will not be able to work in underdeveloped countries as carriers of a higher civilization, of a civilization foreign to the local conditions of life. . . . I foresee a radical change of the structure of missionary work. Missionaries, as carriers of the great message, will not behave also as carriers of a message from a higher civilization, but as brothers and teachers, as well as disciples and students of the local cultures.[66]

These men are not opposed to materially assisting nationals. Papavassiliou speaks of education and medical care as some of the aspects of the living witness of the missionaries. But this is only a part of the witness, a consequence of the presentation of the truth, the message of Christ.

Again the limited resources of Orthodoxy determine the extent of the social services it can provide on its mission fields. It is highly doubtful that it could match the expenditures of Roman Catholic and Protestant missions. Yet, to write off the disavowal of social enterprise by the Orthodox on the basis of their material inability to produce them is to miss the point. For Orthodoxy, above all things, has maintained that it and it alone has been faithful to the truth revealed by God through Christ. Therefore, it should come as no surprise that at the present, as at the high points of Orthodox missions, the truth of God is stressed as the main feature of mission. Culture and social welfare are definitely secondary issues.

While there is indeed both historical precedent and authentic tradition for political and social missionary methodology, responsible representatives of Orthodoxy disavow such techniques for the future of Orthodox missions.

Chapter IX

The Method of Mission:
The Orthodox Presence of the Diaspora

The preceding chapter treated the work of Orthodox missions from the standpoint of a missionary elite going into a country to witness to the gospel. This missionary force is limited in numbers and, consequently, in geographical penetration. But the foreign missionary is not the only "overseas" Orthodox. There is the formidable presence of the Orthodox Church on all six continents. Does this Orthodox presence play any role in the missiology of the church?

Increasingly it is becoming apparent that an important part of the missionary witness of the Orthodox Church is the activity of the Orthodox Diaspora in propagating the faith. This can be termed "the Orthodox presence approach," a concept taken seriously by many Orthodox theologians.[1]

Although this activity might not be considered missionary work, since it does not involve the sending of workers to another country, nor are the target people all nonbelievers (although increasingly in the West a new secular paganism is developing), nevertheless the Orthodox Church sees this presence as a missionary enterprise. Perhaps their viewpoint is more correct than first appears. In terms of location, the West is not the home environment of Orthodoxy. Therefore, there is a sense in which any supposed geographical criterion for "foreign" missions is met. As has been shown above, most of Russia's Orthodox missions took place on Russian territory. The national origins and customs of the Orthodox make at least the first generation a distinct group. This distinction carries on to succeeding generations. However, what really marks off Orthodoxy and gives credence to its claim to be engaged in mission is its theological position. For if, as the Orthodox believe, they are the true Church of Jesus Christ, then it is imperative that they engage in mission. The missionary works that bring the faith to both the heathen in "distant" lands and the non-Orthodox in whose midst the Diaspora finds itself are parts of the same commission.

The similarities in the experience of the Diaspora and the missionary approach to the unconverted are striking. The immigrants settled into their new countries, though most maintained close ties with their homeland and perpetuated their national customs. The succeeding generations, which grew up in their parents' adopted land, took on more of the new culture. In the United States, for example, the descendants of immigrants became assimilated into the American system.[2] While this assimilation took its toll on the Orthodox Churches[3] in that many left the Church, it also forced the Church to introduce English into the liturgy. With this change, the opportunity has arisen for Orthodoxy to break out of its ethnic background and reach both the denationalized descendants of Orthodox immigrants as well as the non-Orthodox population.

It must be clearly noted that the transition to the English language was not primarily for missionary purposes. Second- and third-generation Orthodox, born and educated in America, find themelves more at home in English. Furthermore, many marry spouses from non-Orthodox traditions who find services in the old national language unintelligible. The biggest challenge facing Orthodoxy in America is to recapture the unchurched Orthodox, that is, those who were baptized into the Church as infants but who do not later participate in the life of the Church. However, in their attempt to regain this lost constituency, the Church has created a wealth of liturgical and theological material in English.[4]

The establishment of Orthodox theological faculties in the United States has provided a supply of American-born Orthodox to pastor the congregations whose constituency increasingly has a greater percentage of American-born Orthodox. A number of the priests, in addition to being American-born, are also converts to Orthodoxy from other faiths.[5] The episcopate is experiencing a rise in the number of American-born bishops. Two of the bishops at this writing are converts from other religions.[6]

In all this growth, the pattern of the incarnational methodology can be traced. The cultural environment has been penetrated, the foreignness of the Orthodox Church somewhat reduced, and the awareness of the Orthodox presence by the general population increased. The liturgy is regularly celebrated in English and theological literature is readily accessible. The ranks of the clergy are increasingly filled by indigenous priests and bishops, and full selfhood has been claimed by one of the Orthodox jurisdictions. But in spite of the parallels with traditional Orthodox missionary practice, most of the effort to date has been expended on providing for the immigrants and conserving their descendants in the Orthodox faith.

In the earliest stages of Orthodoxy in the United States, as in other areas of the Diaspora, the services were held in the immigrants' mother tongue. There was no effort to penetrate the non-Orthodox community. This cannot be entirely attributed to a lack of missionary zeal, for the Church also served as a social center for the immigrants. Here in the company of others from their country they could enjoy the sense of community that was denied them by the alien society in which they lived and worked. As in the years of oppression, either by the Mongols in Russia or the Turks in Greece, the Church served as the center of Orthodox culture. Convinced, perhaps even more strongly than today's Orthodox, that theirs was the true faith, the immigrants lacked the means to propagate their faith to non-Orthodox. In any event, the Orthodox Church made little or no penetration into the non-Orthodox world.

However, no study of Orthodox mission theology can ignore the current revival of interest in the missionary expansion of the Church in the Diaspora. Some are raising penetrating questions. "If the Orthodox faith is the only true faith, they argue, have they not a duty to preach it to the non-Orthodox? Must they not bear witness before the entire world?"[7] The answer given by the Orthodox increasingly is Yes. They do have a special mission to the non-Orthodox: to present to them the true faith.

While documentation of this concern of mission abounds, a few selected instances will suffice to demonstrate the point. In December 1967, a "Consultation on 'Orthodox Diaspora' " was held in Geneva, Switzerland. Among the items discussed was the responsibility and challenge that the Orthodox had in sharing their faith in the West.

> Thus the Orthodox Church was placed in a new situation and faced with a new responsibility. Her children were in need of a new type of pastoral guidance, so that their Orthodox faith would not succumb to the powerful social and intellectual pressures of the new environment. At the same time, the Christian West, which finds itself, especially in the last years, in the midst of change and self-examination, was and is in need of an articulate and living Orthodox witness.[8]

It is noteworthy that this consultation was sponsored by Syndesmos, the World Organization of Orthodox Youth Movements. It is the younger generation that both recognizes the need for a vibrant Orthodox witness and is in the forefront of the planning for witness.

Another example of the mission awareness of Orthodoxy is the recent decision to offer a course in Christian missions at the Holy Cross Greek Orthodox School of Theology. Reporting in a non-Orthodox theological publication, Stanley S. Harakas outlines the course:

> In our seminar, the students defined several kinds of mission for the Orthodox Christianity in America. The first was Inner Mission, what one of our theologians has called "Christianizing the Christians." It is the task of spiritual renewal. The second was Home Mission. The students reasoned that if we are truly convinced of the truth of Orthodoxy, then we have no right to "hide it under a bushel" (Matt. 5:15) any longer. Mission parishes should be started wherever an established Parish Community exists. We have a responsibility to preach the pure message of Orthodox Christianity to our next door neighbors. The third form of mission, Foreign Mission, has already begun in a small way. In the Greek Orthodox Archdiocese, funds are collected for this purpose in a national

campaign during the Great Lent. There is some support for Orthodox missions in Uganda, Kenya, Korea and Alaska.[9]

The priorities and mandates developed by the future priests are instructive. The emphasis on renewal is a theme found in other epochs of Orthodox history. One need only think of Macarius Gloukharev's desire to promote spiritual renewal in the Russian Church by Bible translation and distribution or of the efforts of Eusebius Matthopoulos who started the Zoe movement in Greece. While Gloukharev's efforts were frustrated, the enduring legacy of Zoe and the movements founded as a result of it demonstrate the possibility of renewal occurring. The role that spiritual renewal plays in the missionary structure and vision of the local congregation is discussed below.

The concern of the students for proclaiming the truth of Orthodoxy to their neighbors marks a departure from the traditionally ethnic Greek Church. Yet, however strange it may seem to invite non-Greeks into a Greek Church, the evangelistic action follows naturally from Orthodoxy's claim to be the true Church. The application of dogma in this case can only contribute to a rejuvenation of the Church. Here is still another example of the seriousness with which Orthodoxy sees its task in the West.

The relationship of renewal, near-neighbor evangelism, and foreign missions in the thought of the Orthodox theologians is an interesting topic of study. Anastasios Yannoulatos makes a strong case for the interrelatedness of homeland renewal and evangelism, on one hand, and foreign missions, on the other.

> Usually these two efforts are mutually inter-supporting. The heroism of missionaries and their spirit of sacrifice and strong love, always tend to give back to the old Churches new vigor of life, making it possible for them to relive in the spirit of the Church of the martyrs and in the pure but strong spirit of the catacombs, within which our Christianity is re-vigorated and cleansed.[10]

Yannoulatos writes from the perspective of the Church of Greece where the pressures to use the available resources for the reconstruction and uplifting of the national church are great. The Greek Orthodox Church in the United States faces a similar problem with regard to the allocation of funds and personnel. Nevertheless, the renewal emphasis is linked with a fresh interest in foreign mission.

A third example of the seriousness with which Orthodox believers are taking the challenge of evangelism among non-Orthodox can be found in the theme and study document of the Fourth All-American Council of the Orthodox Church in America. The theme of the council was "Mission," in particular the mission of the Orthodox Church in America to America. Under a subsection entitled "Our Responsibility" the following statement appears:

The presence of the Holy Orthodox Church in America is no accident, but the result of missionary activity begun in 1794 and fulfilled in 1970 with the granting of permanent canonical status to the Orthodox Church in America as an autocephalous Church. By virtue of her autocephaly, she is the local Church whose mission in America is to bring all persons to salvation. It is through Her that all may come to the knowledge of the True God and be made partakers of life everlasting.[11]

The impulse to missionary action derives from a theological principle. The opportunity presents itself not by chance but as the result of a strategy laid out two centuries ago and directed by God himself in his concern for the world. The historical reference must be regarded as more than just an attempt to legitimize current Orthodox thinking. Instead it comes from the concept of a continuity of Orthodox history and tradition. Orthodoxy, conscious of the treasure that it has guarded and imparted in the past, is again ready to reveal the treasure of the gospel.

Having established the concern for an Orthodox witness in America, how is the witness to be carried out? Of inestimable help is the development of English as the second (or in many cases, the first) language of Orthodox America. Likewise, the dissemination of Orthodox into all levels of American society means that Orthodoxy need not be confined to one economic level.[12] In short, Orthodox believers have interpenetrated American society. While this puts them in an excellent position to influence their surroundings, it has also led to the abandonment of Orthodoxy by some who were reared in that tradition. These "unchurched" Orthodox,[13] are a special target for the missionary work of the Orthodox.[14]

The organized efforts at mission to the unchurched Orthodox and the non-Orthodox population of America have principally consisted of the publication of books and pamphlets explaining the Orthodox faith.[15] Most are directed to an Orthodox audience with the hope that knowledge about Orthodoxy will result in increased devotion to Orthodoxy. These materials are well written and provide a valuable introduction to the Orthodox Church for the non-Orthodox. At present there is no systematic plan for presenting the Orthodox Church as a religious option for unchurched non-Orthodox.

Whenever mission to America is discussed in Orthodox circles, the involvement of the Orthodox in ecumenical contacts is held up. There are four active dialogues being carried on: Orthodox-Roman Catholic, Orthodox-Anglican, Orthodox-Reformed-Lutheran, and Orthodox-Southern Baptist.[16]

Orthodoxy is both strengthened and enhanced by such contacts. They should be continued and expanded. It is primarily through them that Eastern Orthodoxy witnesses to the apostolic truth to both Roman Catholics and Protestants in our country. Furthermore, the Orthodox presence serves the cause of Christian unity by providing what a Protestant theologian recently called "the balancing wheel" between the two dominant expressions of Western Christianity. The ecumenical movement has provided innumerable opportunities for the One, Holy, Catholic, Apostolic and Orthodox Church to carry on its work of witness and mission. However, we may not have made as much of these opportunities as we might have.[17]

This quotation from Stanley Harakas aptly sums up the current position of Orthodoxy's mission to America. It is mainly being carried on at higher theological levels with tremendous benefits in terms of the recognition of Orthodoxy by the other Churches. The contribution of the Orthodox is being sought in a way reminiscent of the courting of the Greeks by the Reformers and their successors.[18] But the insights gained from the theological dialogues have yet to filter down to the ordinary church member, Orthodox or non-Orthodox. Furthermore, the unique witness of Orthodoxy has yet to challenge the average Western Christian. Orthodoxy is still not generally seen as an alternative to Western Christianity, but is seen as a means of correcting the excesses of the West. Conversions to the Orthodox Church have been individual rather than group conversions. There have been some notable exceptions to this trend, such as the Iglesia Ortodoxa Católica en México, which was formerly an Old Catholic Church founded by Roman Catholics in 1926 as a protest against Spanish colonialism. This church came over to Orthodoxy as a body in 1972. The transfer was not the result of missionary action but came because of self-study on the part of the clergy. It is now an exarchate, or church province, of the Orthodox Church in America.[19]

Another exception was the reception in 1975 of thirty-four converts from the Episcopal Church. They were previously members of the Episcopal Church of the Redeemer (Kansas City, Kansas). When the pastor, disturbed by the recent changes in both worldwide Anglicanism and the Protestant Episcopal Church of the United States, felt he could no longer remain in the Episcopal Church and decided to convert to Orthodoxy, many of his parishioners joined him.

> In his sermon at the end of Vespers, Archbishop John welcomed the new converts, stating that this occasion marked the beginning of a new era in American Orthodoxy. "Until now, with the exception of the mission to Alaska, we have been concerned almost exclusively with the pastoral care of people who were born into Orthodoxy, whose parents and grandparents migrated here. While there have been a significant number of individual conversions to Orthodoxy, this is the first time that a group like this has been received, made up of people who did not have Orthodox ancestors."[20]

There are a number of interesting features in the two cases described above. First, the people involved perceived their move to be toward the original form of Christianity. This is of course in accordance with Orthodoxy's claim to be the one true Church. Second, in both cases, the clergy involved became clergy in the Orthodox Church, though in the case of the Episcopal priest, he was reordained to the priesthood.[21] But by far the most interesting aspect for the purposes of this study is that these conversions occurred without overt missionary work on the part of the Orthodox. The missionary activity was confined to a dissemination of information to inquirers.

If this is the result with little or no extra effort on the part of the Orthodox, what might the result be if a concerted missionary advance were to be undertaken? Opportunities abound for just such an advance. As Harakas has said, the Orthodox have not made as much use of the opportunities as they possibly could.

Full-scale mission to America has as yet to be undertaken by the Orthodox. When they do so, the results of their efforts could change the denominational pattern of the United States. How soon such a mission can be mounted depends on many factors, most of which relate to the ethnic origins of American Orthodoxy. With the advent of an American expression of the Orthodox faith, truly a new era will have begun.

What has been written above concerning Orthodoxy in the United States, in particular the challenges ethnic Orthodoxy faces, is true of the Orthodox Diaspora in other lands. Worldwide Orthodoxy is in a position to proclaim its doctrine. When the barriers of ethnic origin fall, as no doubt they will when the descendants become assimilated into their adopted countries, the door will be open for missionary work.[22]

Chapter X

Motives for Mission

In any discussion of missionary motive the danger of oversimplification is present. "Human motives are always ambivalent. Even the purest motive has a strain of impurity in so far as it is but a faint reflection of the hidden motive which moved God to send His Son into the world."[1] As with the other aspects of Orthodox missiology, the absence of an Orthodox dogmatic definition of missionary motive largely limits the discussion to the plane of *theologoumena*. However, some insight into the subject is provided by contemporary Orthodox writers. It should be recognized at the outset that the discussion of motive is no simple matter and often several motives are at work at once. The purpose of this chapter on motivation is to provide insight into the Orthodox understanding of mission, and not to establish Orthodox dogma by virtue of the arrangement of the topic. This comment does not preclude, however, ranking the topics in an order as is done by some Orthodox theologians. The survey is by no means exhaustive of all possible motives for mission. Only the four motives most frequently raised are here discussed.

THE LOVE OF GOD

That the love of God (God's love for humankind) is a foundational motive of the missionary enterprise will come as no surprise to anyone who reflects on the theological framework of the Orthodox Church. In Anastasios Yannoulatos's words: ". . . The theological thought of the eastern Church moves in a theological and cosmological frame, in which the dominant element is St. John's conception of the love (*agape*) of the trinitarian God, seen in the perspective of eschatology and in doxological contemplation of the mystery of God."[2]

There would appear to be at least two direct consequences that arise from this framework and bear on motivation for mission. The first is the motive of a person's response to the love of God. "What shall I render to the Lord for all the things wherein He has rewarded me?" (Ps. 115:2 in LXX, 116:12 in English versions). Service arises as a natural response to the love shown to

81

humankind by God. This can take many forms. In the Byzantine era, for example, the response to God's graciousness often took the form of philanthropy.[3] In a sense missionary work can be seen as an extension of the concept of philanthropy, though certainly this interpretation does not exhaust either concept.

In the light of the centrality of agape, it is somewhat surprising that the love of God is not mentioned more frequently in the discussion of missionary motive. Paradoxically, it may be the very centrality and givenness of the motive that keeps it from being spoken of. The love of God is there; it exists as the framework of all theological discussion. Therefore, while it remains clear to the Orthodox who operate within the framework, it is obscure to Western observers searching for missionary motives. Typical of this attitude would be the discussion by Efthimios Stylios on the missionary calling to imitate Christ. He asks, "What was it that urged God to fulfill this project of the incarnation of His Son? The answer is given also in a verse of St. John 'For God so loved the world, that He gave His only begotten Son. . . .' " Then Stylios goes on to discuss the incarnation of the missionary into the life of the people among whom the missionary is to minister. "And if one asks how this can be done there is but one answer: only by LOVE. 'God so loved the world. . . .' "[4]

The second direct consequence arising from the theological framework of Orthodoxy is the centrality of love. In view here is the theme of a person's love for humankind, with its basis in God's love for humankind. Both biblically and practically it is difficult to separate this response from the preceding one. It is in the demonstration of our love for humankind that our love for God can be seen (1 Jn. 3:14; 4:20). Even the apparently solitary response to God, as witnessed in monasticism, need not be seen as contradictory. Ample documentation exists on the role of monks in Orthodox missions.[5] The subject of love for one's fellow beings, while prompted by the initial love of God for humankind, demands a separate examination, which will be found below.

In the succeeding discussion, it will be seen that the theme of God's love, while not always in the forefront, is the undercurrent of Orthodox missionary motive. By virtue of the predominance of love in the Orthodox framework, love is the predominant motive. However, there are other motives, logically and theologically secondary, but forced to the fore because of the current situation of Orthodoxy and Orthodox missions.

THE GREAT COMMISSION

The first issue of the journal *Porefthendes* clearly showed a new turn in Orthodox missiological thinking. The masthead of that (and all succeeding issues) carried the Greek text of the first part of Matthew 28:19, *Porefthendes matheteusate panta ta ethne*. The English translation "Go ye" appeared in later numbers of the journal. If the title left any question as to the purpose of the journal, the text explicitly stated the new missionary thrust proposed by the *Porefthendes* committee. A hallmark of the early issues of the magazine was the determined effort to bring the Great Commission of Matthew 28:19 back to the forefront of the Church's life. Under the title "The Forgotten Commandment," Anastasios Yannoulatos tackled the theoretical grounds of why Orthodoxy should engage in foreign missions and the objections generally raised by Orthodox to justify their noninvolvement: "It is not a question of 'can we?' but of an imperative command, 'we must.' 'Go ye therefore and teach all nations.' 'Go ye into all the world and preach the Gospel to every creature.' There is no 'consider if you can,' there is only a definite, clearcut command of Our Lord."[6]

It was the rediscovery of the Great Commission that led to the founding of the journal *Porefthendes* in 1959. As a result of the interest and support generated by the journal, in 1961 the Inter-Orthodox Missionary Centre, known as Porefthendes, was established.[7]

THE MOTIVE OF LOVE

Another frequently mentioned missionary motive is that of love.

The natives must understand that we love them and their country, their souls and their worldly problems and that it is only because of love that we are among them. . . . The whole tradition of Orthodoxy could well be summarized in the words that the Metropolitan of Moscow Macarios said to the Archbishop of Kajan Gouri in 1555 in connection with the subject of christianizing the Tartars: "Win the confidence of the Tartars' hearts and do not guide them to baptism out of any other motive than love alone." This must be the motto of the new Orthodox missionary movement too.[8]

In the article from which the quotation was taken, the author refers to the fact that in the modern age Greece has not been a colonial power. This freedom from colonial connections means that the motives of Greek missionaries are not associated with the regimes of the past. Their motive, love for their fellow beings is thus thought more likely to be believed by the national. As has been pointed out, the relative lack of funds available for foreign missions has produced a mentality and practice in keeping with ancient Orthodox practice and current Western missiological thinking. The indigenous church is free to develop on its own with aid from other Orthodox Churches. In this "evangelical poverty"[9] the nationals are able to see what Orthodox missionaries mean when they say that they are among the nationals only because of love for them.

THE MOTIVE OF INNER NECESSITY

Closely connected with the preceding motives is the concept of mission as an inner necessity of the Christian. This differs somewhat from the Great Commission motive in that the obligation is internalized by the missionary and becomes part of one's very being.

> The question of the motive of mission can be studied from several angles: love for God and men, obedience to the Great Command of the Lord (Matt. 28:19), desire for the salvation of souls, longing for God's glory. All these, surely, are serious motives; and the last especially is in perfect harmony with those that have been developed already. However, we think the real motive of mission, for both the individual and the Church, is something deeper. . . . It is inner necessity. "Necessity is laid upon me," said St. Paul, "Woe to me if I do not preach the gospel" (1 Cor. 9:16). All other motives are aspects of this need, derivative motives. *Mission is an inner necessity (i) for the faithful and (ii) for the Church. If they refuse it, they do not merely omit a duty, they deny themselves.*[10]

The argument advanced by Yannoulatos to support this position, in the foregoing quotation from him, revolves around the incorporation of the believer with Christ. It is impossible for the person who is truly united with Christ to think or act in a manner different from that of Christ. It is perhaps helpful to point out that the author is conscious he is discussing the ideal and not the actual. Therefore, the real situation is sadly somewhat different, as Yannoulatos has noted in his meditation "A Difference of Opinions."[11] Nevertheless, Yannoulatos and those other Orthodox who write in the same vein[12] recognize that the claims of Orthodoxy make sense only if there is missionary activity. How can one claim to hold the truth and yet not feel a duty to share it? How can one be united to Christ and fail to share the vision of the Christ? How can one speak of Orthodox spirituality, a spirituality that dwells on mystical union with Christ, and not manifest a concern for the salvation of those not so united to Christ? Questions like these are being asked in Orthodox circles, questions that challenge the (recent) tradition of Orthodoxy, which is to be concerned with its own affairs and not with the propagation of God's truth that it claims to possess. To this attitude, Yannoulatos issues a warning: "Let us not deceive ourselves. Our spiritual life will not acquire *the fervor, the broadness, the genuineness, that it should, if we continue to regard and live Christianity limited within the narrow boundaries of the community to which we belong,* forgetting its universal destiny, even if this community is our town or our country."[13]

It is not at all difficult to recognize the prophetic nature of what is expressed here. Perhaps because in the plurality of the West the conviction of the uniqueness of the Christian faith, or in the very least the uniqueness of any one version of the Christian faith, has been lost, the call from the Orthodox world sounds all the more clear and certain. Again in the examination of the Orthodox perspective, one can find new light on the Western Churches' situation. Particularly in the area of missionary motivation, there is to be found a view of missionary involvement that may serve as both challenge and inspiration to the Church at large.

> When, in this perspective [writes Yannoulatos], we make a theological study of the purpose and motive of mission, it becomes clear that our Church's call to mission must be preached not only, or not so much, in terms of external reasons (such as the existence of still uncivilized tribes, the spread of hunger, the expansion of illiteracy), but explicitly as a *call to repentance,* to the rediscovery of the real meaning of the Church; to the living out of the mystery of our incorporation into Christ; to a true orientation in the face of both the immediate and the ultimate future, and to the right doxology *(Orthodoxos)* of God.[14]

Chapter XI

The Liturgy in Orthodox Missiology

THE LITURGICAL ORIENTATION OF ORTHODOXY

It is no exaggeration to state that the chief feature of the Orthodox Church is its liturgical orientation. Above all else, it is a worshiping church. Writing of the Orthodox Church, George Florovsky states: "Christianity is a liturgical religion. The Church is first of all a worshiping community. Worship comes first, doctrine and discipline second."[1] That should not be interpreted to mean that worship can proceed without regard for doctrine, for correct worship is the expression of correct doctrine. Indeed, one does not properly understand Orthodox worship unless one sees it as a proclamation of Orthodox belief. The two are "inseparable."[2]

This close connection between right doctrine and right praise is the key that explains the importance of the liturgy in the proclamation of the gospel. This proclamation is in the first place to the believers themselves. As Peter Hammond has observed:

Nobody who has lived and worshiped among Greek Christians for any length of time but has sensed in some measure the extraordinary hold which the recurring cycle of the Church's liturgy has upon the piety of the people. Nobody who has kept the great Lent with the Greek Church, who has shared in the fast which lies heavy upon the whole nation for 40 days; who has stood for long hours, one of an innumerable multitude who crowd the tiny Byzantine Churches and overflow into the streets, while the familiar pattern of God's saving economy toward man is re-presented in psalm and prophecy, in readings from the Gospels and in the matchless poetry of the canons; who has known the desolation of the Holy and Great Friday, when every bell in Greece tolls its lament and the body of the Savior lies shrouded in flowers in all the village Churches throughout the land; who has been present at the kindling of the new fire and tasted of the joy of a world released from the bondage of sin and death—none can have lived through all this and not realized that for the Greek

86

Christian the Gospel is inseparably linked with the liturgy which is unfolded week by week in his parish Church. Not among Greeks only but throughout Orthodox Christendom the liturgy has remained at the very heart of the Church's life.[3]

There is another dimension to the proclamation of the gospel by the liturgy, a dimension at times obscured even within Orthodoxy. This is the extension of the Orthodox faith because of the liturgy, by means of the liturgy, and with the result that the liturgy will be celebrated in the whole earth. Or in other words, the liturgy contains the motivation for mission, is a method of mission, and is the aim of mission. This does not negate what was said in the preceding chapters, but gives a particularly Orthodox understanding to the subject. For example, it was noted that the immediate aim of mission was the establishment of the Church. But what does the Church that has been established do, if not worship God? Likewise, the motivation for mission is found in communion with God, the high point of which, for the Church as a corporate body, is its worship of God. Finally, in Orthodox missionary methods the repeated emphasis has been on the translation into the vernacular of the Scriptures (used extensively in Orthodox worship) and the liturgy, so that the people could praise God in their own tongue.

That there is a close connection between the liturgy and the mission of the Orthodox Church should not be regarded as curious. What else would one expect from a Church in which the liturgy plays so central a role? What would be strange and out of character would be no mention of worship in the mission of the Church. This emphasis provides a convenient entry into the thinking of Orthodoxy on the missionary task and at the same time serves as an example to the Western Churches, which might discover new motivation and power for mission.

By way of introduction, a comment on terminology is in order. The word "liturgy" means, in Greek, a public work or service. Hence all services of the Orthodox Church that are public and designed for the worship of God could be classified as liturgies. This is the general use of the term in the West. In the Eastern Church, however, the term is generally reserved for the chief worship service, and if prefaced by the word "holy"[4] or "divine,"[5] refers to the Eucharist. While the Orthodox usage will be generally followed below, the theology elucidated should not be considered unique to this one service. The other services of the Church, namely the divine offices of matins, vespers, and the hours, and the occasional offices (such as baptism, marriage, etc.), also bear witness to the union of doctrine and practice. It would be false and misleading to truncate the worship of the Orthodox into one service. The quotation referring to the liturgical cycle in Greece should make this abundantly clear. The whole of the liturgical experience shapes Orthodoxy. The thoroughness of the integration of Orthodox worship into the totality of human life accounts for the survival of Orthodoxy under persecution and for the deep penetration of the faith into the peoples who have been traditionally known as Orthodox.

THE LITURGY AS MOTIVATION FOR MISSION

The Missionary Structure of the Liturgy

It is not the purpose of this section to undertake a general structural analysis of the Orthodox liturgy. This has been adequately treated by a number of Orthodox authors.[6] Nor is it an attempt to provide a commentary on the liturgical actions of the priest. Allegorical interpretations of these abound, some of which merit more consideration than others.[7] Similarly, straightforward explanations of the liturgy have been published in recent years so that the laity might be better informed. These can be readily consulted by anyone interested in the explanation of the service.[8] The purpose here is to record and comment on the Orthodox understanding of how the structure of the liturgy serves the missionary cause.

The Sermon

There is a tendency among Western authors to set the liturgical emphasis of Orthodoxy in opposition to the homiletical emphasis of Protestantism. An example is the title of a book, *Icon and Pulpit*.[9] The subtitle explains its theme as "The Protestant-Orthodox Encounter." By virtue of the elements chosen to represent the respective positions, one would expect that since there are no icons in Protestantism, there is no pulpit in Orthodoxy. While admittedly this juxtaposition of key elements produces a striking title, it obscures the true position of Orthodoxy and hinders the encounter the book seeks to promote. For indeed, Orthodoxy has a pulpit, prominent at times in the history of Orthodoxy, though at other times slipping into disuse owing to the theological poverty of the clergy.[10]

Perhaps the greatest sign of life in the Orthodox Church today is the revival of the pulpit and the restoration of the former place of honor to the sermon. The Zoe movement in Greece was largely responsible for the renewed stress on preaching in that land, while at the same time stressing the importance of the liturgy.[11] In America the sermon is an important part of the liturgy, used for the instruction and exhortation of the people of God.[12] From Russia, however, comes the most important testimony to the inherent compatibility of the icon and the pulpit. In a land where religious instruction is forbidden, the sermon in the worship service has taken on a dimension unmatched in Western Protestantism.[13]

It must be recognized therefore that

> The liturgical sermon, which was considered by the Fathers to be an essential and integral part of the Eucharist, is the main expression of the *teaching ministry* in the Church. It must be neither neglected . . . nor deviated from its unique purpose: that of conveying to the people the Word of God, by which the Church *lives* and grows. It is also wrong to

preach the Word *after* the Eucharist—it belongs organically to the first, the teaching part of the service, and fulfills the reading of the Scriptures.[14]

The emphasis on the teaching ministry of the sermon is further strengthened, as Schmemann has pointed out above, by its position in the Liturgy of the Catechumens. The sermon comes just before the dismissal of the catechumens and would serve as a vehicle for the instruction of the unbaptized. At the same time it could be used as a time of reflection and preparation for the baptized believers who were to partake of the Communion elements. It is therefore a false antithesis that would ignore the place of the sermon in the Orthodox liturgy.

The Scripture Readings

There exist a regular order and standard readings from the Epistles and Gospels for all the Sundays of the Orthodox liturgical year. The liturgical year is composed of two overlapping cycles, one fixed by the earth's orbit around the sun, that is, the fixed date of the Lord's nativity, the feasts connected with the saints; the other, dependent on the movable feast of Easter. The standard readings are based on their proximity to the date of Easter, so that the dates of the standard readings vary from year to year. Furthermore, when a special event in the life of Christ (mostly fixed days, like the transfiguration) or one of the saints falls on a Sunday, the standard reading is replaced by the reading for the particular celebration. Lists of the readings can be found in several different service books.[15]

It is not the purpose of this section to comment on or to analyze the various readings; this has been admirably undertaken by George Barrois in *Scripture Readings in Orthodox Worship*.[16] Rather, the purpose is to point to the regular cycle of Scripture readings throughout the church year. To the Epistle and Gospel readings, one must add the repetition of Psalter selections and the Old Testament readings connected with Lent and other occasions during the year.[17] While the entire course of readings is intended for the edification of the faithful, the readings around Easter, bound on the one side by the beginning of Lent and on the other by Pentecost, preserve the instructional character of the lectionary.

> The New Testament lectionary for the time extending from the beginning of the Lenten Triodion to Pentecost demonstrates the special concern of the Church with the preparation of the faithful for the celebration of the paschal mystery. The instruction of catechumens preparing for baptism and of the newly baptized had been the common practice of all the ancient Churches, Rome, Jerusalem, Antioch, Constantinople, the Orientals and the Africans.[18]

The Scriptual Phraseology of the Liturgy

In addition to the formal use of Scripture in the readings and the sermon, the Scriptures have an even wider use in the text of the liturgy itself. For the

Orthodox Church, "her various liturgical acts and her prayer life, hymns, and services are imbued, one might almost say immersed, with Scriptural verses and allusions."[19] There is as yet no exhaustive study on the Scriptural content of all the Orthodox services. However, Demetrios Constantelos has produced a study of three liturgies and four sacraments.[20] His purpose was to demonstrate scientifically the claim of the Orthodox Church to be the "Biblical Church par excellence."[21] In his study Constantelos did not consider the various readings from the Bible that are a part of every service of worship but concentrated on the scriptural elements found in the prayers and petitions of the service.

Of the seven services he examined, "more than twenty-five percent of the services are made of Scriptural material. With the allusions and the Biblical proper names the percentage is still higher."[22] Of course, not all services have this percentage, as "some prayers or even services are more Scriptural than others."[23] As might be expected, Psalms is the most alluded to, followed by Matthew and Genesis. Of the canonical books, only nine in the Old Testament and one in the New Testament are not cited.[24] Constantelos also found allusions to the Deuterocanonical books of 1 Esdras, Tobit, Judith, Wisdom of Solomon, Ecclesiasticus, Baruch, Song of the Three Children, Susanna, and 1, 2, 3, and 4 Maccabees.[25]

All this leads Constantelos to conclude that "The Word of God was in the early Church and continues to be the inexhaustible source of spiritual instruction and nurture in the Orthodox Catholic Church today. The Holy Scriptures, which have penetrated the liturgical books and the hymnology of the Church still occupy a central place in the life and worship of Orthodox Christians today."[26]

Constantelos's study is important for the study of Orthodox mission theology because it demonstrates the link between the Bible and Tradition. It further explains, in part, the biblical mindset Orthodoxy imparts to the believers. "Scriptural sayings and elements are in the mouth of the faithful like proverbs and mottoes."[27] This would be true even where the population was illiterate. "The study of the Bible has always been encouraged to such an extent that even the illiterate in the Orthodox world have learned by heart whole Psalms and other portions of the Scriptures."[28] It takes no great reflection to note that the scriptural elements in the liturgies and major sacraments form a powerful tool in missionary work. The biblical material and thought-style is able to be better impressed on the minds of the new converts. In areas where oral tradition is a cultural pattern, the liturgy can be assimilated in the same manner. It can therefore become not just a weekly period of worship but a vital element in the expression of one's faith.

Motivational Factors in the Liturgy

Whereas the liturgy can and has served as a method of educating new converts in the faith, it has at times been ignored as a missionary element by the established Orthodox Churches. Seen solely as a means of worship, the potential of the liturgy to motivate the Church to mission was long neglected. As will be shown below, this has recently been rediscovered by Orthodox writers. The establishment of the Church in the Diaspora has permitted time for reflection on the nature of the Church's task. Ecumenical contact, both in official meetings and on the individual level, has challenged the Orthodox to examine their tradition for its missionary emphasis. This did not go unheeded. The response has provided the West with a challenge of its own.[29] The motivating factors in the liturgy can be considered in two aspects. The one is the missionary elements, or calls, within the texts themselves. The other is the overall thrust of the liturgy and its affect on the believer.

Missionary Elements in the Liturgy

That the Orthodox liturgy contains a missionary element can be simply demonstrated by reference to the prayers for the catechumens. Preserved in the liturgy, it indicates the interest of the early Church for those outside the Church. During the first centuries of the Christian Church's growth and before the official recognition of Christianity by Constantine, adult baptism was the "prevailing custom."[30] Baptism was only administered after a long period of instruction. Those undergoing this instruction, the catechumens, were not permitted to take part in the Eucharist. In the Orthodox liturgy the prayers for the catechumens were immediately followed by their dismissal from the service.[31] In some Orthodox Churches these prayers are said inaudibly by the priest inasmuch as there are no catechumens, the class having disappeared with the widespread establishment of infant baptism.[32] Yet the prayers need not be considered as only an archaic remnant. Especially when the prayers are said audibly, as in the liturgy of the Orthodox Church in America, they serve a missionary purpose.

> The *Prayers for the Catechumens* remind us of the golden age of the Church when *mission,* the conversion to Christ of non-believers was considered the *essential* task of the Church. . . . They are an indictment of our parishes as static, closed and self-centered communities, indifferent not only to the mission of the Church in the world, but even to the general interests of the Church, to everything which is not of immediate interest to the parish.[33]

A similar and even stronger denunciation of the inactivity of the Church in missionary witness comes from a sermon preached by Anastasios Yannoulatos at the Athens University Church: "Can a Church that for centuries now has had no catechumens, but jealously guards the treasure of faith for itself, totally indifferent to whether other people are being born, breathe, live and die, within the Lie—which therefore is alien to the feelings of world love and justice—be really 'Orthodox'?"[34]

Both these authors are calling the Church to task for missing the missionary call present in their worship services. Far from regarding the purpose of the worship service as antithetical to evangelistic outreach, they see it as a motivating factor. Yannoulatos continues:

> The atmosphere of the Liturgy of the Presanctified Gifts is particularly helpful for meditating and praying for External Mission; it constitutes the most suitable climate for the development of the ecumenical, Missionary spirits of our Church. For, firstly, it brings us into a mystical contact of prayer with the life of the ancient Church, with the forgotten classes of the "catechumens" and the "illuminated," and it reveals to us in a soft but stirring way the shortcomings (or more precisely, the guilt) of our Church in the contemporary era. Secondly its whole atmosphere throbs with a feeling of repentance and contrition in front of the sacrifice of the Cross, towards which the entire Lent is orientated.[35]

What the prayer for catechumens does is to focus the contemporary congregation's attention on the missionary tradition of Orthodoxy, a tradition which, however strongly professed, needs to be manifested in the present age. Why are there no catechumens? Why is their absence not generally seen as a lack in Orthodoxy? What factors of the celebration of the Eucharist have been lost by the lack of a catechumen class? The tradition remains, but the Orthodox must face the question of their possible betrayal of the tradition with which they have been entrusted. Has, as Yannoulatos suggests, the Church without catechumens, without mission ceased to be Orthodox? One thing is clear, the tradition till now preserved testifies to the concern of the early Church.

The search for missionary elements is not confined to the prayers for the catechumens. There are other elements that can be seen in this light. An example of a missionary interpretation of liturgical elements is found in an article that meditates on parts of the Triodian, a liturgical book.[36] Efthimios Stylios traces the parallels of the troparions (a troparion is a stanza of religious poetry)[37] with the stages of missionary preparation and service. It is Stylios's contention that the liturgical books contain a wellspring of missionary ideas. Due to the general lack of interest in mission, this treasure has been unexplored. An extensive study of the issues is long overdue. Stylios expresses the hope that "the revival of interest in Orthodox missions . . . will soon bear considerable fruit on this point as well."[38]

The Missionary Thrust of the Liturgy

In addition to selecting the elements of the liturgy that are mission oriented, the entire liturgy itself can be seen as a motivating force for mission. This is brought out clearly in an article by Alexander Schmemann, where he speaks of the "missionary imperative" that is a part of the Orthodox tradition. "Nothing reveals better the relation between the Church as fullness and the Church as mission than the Eucharist, the central act of the Church's *leiturgia,* the sacrament of the Church itself."[39] It is in the Eucharist that the Church rises up to heaven and is separated from the world.[40] But it is also in the Eucharist that the Church returns to earth and to its mission.

The Eucharist is always the End, the sacrament of the *parousia,* and, yet, it is always the *beginning,* the *starting point:* now the mission begins. "We have seen the true Light, we have enjoyed Life eternal" but this Life, this Light, are given us in order to "transform" us into Christ's witnesses in this world. Without this ascension into the kingdom we would have had nothing to witness to; now, having once more become "His people and His inheritance," we can do what Christ wants us to do: "You are witnesses of these things." (Lk. 24:48). The Eucharist, transforming "the Church into what it is"—transforms it into mission.[41]

Just as mission can take place because Jesus came from the Father into the world and witnessed to the truth of God, so in like manner the Church can only witness to what it knows of God. It is the communion with the Godhead that motivates and enables the Church to carry out its divine calling. The Eucharist becomes the source of the Church's strength for mission.

This concept of the Eucharist does more than reveal the liturgy as a factor in missionary motivation. It demonstrates the corporate character of the Orthodox Church in sharp contrast to the Western Churches' individualism. Worship in the Orthodox Church is essentially corporate in nature.[42] The liturgy is never celebrated by a priest alone.[43] There must always be a congregation present, however small that congregation be in actual fact.[44] It is the Church that joins together in the liturgy; it is the Church to whom the mission of God is entrusted.[45] The communion with God brings the congregation together in the sharing of outpoured grace. Thus in Orthodox theology the theme of the Church as the body of Christ, to which one is joined by Christian initiation and apart from which one will not be saved, is borne out in the experience of worship. In *The Church Is One,* Khomiakov wrote:

We know that when any one of us falls, he falls alone; but no one is saved alone. He who is saved is saved in the Church, as a member of her, and in unity with all her other members. If anyone believes, he is in the communion of faith; if he loves, he is in the communion of love; if he prays, he is in the communion prayer. Wherefore no one can rest his hope on his own prayers, and every one who prays asks the whole Church for intercession, not as if he had any doubts of the intercession of Christ, the one Advocate, but in the assurance that the whole Church ever prays for all her members.[46]

From the emphasis on the corporate experience of salvation in the community of faith, the centrality of the communal worship clearly stands out. The individual is not saved in isolation, nor lives in isolation. The individual is saved and lives in the community of faith. In community, specifically in the

Eucharist service, the individual obtains the needed spiritual nourishment. It is important to stress this point, for the unity of the Church and its union with Christ is a key to the understanding of Orthodox theology. During the Eucharist, the Church unites with Christ. After the Eucharist, the Church returns to its mission in the world. But it is not simply a return. The Church, which has been called by God to the presence of the Trinity—a presence celebrated by the Communion in the body and blood of Christ—is then sent by God to the world. The Eucharist ends in mission, the Godhead sending the Church as the Father sent the Son.

Having spoken of the communal aspect of the Eucharist, it must be pointed out that what is shared in mission is nothing less than a new life, the new life in Christ Jesus. Since this new life is not merely intellectual knowledge but a real participation in Christ, the question arises as to how this life is communicated. For the Orthodox, it is not a communication comprised solely of intellectual ideas and propositions. Doctrine, without the experience of the living Christ, is useless. By participating in the Eucharist, by partaking of the life Christ provides in the communion in his flesh and blood, one finds real life. The one who eats is also the one who is sent. "As the living Father sent Me, and I live because of the Father; so he who eats Me, he also shall live because of Me" (Jn. 6:57 NASV).

> This internal relation of "eating" with "sending" must be stressed. Christ is not a prophet or a theory. He is *life, the life!* The transmission of life is not realized so much by words or by thoughts. It reaches its fulfillment in Holy Communion. Every part of our being—one human being that is body and soul—must be holy. It is for this reason that we receive His blood and His body: so that everything in our body may be transformed, so that we may "become partakers of the divine nature" (2 Peter 1:4).[47]

The liturgy, then, serves not only as a motivating factor but also as the source of spiritual strength. A correct understanding of the centrality of the eucharistic experience in Orthodoxy provides one with a key to the role of the Eucharist as a motivating and enabling factor in missionary outreach.

THE LITURGY AS A METHOD OF MISSION

In the discussion of missionary aims in chapter 7 the point was raised concerning the role of the liturgy in witness as well as worship. It will be recalled that the traditional story of the conversion of Vladimir pivots around the liturgical witness of Orthodoxy. Whatever credence is attributed to the traditional account, the liturgical witness of Orthodoxy is still considered a part of the witness of the Church.

"Although the sacrament of the Eucharist, since the very origin of the Church, was a celebration closed to outsiders, and full participation in the

Eucharist remains reserved for the members of the Church, liturgical worship as a whole is an obvious form of witness and mission.''[48] This statement from a report by the Orthodox Consultation on Confessing Christ (1975) would appear to be contradictory. How can an act of worship that is reserved for the Church be a form of witness to outsiders? The answer lies in the nature of the eucharistic celebration itself. It is a memorial, or remembrance, for the Church and at the same time a proclamation of the gospel (1 Cor. 11:23–26). The remembrance aspect of the Eucharist serves as a motivating and strengthening force in missionary work. This was the thrust of the previous section. In the next section the witnessing, or proclamation, aspect of the Eucharist will be discussed.

The Proclamation of the Gospel in the Eucharist

Two consultations of Orthodox theologians held in the 1970s dealt with the issue of confessing Christ in the liturgy. Both were organized by the Commission on World Mission and Evangelism's Desk for Orthodox Studies and Relations. The first, held at the Monastery of Cernica, near Bucharest, Romania, in June 1974, dealt with a broader range of issues involved in the Church's witness.[49] The second consultation, held at Etchmiadzine, Armenia, in September 1975, was especially concerned with the question of liturgical witness.[50] Since both meetings were consultations, the reports cannot be considered authoritative statements of the Orthodox position. However, they are working statements of what Orthodox theologians are thinking, and as such serve to further the study of the subject.

In the Cernica Consultation, the topic was of much wider scope than that of the liturgy in mission. However, several references to the evangelistic nature of the liturgy appear in the report. M. V. George, of India, presented a paper on "Confessing Christ Today through Liturgy as a Form and Experience of the Fullness of Salvation" in which he gives several examples of the connection between liturgy and mission.

We confess Christ today through the Liturgy in multifarious ways. There is first of all the combination of the pulpit and the altar in liturgical worship. The sermon is a part and parcel of liturgical worship. The homilies of the Fathers were mostly delivered in the liturgical context. Most of the Christian preaching and teaching in the Orthodox Churches in the Soviet Union takes place in the liturgical context even today. Then, the transformed lives of the faithful who partake of the mysteries regularly is an eloquent witness to the whole world that Jesus Christ is still the greatest deifying force on earth. Though there are exceptions, of course, regular communicants manifest their deified lives in the so-called secular vocations of life and they sanctify everything they touch. Thirdly, we confess Christ today to the non-Christians who attend the Liturgy casually at first. Conversions still take place through the magnetic attraction of the Eucharistic service. The casual visitor slowly becomes a regular attendant and then studies the faith of the Church and asks for baptism.[51]

The close relationship between the sermon and the liturgical rite has already been discussed above. Likewise, the emphasis on regular communicants being a source of Christian witness stems from the Eucharist being a source of spiritual power. One wonders if the lives of the communicants point specifically to the Eucharist; that is, Do non-Christians know that the difference they are observing can be traced to the liturgical participation of the believer or do they simply notice a "Christian" difference?

Another way of expressing this thought would be to ask if the liturgy can witness secondhand to the non-Christian without a verbal explanation given on the part of the Christian. Is the connection between regular eucharistic communion and sanctity of life directly transparent to the outsider? Certainly the liturgy becomes a testimony to the non-Christian when the latter asks the Christian for the secret of the source of the Christian's holiness. In either case, the thing that first attracts the unbeliever's attention is the "transformed life." The source of strength and power that produces a transformed life is found in regular communion with Jesus Christ. Here, as one would expect, the motivational and methodological aspects of the liturgy are closely joined. The power communicated in the Eucharist is at the same time a motivation for mission and a witness to the truth of the gospel. Therefore, from the standpoint of the Christian, the Eucharist is an important facet of the evangelistic mission to which the Lord calls the person.

But the liturgy is a testimony to the non-Christian as well. M. V. George noted above that conversions still occur because of it. Two points immediately arise. First, can the liturgy be legitimately used in this way? Is not the liturgy a closed event for the Church?[52] Second, what or who does the witnessing? Is it the pageant of celebration: the signs, symbols, and sounds of the service? Or is it the testimony of the Holy Spirit, convicting of sin and convincing the unbeliever that what is happening is the commemoration of the real event in history?

The first point is the easier to deal with. N. A. Nissiotis remarks in his introduction to the reports of the Cernica Consultation:

It is also interesting to note in Reports No. 2 and 3 the Orthodox attitude that the Eucharist should not be used as a tool for confessing Christ or as an instrument for mission, but as the focal event of the Church community, and as such must be seen as the springboard, the starting event of Christians for confessing Christ in today's world.[53]

And yet, the element of liturgical proclamation is still recognized as valid, as can be seen from a quotation from Report No. 3.

Though the Eucharist is only for the Assembly of the faithful, for their sanctification, non-Eucharistic liturgical expressions, non-Eucharistic liturgical prayers, liturgical Bible reading, icons, hymnology etc. can and should be also used for proclaiming the Gospel and confessing Christ to the world. . . . Matins and Vespers as well as the liturgy of the Catechumens can give a framework for the Church in new creations in this field.[54]

The tension between the use of liturgical acts as proclamation to unbelievers and their reservation for the faithful is evident here. Not in the sense that the nature of the Eucharist is open to debate, for it is not. There is universal agreement that it is a service for the Church, not for outsiders. (Although as a point of fact, this writer knows of no place where the ancient prohibitions concerning the presence of the uninitiated, meaning unbaptized, or non-Orthodox, is enforced.) Nevertheless, there is considerable agreement (though perhaps not as universal as that concerning the nature of the eucharistic gathering) that testifies to the evangelistic value of the liturgy. What makes this so? Without anticipating the second question of who or what does the witnessing in the liturgy, the nature of the liturgy that gives it this evangelistic aspect must be briefly examined.

When one says the Eucharist is for the Church, that is correct. But if one means *only* for the Church, then a key element in Orthodox liturgical theology has been missed. For the Orthodox liturgy is not simply for the Church but for the world as well. "Liturgy is our thanksgiving for—and on behalf of—the created world; and the restoration in Christ of the fallen world."[55] "The eschatological nature of the Church is not the negation of the world, but, on the contrary, its affirmation and acceptance as the object of divine love."[56] Therefore, the liturgy is for the Church, but not exclusively for the Church. It is for the world as well, that the world might be saved. The sacrament is not for the world to partake of, but it is for the salvation of the world. As Christ gave his flesh "for the life of the world" (Jn. 6:51), so the Church gives that life to the world. In the sacraments the fullness of the life that God designed for the world is revealed. "The Church thus is not a 'self-centered' community but precisely a missionary community. . . ."[57]

All this may seem strange to the Western observer who sees the sacraments as internal, or community-centered, events with no reference to the world.

The Western Christian is used to thinking of sacrament as opposed to the world and links the mission with the Word and not the sacrament. He is, moreover, accustomed to consider the sacrament as, maybe, an essential and yet clearly defined part or institution or act *of* the Church and within the Church, but not of the Church as being itself the sacrament of Christ's presence and action. And finally he is primarily interested in certain very "formal" questions concerning the sacraments: their number, their "validity," their institution, etc. Our purpose is to show that there exists and always existed a different perspective, a different approach to the sacrament and that this approach may be of crucial importance precisely for the whole burning issue of mission, of our witness to Christ in the world. For the basic question is: *of what are we witnesses?* What have we seen, touched with our hands? Of what have we partaken, been made communicants? Where do we call men? What can we offer them?[58]

It is, then, Orthodoxy's understanding of the sacramental nature of the Church that makes the liturgy a part of the Church's evangelistic witness. The situation may be summed up as follows: Orthodox Tradition dictates the closed nature of the eucharistic gathering; Orthodox theology recognizes the proclamatory nature of the eucharistic event. In attempting to balance both truths, Report No. 3 of Cernica recommended the use of noneucharistic liturgical expressions as an evangelistic tool.

The issue was dealt with more fully by the consultation held at Etchmiadzine. This consultation noted that "liturgical witness as a whole is an obvious form of witness and mission."[59] Under the heading "To Whom to Proclaim?" the consultation listed several groups.

> . . . The following categories of people should directly or indirectly hear the message of the Holy Eucharist.
> a) The members of the Church who try sincerely to practice the faith should be made true evangelists by the Gospel proclaimed to them. . . .
> b) The nominal Christians. . . .
> c) The mobile population, migrant workers, refugees, etc., some of whom have no permanent roots anywhere under the sun.
> d) People of the diaspora of our modern age.
> e) The non-Christians in the vicinity of our congregations and Churches. . . .
> f) The fields where no one ever preached the Gospel.[60]

It is difficult to think of people who do not fit into one or more of the groups above. The world needs to hear the message of the gospel as proclaimed and acted out in the eucharistic celebration. Whatever theological distinctions are made in regard to the closed nature of the celebration, the need for its universal proclamation is clear. In the liturgy there is the encounter with "a real Presence of Christ."[61]

In discussing how the gospel should be proclaimed, emphasis is placed on new forms of worship (which, however, follow the old pattern) to meet the needs found in "contemporary society." Therefore, it remains true that the Orthodox Church still considers its worship as an evangelistic tool, both for its own nominal members and for society as a whole. "The Incarnation was for the whole people of all ages and redemption of the whole cosmos. The Holy

Eucharist was instituted, among other things, to proclaim the death and resurrection of our Lord 'until he comes again.' "[62]

Having thus dealt with the first point raised above, whether or not it is legitimate to consider the liturgy an evangelistic method, the second point must now be discussed. Who or what does the witnessing when the liturgy is the method? The first answer is that the witness is given by those whose lives have been transformed by their ongoing participation in the Eucharist. ". . . our own availability to the Gospel, and our own opening to the Spirit through the Communion of the Divine Body and Blood, our own sanctification remain the best method of Mission."[63] Second, the witness of the Spirit in testifying to the reality of Christ must not be overlooked. The Holy Spirit is invoked by the Epiclesis to change the gifts of bread and wine into the body and blood of Christ. This central role in the eucharistic celebration is indicative of the Spirit's importance in the Orthodox Church.[64] Furthermore, it is not only upon the gifts that the priest prays the Spirit will descend, but upon the congregation as well.[65] Therefore, it is only natural that the Holy Spirit is the interpreter of the sacrament.[66]

But the answer most frequently given as to how the liturgy is a witness to the gospel is that the beauty of the celebration testifies to its truth. "The Orthodox cult, by its beauty and variety, is unique in all Christianity. . . . This, 'heaven upon earth,' is the manifestation of the beauty of the spiritual world."[67] Orthodoxy witnesses to the spiritual reality that the world without Christ does not know. In the liturgy the church ascends to the throne of God.[68] Thus the witness of the liturgical celebration is the witness of the courts of heaven, the heaven-on-earth theme so frequently found in Orthodox literature.[69] Perhaps this insight into heaven provides the most compelling reason why the liturgy is an obvious evangelistic method. In the liturgy is demonstrated the beginnings of the new order, the kingdom of God.[70]

The Foreignness of the Liturgy

The beauty of the liturgy can be interpreted in another way from that outlined above. Rather than seeing it as the truth of God brought near, it can be superficially regarded as merely exotic or strange. It may seem to be a relic from the past, with no relevance to the contemporary situation. To many non-Orthodox, the liturgy seems to be too long, too repetitious. (Certain Orthodox also share this view.) How can something so out-of-date convey the truth of God?

As remarkable as it may seem, it is this out-of-dateness, this foreignness that gives the Orthodox celebration its enduring value. The Eucharist remains a link with the past; but more than just the past, it remains a link with another type of reality that stands in sharp contrast to the material world.[71] The liturgy witnesses to a different order. And precisely this aspect of the liturgy makes it attractive to non-Orthodox. Thus, while remaining in a sense foreign, Orthodox worship is by no means unpalatable to non-Orthodox. Yannoulatos explains:

Orthodox worship, as many scholars observe, can be easily comprehensible and acceptable to the Asian and African world. Its mystagogic atmosphere, ever rendering vivid the mystery of the Word's Incarnation and of man's theosis (becoming divine), affects man's whole being. As the recent instance of the Kenya Orthodox communities bears witness, it is a primary power in disseminating and consolidating Orthodoxy.[72]

When one considers the corporate nature of African worship, the foreignness of Orthodox worship to a large extent disappears. Perhaps it is only in the West, where individualism has prevailed over the group experience, that Orthodoxy seems strange. In many countries of mission, the Orthodox way fits in far better than the Protestant or Roman Catholic forms that are there now.[73] Wentink writes:

> The greatest contribution which the Orthodox Church can make to the African Churches is the Holy Liturgy. This central element in the Orthodox Church has already found ready acceptance among the African Orthodox. It is interesting to see how soon former hardcore independence-fighters have been won over to the liturgy of St. John Chrysostomos which dates from the third century. Unlike the Roman Catholic Church, the first task undertaken by the African Orthodox *in their mission to other tribes* was the translation of the liturgy into the vernacular.
>
> It is fascinating to witness the Incarnation of Christ on an ordinary Sunday morning in a small Church somewhere in Kikuyuland. With a minimum of training or education every Church member understands the symbolism and the Mystery of the Word that becomes flesh. The Congregation stands for three hours and participates fully in the Worship service. Hundreds line up to receive the Holy Communion which is the most important part of the service. Not only for the Greek Orthodox but also for the African Orthodox the liturgy is the strongest appeal of the Church. African members regard the Sacrament as a substitute for the old Kikuyu sacrifice and baptism as their initiation. For them Orthodox Faith and symbolism have replaced their old religious customs, not as something completely strange and new but as something familiar which they had dimly perceived and humbly revered as non-Christians for a long time.[74]

This does not mean that Orthodoxy need be exactly the same in its African or Asian manifestations, because the history of the Orthodox Church demonstrates that a variety of liturgies can exist together.[75] The tie that binds the Orthodox is not liturgical uniformity. This is borne out in the present day with the linguistic and liturgical variants present in worldwide Orthodoxy.[76] What remains constant is the common faith confessed by those who are Orthodox.

"The unity of the Orthodox Church does not center in a superficial uniformity, but in one faith and one sacramental life."[77]

While prepared to accept an African Orthodoxy that worships God "in drum and dance,"[78] the liturgical form is strikingly similar in all the Orthodox Churches. No doubt the reason for this goes back to an imitation of the ways and practices of the original transmission of the gospel to the new areas of Orthodoxy. Yet the universality of the Orthodox sacramental order is in itself a testimony to its transnational character. For though it originated in an Hellenistic environment, the liturgy is no longer Hellenistic. It has been adopted by world Orthodoxy as its own. In a sense the liturgy remains foreign, not because of its Greek origin, but because in a real way it is not of this world. As has been said above, it testifies to another world, one foreign to this world, which it will someday supersede.

THE LITURGY AS THE AIM OF MISSION

It is hardly necessary to belabor this aspect of the liturgy with regard to the mission of the Church. Right praise of God is one of the ways that the ultimate aim of mission, the glory of God, is accomplished. Thus the worship of God is an intermediate aim of mission. Even as such, it is not really an aim within itself, since, as has been shown above, the goals are the founding of churches and the conversion of those who do not know the Christ. The liturgy results from the accomplishment of the intermediate aims of mission.

However, there are two valid liturgical observations that can be made under this heading. The first is that the worldwide spread of the gospel should also signify the extension of the praise of God. This should not be thought of as solely quantitative growth, but as qualitative as well. The result of the planting of truly local churches is that each church is free to fulfill God's calling for it. "In each country, the Church is called to glorify God with her own voice . . . and [the people of each country are called to] add their contribution to the common doxological hymn."[79] The nations have a contribution to make to the universal praise of God. Their voices must be developed. The praise of God is not complete until all "the great multitude from every nation and all tribes and peoples and tongues" (Rev. 7:9) raise their voices in praise.

Viewed in this manner, the liturgy celebrated in many different languages becomes an eschatological sign. And indeed it should be seen in this way inasmuch as Orthodoxy is oriented toward the future completion of all things in Christ. This eschatological fulfillment can be seen in two modes, that of the believer's union with Christ, or *theosis,* and that of the Church as a whole taking part in "the doxological symphony that the universe is called to offer to God."[80] Just as the preaching of the gospel to all the nations is a sign of the end times (Mt. 24:14), so is the extension of the liturgy into the world an eschatological sign.[81]

The second observation is simply that the aim of having the liturgy celebrated in the language of the new Orthodox churches serves as an inspiration to the established Orthodox Church and as a testimony to the non-Orthodox. Because of the emphasis on liturgical translations into the vernacular, the celebration of the liturgy is definitely an aim of mission. But in addition to the effect of the liturgical celebration on the fullness of praise for the Godhead, the effect of a joyous celebration on those outside is not to be minimized. It is the witness of the local church to its neighbors and to worldwide Orthodoxy. The horizontal dimension of the praise of God forms a backdrop to the Church's life in the world and for the world.

Chapter XII

Missiological Dimensions in Orthodox Ecclesiology

Any exploration of Orthodox missionary thinking inevitably must arrive at a consideration of Orthodox ecclesiology. Indeed, the assumed factor throughout this present study has been the centrality of the doctrine of the Church to Orthodox missionaries. Converts were always converts to the Church; the incorporation of the believers into Christ's body has been shown to be the immediate aim of mission. Before undertaking an examination of how the Church is involved in mission, it is appropriate to look at the Orthodox doctrine of the Church.[1]

ORTHODOX ECCLESIOLOGY

The matter of first priority would appear to be to define "the Church." However, as Florovsky points out: "It is impossible to start with a formal definition of the Church. For, strictly speaking, there is none which could claim any doctrinal authority. None can be found in the Fathers nor in the Schoolmen, nor even in St. Thomas Aquinas. No definition has been given by the Ecumenical Councils, nor by the later Great Councils in the West, including those of Trent and Vatican."[2]

Some writers view this lack of a definition from the past as an indication that no definition of the Church is possible. For example, Sergius Bulgakov can state that "There can thus be no satisfactory and complete *definition* of the Church. 'Come and see'—one recognizes the Church only by experience, by grace, by participation in its life."[3]

While this would apparently present an insoluble problem, the lack of a formal definition does not mean that nothing can be said about what the Church is. The explanation given by Florovsky is that the Fathers did not bother to define the Church because they beheld its reality. "The lack of formal definition does not mean, however, a confusion of ideas or any obscurity of view. . . . One does not define what is self-evident."[4]

From what has been said then, it should be clear that in Orthodox theology, one does not find definitions but finds descriptions of what the Church is. When considered this way, there are any number of sources to which one can refer. Some, like Bulgakov, emphasize the union with the living Christ. The Church is primarily where the believers share the reality of the divine life. One could perhaps speak of an existential perception of the Church, though without at any time denying the objective character of the outworking of the incarnation and of Pentecost.

Another view, which complements this dynamic expression, speaks of the marks of the Church. These are found in the Nicene Creed,[5] which is used in the Divine Liturgy of the Orthodox Churches.[6] There are four marks, or notes as they are often called: the Church is one, holy, catholic, and apostolic. These marks are by no means unique with Orthodoxy as they are recognized by other Christian traditions, in particular the Roman Catholic and Anglican. It is around these points that Orthodox theologians have discussed the nature of the Church.

It is understood (or at least it is felt, dimly but firmly) that the Church no longer would be the Church were she deprived of one of these attributes, that only the consensus of these four qualities professed in the Creed expresses the fullness of her being. . . . It is clear that the harmony of the four marks of the Church is of such a kind that to suppress or change the character of one member of this fourfold distinction would suppress the very concept of the Church, or at least would transform it profoundly, changing in their turn the characteristics of the other marks.[7]

That these two perspectives are complementary becomes obvious on reflection. The marks of unity (the Church is one) and holiness (the Church is holy) are only what would be expected from an organism that was sharing the new life in Christ. If Christ is not divided (1 Cor. 1:13), then the Church cannot be divided. If Christ is holy (Hebrews 7:26), then his body must be holy. Thus one can see in the first two marks the correspondence to living the new life in Christ.

An interesting comparison is drawn by Nicholas Zernov between Protestant and Roman Catholic views of the Church. For the Roman Catholic, "the Church is a visible institution established by Christ Himself and endowed by Him with the right doctrine and an inexhaustible fountain of Grace."[8] Only within the institution is salvation available.[9] Furthermore, it does not depend on the worthiness of the celebrant of the divine mysteries, save that the minister has received the correct ecclesiastical authority and performs the prescribed ritual correctly. As Zernov points out, the human elements are not important except as the instruments used to transfer the grace. "The Church, then, is a Divine Body which exists independently of the efforts and conditions of its earthly members. Its doctrines can never be corrupted, its unity can never be broken, its ministry can never cease to exist."[10]

By way of contrast, the Protestant conception is that the Church "is not the means of salvation, but the body of the already saved, the sphere wherein the Saints find their comfort and rest."[11] Therefore the worthiness of both the minister and the community is an issue.

> A modern Protestant, for instance, is exclusively concerned with the spiritual state of his local congregation. He is not concerned or interested in the question of what kind of ordination his presiding pastor has received. . . . But he is sure that peace and love must crown a liturgical gathering and he would probably refuse to receive the Holy Bread and Wine from the hands of an immoral pastor or in the company of people for whom he has neither trust nor brotherly feelings.[12]

Having outlined the Roman Catholic and Protestant conceptions of the Church, Zernov compares them with the early Church's understanding and finds these Western interpretations lacking because of their individualistic bias. Both concentrate on the person's private relationship to God. Zernov sees the focus in the early Church to be the "living organism composed of all the regenerate people of God."[13] It is the fact of the Church being a living organism or body that distinguishes it from the concept outlined above. According to Zernov, this focus means that the salvation of God was a salvation in community. To repeat again the phrase of Khomiakov, "when any of us falls, he falls alone; but no one is saved alone. He who is saved is saved in the Church, as a member of her, and in unity with all her other members."[14] This forms in the eyes of Orthodox theologians one distinct, perhaps *the* distinct, difference between Eastern and Western conceptions of the Church.

Therefore, what was meant by the mark of the Church being one was nothing less than total identification with the other members of the body of Christ.

> A Christian became a new creature in that he knew all men to be brethren, members of the same Body of Christ, all of whom could become the temples of the Holy Ghost. He became aware of the fact that his destiny was essentially bound up with the salvation of his fellow Christians. . . . To be a Christian meant to love one's brother as oneself, to identify one's own salvation with the salvation of one's neighbors. . . . This conception of the Church, which might be called a "corporate" conception, ascribed a unique importance to Christian unity; every division, every split among the members of the Church was the violation of the bond of love and was inevitably followed by their separation from the Holy Ghost. Whatever the reason of the division might be, everyone who was involved in it endangered his salvation; because he failed to preserve the unity of Christ's Body.[15]

This concept of the early Church did not survive in the Constantinian era. Two forces destroyed it. One was, as might be expected, the alliance of the

Church with the state, which led to secular authority being used to carry out ecclesiastical mandates. The wedding of Roman legal forms to the gospel of Christ was a disastrous union. It was a case of the law killing that to which the Spirit had given life. Zernov claims the legal forms of church governments that arose "are still a source of continual embarrassment to modern Christianity."[16]

The second force, which acted to modify the early Church's conception of itself as a community in communion with God, was the revolt against the very freedom of the gospel itself. With the freedom of the gospel came an incredible responsibility in the brotherhood of the Church. "A Christian became free but he received a burden of responsibility which was till then unheard of, and very soon an unconscious but hard struggle against the gift of freedom arose within the Church."[17] Areas in which decisions were made by the community of faith were codified or, as Zernov expresses it, "petrified" in church law. The control and guidance of the Holy Spirit was replaced by formulae imposed by an external force (external to the local fellowship that is, not to the wider body).

Zernov sees this trend commencing before the Constantinian era, but reaching its full potential only when the Church was officially recognized and supported by the Roman state. Therefore the Christians moved away from freedom and responsibility to law and individuality, which is reflected in the understanding of Western Christendom to this day. The purpose of Zernov's paper is not to castigate the Western Churches but, rather, to show a way forward in the problem of Christian disunion. As with so many other problems, before one can go forward, one must first go back and correct the wrongs and put right the false directions that have been pursued. The modest proposals he puts forth are worthy of consideration.

However, the topic in this section is not the unification of the Church, but the nature of the Orthodox Church. In keeping with Orthodoxy's claim to be in a direct lineal descent from the early Church, Zernov sees the essential characteristics of the early Church preserved in the Orthodox Church.

> The Eastern Orthodox Church has preserved many ancient and valuable features of Church life in their integrity, the corporate conception of the Church is still a living reality for many of her members; although the Orthodox Church has been externally paralyzed for many centuries, the harm done to it by its numerous oppressors has been far less destructive than has been the case in Western Christendom. The Orthodox Church has had to live under an external yoke, but it never compromised inwardly its true nature by accepting legal and compulsive forces from the Civil Powers.[18]

A statement such as this one is open to debate. Before entering the fray, one should first clearly understand what Zernov is saying. The Church has been affected by the relationship to the civil government and affected in such a way as to produce a diminishing of its pure Christian witness. The net effect was, however, less on the Orthodox Church than on the Western Churches, in that the Orthodox Church never took the civil power to itself as did the West. In any case, the point at hand is not whether Caesaropapism compared favorably with the situation in Rome or Geneva. Instead the issue here is the nature of the Church as understood by the Orthodox. To this end, Zernov provides a useful guidepost by calling attention to the nature of the Church as "a brotherhood of persons who are in Communion with the Holy Ghost."[19] This corporate conception of the Church is the most valuable contribution Orthodoxy can make to the contemporary ecclesiological debate.

Moving on to other theologians' contributions to the definition of the Church, their understanding of the word "catholic" needs to be considered. The reason for this is not just to explore fully the doctrine of the Church, but because their understanding of the word contributes to their missionary thought. In an article by John Meyendorff, the meaning is discussed in reference to the Eucharist. Since in "the Eucharist, Christ and the Church are truly one Body . . . it is there that the Church is truly the one, holy, catholic Church of Christ."[20] The centrality of the Eucharist to mission has already been mentioned. Here is seen the centrality of the liturgical act to the very definition of the Church. However, this in itself is not a significant expansion over the insight gained from regarding the Church as the brotherhood of faith in fellowship with others and God.

The important thing that emerges out of the eucharistic understanding is that every local assembly gathered in the name of the Lord Jesus Christ is in fact "the *one Church catholic*."[21] Or as St. Ignatius of Antioch wrote: "Wherever Christ Jesus is, there is the catholic Church."[22] The idea presented here is a catholicity that is realized in the local assembly. Because in each eucharistic gathering the fullness of Christ is present, the gathering has what it requires to be fully the Church. To derive this theological concept requires a particular understanding of the word "catholic" (Greek: *katholikos)*. Taken in this sense, it does not mean universal in a geographical sense, but what Meyendorff calls a philosophical connotation. The root idea would then be fullness, the fullness of the apostolic doctrine that is received by the whole Church. A catholic church (with lower-case *c*s) would be one that holds to the fullness of the revealed truth and is a witness to the apostolic truth. Lossky speaks of catholicity as a quality of the truth, or "a mode of knowledge of the Truth proper to the Church, in virtue of which this Truth becomes clear to the whole Church, as much to each of her smallest parts as to her totality."[23]

In this sense the whole Church, not simply the clergy, is the guardian of truth.[24] While the clergy, and especially the bishops, are the guarantee of the apostolicity of the Church, the *laos tou Theou* embody the fullness of the faith.[25] This theme has been seen above in the discussion of the liturgical role of the laity. In the defense of truth a layperson is obligated to oppose even a bishop who is not holding the truth.[26] Relating this to the mark of catholicity means that "catholicity is not the abstract universalism of a doctrine imposed by the hierarchy, but a living tradition always preserved everywhere and by all—*quod semper, quod ubique, quod ab omnibus.*"[27]

The recognition of the fullness of doctrine received and guarded by the full Church leads to another aspect of the understanding of the adjective "catholic." For, as seen above, this adjective can be properly applied to the local church. Meyendorff writes:

> . . . a local Church, gathered around its bishop for the celebration of the Eucharist: this assembly *is* the Catholic Church. . . . A local Church is not a *part* of the Body, it is the Body itself, which is symbolized most realistically in the Byzantine rite of the preparation of the elements, when the priest places on the paten parcels of bread commemorating Christ Himself, His Mother, all the saints, all the departed and all the living: in this Bread the whole Church is really present together with the Head.[28]

This local fullness is not at the expense of the universal unity of the churches. How could it be? For the same Christ in his fullness is present in all the other local churches, if they share the same faith and sacramental life. Herein lies the reason why the Orthodox could not subscribe to a branch theory of Christendom. Each local church, to be authentically catholic, must possess the fullness of the faith. Catholicity is lost if the fullness is lost. This should provide an insight into a theme developed more fully below, namely, why the Orthodox see the prospects for unity in a different way from which most Protestants see the prospects for unity. Therefore, when used geographically, catholicity means more than just location; it signifies a "doctrinal, cosmic and moral universality"[29] as well.

To sum up the argument thus far, the Church is a living organism, which has certain marks that identify it but are not external to it. Two of the marks have been discussed, oneness and catholicity. This is not intended to imply that the other two marks are not as important, for most certainly they are vital to a true understanding of the Church. But the marks of holiness and apostolicity are, in this case, more self-evident. The Church, to be the body of Christ, must be holy, as he is holy. The Church must also still possess the unique witness of the apostles to be truly Christ's body. No foundation other than that of the apostles and prophets is possible (Eph. 2:20f.).[30]

Therefore, this leads to an understanding of the Church that can be called dynamic. This presents an ecclesiology different from the static concept generally associated with the Orthodox Church. The reason the Orthodox Church has been seen as static is twofold. On the one hand, there is a great deal of ignorance about Orthodoxy, as was pointed out in the first chapter. On the other hand, what is known and observed is a Church that preserves a large amount of tradition, practiced, it seems, unknowingly and unthinkingly by the congregation. The opportunity will arise to discuss how true this impression is when considering the missionary involvement of the Church as a whole and, in particular, the congregation's role in mission. It has been the purpose of this section to work toward a definition of the Church and to examine some Orthodox thinking on the subject.[31]

CHURCH UNITY AS A MISSIONARY FACTOR

The discussion on the marks of the Church naturally leads to the question of the disunity of the churches. It is not within the scope of this study to examine the Orthodox contribution to the problem of church unity. Nor is there any need, since several works on the subject have already appeared. A most useful compendium, *The Orthodox Church in the Ecumenical Movement,*[32] includes the encyclicals issued by Orthodox patriarchs and reports of Pan-Orthodox conferences. Over half the volume is devoted to what is termed "personal statements," that is, articles, sermons, and papers that were presented by individuals and do not bear the authority of a particular national church. However, in most if not all cases these contributions reflect the state of the Orthodox Church.

In additon to the articles printed in the above-named volume, other significant literature has appeared in *The Ecumenical Review,*[33] *Contacts,*[34] *Porefthendes,*[35] *International Review of Mission,*[36] *The Greek Orthodox Theological Review,*[37] *St. Vladimir's Theological Quarterly,*[38] *Journal of Ecumenical Studies,*[39] and *The Christian East.*[40] To this list must be added a good number of books, both for and against Orthodox participation in the ecumenical movement.[41] A fine dissertation that examines the field in depth was produced by Robert Stephanopoulos.[42] His bibliography is one of the best developed on the subject, though it is limited to material appearing before 1970. Passing mention must also be made of the vast amount of literature that has grown up because of the contact over the centuries between the Anglican Communion and the Orthodox Churches.[43] In light of the evidence it is impossible to maintain that Orthodoxy was not interested in the question of Christian unity. As was pointed out in the first chapter, Orthodox churchpeople and theologians have pioneered ecumenical contact and discussion.

Of concern here is the question of unity insofar as it affects missionary work and the theology of mission. Like so many points of doctrine, there is no defined Orthodox dogma on this subject. Therefore, one can discern two or possibly three different approaches to the subject of mission and unity, although in the final analysis there does seem to be a common Orthodox view on the Church that comprehends all alternative views.

In a Festschrift in honor of Walter Freytag, Metropolitan James of Melita (now Archbishop Iakovos) argues that without church unity there can be no missionary work. While admitting the vast scope of Byzantine missions, the metropolitan sees the eleventh-century schism between East and West altering the course of missions. Since he finds the guiding principle of missions in John 17:18–22, Metropolitan James sees sanctification and unity as key elements in mission. "*Sanctification* through truth as a *means* and perfection in oneness as an *identification* mark are acclaimed to be the main and most important requirements of those sent so that the world may know Christ and believe on Him."[44] Therefore, when the unity was broken, and even though the Roman Church was responsible (from the Orthodox point of view) for the schism, the Orthodox Church saw its mission altered from evangelism to a search for Christian unity. Metropolitan James sees the history of the Byzantine Church bearing this out in terms of the reunion councils of Lyon (1274) and Ferrara-Florence (1438–39), and the correspondence and contacts with the non-Roman Catholic[45] Churches of the West. He also sees support for his thesis in the Orthodox involvement in the ecumenical movement.

It is because division is so incompatible with mission that unity must be sought before anything else. The Orthodox Church, according to the metropolitan, "believes therefore that oneness in the Church is an absolute prerequisite for the proper discharge of the mission of the Church."[46] Without unity the Church dishonors its Lord.

> If it is agreed that the Church is "Christ Himself in our midst continued into eternity" then it can have no other mission but the threefold mission that He had, i.e., the prophetic, the sacerdotal and the royal. . . . Oneness in both mission and goal is far more important than modern missionary ventures. . . . Unity amongst Churches engaged in missionary enterprise is of incomparably greater value than disunion even in its most justified form. Mission is far more important to an Orthodox than missions.[47]

Lest the wrong impression be given with regard to the preaching of the gospel, the metropolitan does not disparage the fact that fruit has been gained through evangelism. "The Orthodox Church, however, will never permit itself to condemn missions."[48] Even missions that, because they are done in disunity, are done in envy and strife, namely, for partisan reasons, can bear fruit. But while he does not condemn, neither can he believe that missions are either the theologically correct or the most effective way of evangelism. He lays out the challenge that "the millions that were driven into the fold of Christ by the Church of the first ten centuries can in no way be encountered by the missionary achievements of the divided Church."[49] Therefore, the Orthodox Church must press for unity so that missions can flow out. The metropolitan is not persuaded that missions can lead to unity. "Missions can probably lead to mergers or limited schemes of unity, but it would be more than audacious to think that they can lead to unity."[50]

It is an interesting concept provided by Metropolitan James. The concept of unity as being the key to the successful spread of the gospel must not be underplayed. As the metropolitan points out, this is a dominical saying, which Jesus links to his goal for his disciples. However, what is not clear in the metropolitan's presentation is how this search for unity is connected to the Orthodox concept of the one true Church being the Orthodox Church. Metropolitan James hints at this when he castigates the Roman Church for cutting itself off "from the one Church."[51] If it was so cut off, then was it unity that needed to be sought or repentance and restoration? Presumably those Churches, which then in the sixteenth century separated from Rome, also needed to be restored to the one Church that remained. Therefore, while the metropolitan's structure is attractive, it would appear to be more suited to Anglican branch theory than to Orthodox ecclesiology. For it is difficult if not impossible to reconcile the search for unity unless it is first a return to unity, albeit a unity without uniformity.

Apart from the problem of Orthodox ecclesiology, Orthodox missiologists do not agree with the metropolitan's judgments.

> The unity of the Church, like her holiness, is not a truth of human reason, but a dogmatic truth; in other words, it is not something which can be proved, but it is an object of faith. . . .
>
> This certainty that the Church is one . . . implies the duty of further *kenosis*. In spite of some opinions to the contrary among the Orthodox and in spite of divisions, the mission must be continued.[52]

If Metropolitan James represents the view that without unity mission cannot take place, then Elias Voulgarakis, in an article from which the quotation above was taken, maintains that unity is a result of mission. Working on the basis that the Church's mission must be of the same type as the mission of Christ, he asks what the mission of Christ was like. In the first place, Christ's mission had its basis in love.

> For us men, the highest form of God's love is expressed in the offering of His only begotten Son. . . . The only word which comes at all close to this idea of love is *kenoun,* in the well known passage . . . (Phil. 2:6–7) . . . it takes on fresh significance, and a new word is coined which has become a Christian technical term. In this sense, the meaning of *kenoun* and of its substantive *kenosis* is most nearly expressed by the words: abdication, renunciation, abandonment, outpouring.
>
> The essential characteristic of love, then, is the *kenosis* of the subject; that is, this inner voluntary self-denial which makes room to receive and embrace the other to whom one turns.[53]

The character of this *kenosis* is one of action for or toward the other person. It does not matter what the intended receiver's attitude is. "Love does not presuppose dialogue."[54] This much is clear concerning the nature of love, especially the redemptive love of the Son of God. Voulgarakis goes on to describe what occurs because of *kenosis*.

> The immediate result of *kenosis* is unity. This unity exists objectively, even if only one party loves. The connection with *kenosis* makes unity

active, because it leads to a dynamic identification. The mystery of the hypostatic unity of God in Trinity and the union of the two natures in Christ are acceptable and more easily intelligible by human standards, if one considers that here we have love in its perfect form. Complete union is achieved in perfect mutual *kenosis,* yet this does not lead to any confusion of persons. . . .[55]

While it is understandable how identification takes place in spite of the lack of response from the one who is loved, it is not quite as clear how objective unity emerges. For real love does not depend on response, but real unity must. Sharing can only occur when both share, not when the sharing is one-sided. While the incarnate Son of God can through *kenosis* identify with a fallen humankind, the human being cannot be united to God without undergoing a similar *kenosis.* It is difficult to see how any objective unity is attained without at least a partial *kenosis* on the part of the receiver. In spite of this criticism of Voulgarakis, his analysis is helpful in understanding a key element in Christ's mission. A side benefit is the light it sheds on some aspects of the Christian doctrine of God.

Moving on from the relationship between *kenosis* and unity, Voulgarakis deals with the relationship between mission and unity. The mission of the Son of God and his *kenosis* "and sinful man's response to Him through the Spirit, result in their mutual union; that is, the Church."[56] Therefore, the mission of Christ leads to unity between God and the human being. When the relationship between Christ's mission and the Church's mission is examined, the latter is found to be an extension of the former. "The analogy between Christ's mission and that of the Church is valid not only for the form and manner of that mission but also for its operation. The Church exercises a mission out of love."[57] The Church then must follow the *kenotic* method of mission to be faithful to its Lord, and it follows this method because of the motivation of love. Now love leads to unity; therefore, the relationship between mission and unity can be drawn out from an understanding of the *kenotic* action.

> Mission and unity are not two great, independent concepts that must be reduced to a common denominator, but rather two allied and interlocking forms of the same principle—love. . . . The direct product of mission in its widest sense, as the *kenosis* and outpouring of God, is unity—not only as an eschatological end, but also as a reality wherever it is partially expressed. Unity, once it is exalted in its dynamic identification, turns out to be the beginning of a new *kenosis,* and so on.[58]

Here Voulgarakis identifies mission with *kenosis,* so that mission, or *kenosis,* results in unity. While it is clear that the mission of God results in the unity between God and individuals that is called the Church, it is not quite so clear why the unity that results from the Church's mission should result in further mission. What seems to be missing is a theological understanding of the unity that results from the Church's mission. How does the unity between Christ and individuals in redemption become a unity between individual people in the Church?

From the Orthodox doctrinal perspective of the Church as community, the answer is that there is unity between human being and human being because of their common bond to Christ and because Christ is present in the Church working through the Church. In one sense identification with the Church is identification with Christ. Therefore, as people join the Church through the enabling help of the Holy Spirit, they come to a position of being able to love God and others with a form of *kenotic* love. This leads the Church to love those outside its boundaries as God in Christ loved, and still loves, those who are outside the trinitarian fellowship. Love then spurs on mission to find fulfillment in unity. But the unity, while complete, is never finally finished as long as there are ununited objects of love.

With regard to the theme of the unity of the Church, Voulgarakis sees mission as an essential expression of the Church's unity. If there is no mission, or if mission is constantly needing to defend its right to exist, then the type of unity being maintained comes under question. "The Church which hesitates to undertake missionary work in the name of unity—that is, of her own nature—testifies that she is deficient in unity."[59] To be truly the Church means that the Church imitates and continues Christ's work. Without a mission of love, the claim of identification with Christ suffers. Therefore the mission of the Church must continue, despite the divisions that mar the oneness that should mark those who confess Christ.

In spite of Voulgarakis's disagreement with Metropolitan James, he does agree that the mission advocated by the metropolitan is indeed a valid and necessary one: "In the same way, mission must be expressed in two ways, according to 'actual need': first, as the word is commonly understood, as the Church's *kenosis* towards those outside her; and secondly, as the Church's *kenosis* towards the confession united with her by the sacraments but separated by doctrine."[60]

In both authors quoted above, the connection between unity and mission is clearly drawn. Both see the humbling of oneself in love as the only true basis for unity. For one, church unity must precede mission; for the other, mission leads to unity, which leads in turn to mission in a cycle that only ends in the eschatological age to come. Therefore the area of agreement would seem to be larger than the area of disagreement.

A third variant view is that developed by Nectarios Hatzimichalis in his series of articles in *Porefthendes* on Orthodox ecumenism.[61] His main point is that the Bible, in both Old and New Testaments, and the Patristic Fathers all testify to a universal concern that is not limited to racial or national boundaries. God's love is not limited to one or more groups to the exclusion of the other nations. By ecumenicity, he understands the need to draw all the nations, the entire world, into the fellowship of the Church. Because Orthodoxy has been attacked on the point of nationalism and supposed racialism, and because some Orthodox oppose the formation of a Pan-Orthodox (as distinct from a particular national Orthodox Church, e.g., Greek or Russian) mission, Hatzimichalis felt compelled to present the evidence not only for the goal of ecumenism but the method of ecumenism that supersedes national identities.[62] For inasmuch as God's love is not limited, neither should the love and mission of the missionaries sent out by Christ's Church be limited. To go only to one's own kind, or to go to another nation and attempt to make them like oneself, is foreign to the Bible's concept of mission. But it is also foreign to the scriptural teaching on the purpose of God for the human race. This is demonstrated in the New Testament when in the *eschaton* the nations will be represented in both judgment (Mt. 23:31–46) and redemption (Rev. 7:9–10). Therefore the Church needs to reach out to all people and must be comprised of people from all nations. From his biblical analysis, Hatzimichalis moves to his thesis for Orthodox missions: "If we find in God the will for ecumenical salvation, if in Christ lies the salvation of all the human race, if mankind feels a nostalgia for salvation and redemption, then Christianity and especially Orthodoxy ought to be an ecumenical religion."[63]

It must be kept in mind that Hatzimichalis uses the term "ecumenical" in the sense of universal and world-encompassing, in distinction to a religion that is culturally or geographically bound. In the development of this theme in the Patristic age, the traditional Orthodox interpretation of Pentecost as the reversal of Babel is brought out. The intended unity of people is realized in the Church. "Maximus the Confessor sees one mankind, which is organically one from its very origin and the purpose of the Church is to reveal through Mission the re-establishment and completion of this unity to men who have lost their intuitive unity."[64]

Having made his point about the universality of the gospel and the cultural, linguistic, and racial differences this will mean in the Church, Hatzimichalis moves on to his application. One has perhaps suspected throughout the book that Hatzimichalis is addressing primarily his own Church. However, in the application this becomes clear. For in his conclusion, he attacks the nationalism that has sometimes marked Orthodoxy.

> . . . There exists a "tragic division" within the bosom of the Church, as to the supernationalism and universality of Orthodoxy.
>   But nationalism is a natural evil rooted as a parasite in the fallen human nature and was never absent from any Church; from the Churches of the Byzantine dominion, . . . the Pan-Slavic messianism. . . . Nationalism, therefore, is the tragedy of every Christian Church. . . . [65]

Hatzimichalis is calling for a repentance and turning from the nationalistic conceptions of the Church that are a barrier to Christian mission. From his own communion he seeks an Orthodox ecumenism that will enable their missionaries successfully to plant new Orthodox Churches. He argues this point on the basis of Orthodox Tradition, the times in which the Church finds itself, and the need to manifest unity, not only a Pan-Orthodox unity but one with other Christian traditions. Speaking of Chrysostom in actively seeking the return to the Orthodox Church of some who had gone into heresy, he connects this retrieval of Christians to Orthodoxy with the current ecumenical dialogue. "It is because of this tradition that the Orthodox Church, considering external mission as inseparably connected with the ecumenical dialogue, approved of its connection with the World Council of Churches. . . . "[66]

To sum up Hatzimichalis's position, it means that church unity finds a threefold base: Tradition,[67] the needs of the unredeemed world, and unity as the best missionary method. Therefore, unity is again directly related to the missionary work of the Church, although the reader is confronted with a plea for unity and joint action primarily within the Orthodox Communion. Hatzimichalis's argument is a salutary reminder that the question of the unity of the Church must be tackled on more than an interdenominational level. One can easily think of examples of competition between Roman Catholic orders or between different national branches of certain Protestant Churches, which will cause one to realize that the warning sounded is not merely one of value to the Orthodox.

At the beginning of this section it was stated that beneath the apparently conflicting viewpoints, there appeared to be a common Orthodox position. And while it is not in the interests of truth to minimize the real differences that have been pointed out above, nevertheless the common view has emerged. The Orthodox Church places a high value on unity. Furthermore, in every case this unity is related to the witness of the Church. The claim of the Orthodox Church to be the one, true, undivided Church naturally finds expression in missionary activity. As has been shown above in the discussion of missionary motives and aims, a denial of the missionary task of Orthodoxy is taken by some Orthodox writers as a denial of Orthodoxy.[68] In fact, the same could be said of the three theologians cited in this section in that their view of the Orthodox Church compels them to missionary work. To conclude as one would expect from a study of Orthodox ecclesiology, unity as a theme relates to every aspect of the witness of Orthodoxy.

Chapter XIII

The Missionary Nature of the Church

In the historical overview of missions it was demonstrated that the Orthodox Church throughout its history was engaged in missionary work. In that section and in the one on methods, the link between mission and the Church was sketched lightly. It remains to spell out in greater detail how the Church is involved in missionary work. One might phrase the problem thus: If the extension of the Church is the goal, how does this extension take place? In the West the traditional answer would be through a missionary society, either a monastic order in the Roman Catholic Church or the mission agency or board in the Protestant Churches.[1] But the Orthodox Church knows no such enterprise as a missionary order.

> The missionary work of the Russian Orthodox Church began a long time ago, and was on the whole directed to the same ends as missionary activity in all other Christian Churches. But it was much more closely related to the work of the Church as a whole than was the case in the West. From the start it was free from that disintegration which gave a doubly professional character to missionary service in the Western Churches. There were indeed some attempts along these lines, due to Western influence, but in spite of them our missionary work did not become a separate profession, and the word "missionary" did not gradually acquire the narrow professional sense that it seems to have in the Western Churches. From the Orthodox point of view, the Church *as such* is mission.[2]

"The Church *as such* is mission." How does this watchword translate into the reality of the missionary structure of the Orthodox Church? The answer lies with an examination of the doctrine of the Church in all areas. As was pointed out in the first chapter, the theological frame of reference for the Orthodox Church is different from that of the Western Churches. There is in Orthodoxy a greater emphasis on the corporate character of salvation. The goal of salvation, *theosis,* also affects the presentation of the gospel. Salvation is not a

116

midway point in the person's pilgrimage from being without Christ to the final consummation in glory. Instead salvation encompasses the entire journey from darkness into the new light of eternity.

The role of the laity also features largely in the Orthodox ecclesiological framework. The clergy, and especially the bishop, may represent the Lord Jesus Christ,[3] but the people comprise the Church, and without the people the clergy cannot officiate.[4] This should begin to provide a clue to the understanding of the statement "The Church *as such* is mission." It is analogous to the statement; the Church as such is the liturgical community. While on first examination this latter statement seems trite, if not tautological, yet the point is that the whole Church must be involved in worship. All celebration is for the Church and is real celebration of the community. The liturgy is not the prerogative of the clergy with the congregation as merely observers.[5] All participate in the service of the Lord.

It is in the corporate character of the Church that one finds the key that unlocks the Orthodox understanding of the missionary involvement of the Church. As in worship, so also in mission, all participate in the service of the Lord, even if not all perform the same task of service.

> . . . Mission work is not exactly an individual duty but pre-eminently a collective one, which falls exclusively under the competence of the Church. So if and when each one of us does missionary work, he acts not merely as an individual but as a member of the Church or as the son of the Kingdom of God, as Christ's agent, aiming to reinstate others too on the road which leads to salvation through the Church.[6]

In exploring the concept of mission as a collective task of the Church, there are two areas to examine. The first is what has been done on the level of the whole Church to promote mission. By the whole Church, one would understand either efforts by a particular national church, for example the Church of Greece, or two or more national churches in some type of Pan-Orthodox effort. If one is to take seriously the claim that mission is the task of the whole Church, the second area that needs to be considered is the individual congregation's involvement with mission. To the study of these two areas we now turn.

THE CHURCH AS A MISSIONARY AGENCY

In view of the historical survey presented above, it should not be necessary to repeat the details of Orthodox mission expansion. What is needed here is to clarify some points that were not expanded on or whose full significance was not noted above.

The Hierarchy as the Initiator of Mission

Even a cursory glance at Orthodox mission history is sufficient to show that most missionary expansion resulted from missionaries being sent by the ruling clergy of the Church. This statement might seem to be refuted by the example of the Slavic mission of Cyril and Methodius. They were sent out by imperial decree on what was a dual-purpose embassy, namely, with both political and religious objectives.[7] However, as Dvornik points out, in such an undertaking the patriarch, in this case Photius, would certainly play a part.[8] The same type of relationship existed in Russia under Peter the Great and his successors. The tsar would direct the Holy Synod to secure the candidates for missionary service. In most cases the Holy Synod either drew up the plans for expansion or approved plans drawn up by others and then submitted these to the tsar for his approval.[9]

Beyond the role of the political ruler in the establishment of mission work, a topic dealt with above, the majority of work was carried out by bishops who had a zeal for the expansion of the faith. In the literature on missions in the Patristic period, John Chrysostom is constantly held up as a model of one who had a burning missionary zeal.[10] Bishop Innocent, in a different class because he was in charge of a missionary diocese, serves as an example of the positive effect a person in his position could have to advance the growth of the Orthodox faith.[11] In the present age Bishop Anastasios Yannoulatos has been and still is an ardent supporter of external mission.[12]

It is not the purpose here to hold up various Orthodox prelates as models to be adopted by all bishops. It is solely to call the reader's attention to the role the hierarchy has played in Orthodox mission work. While this should be obvious in that the Orthodox Church is governed by an episcopal structure, yet the focus on the individual missionaries tends to obscure the backing they received from the church authorities. However, having understood the line of argument thus far, it may still not be clear to the reader why the subject need be discussed at all. Certain bishops, the patriarch of Constantinople, the metropolitan of Moscow, and other eminent personages have supported missionary work. Of what relevance is this fact to the issue of the Church as a whole being involved in mission?

Again the discussion must refer back to basic Orthodox ecclesiology. The bishop is the representative head of the community. Not only does he represent Christ in the Eucharist, he also represents the people.[13] The prayers the celebrant offers up in the liturgy are all prayers in the first-person plural except when the celebrant prays for the forgiveness of his own personal sin.[14] When one fully understands the role of the bishop as speaking for the church, then the action of the bishop is an action on behalf of the whole local church. To change the terms slightly to provide another illustration, it is the whole Church, laity and clergy, which is responsible for correct doctrine, yet normally it is the bishop who is the authoritative teacher of the truth.[15] Therefore the church, in the person of the bishop, can be said to be involved in mission.

While this reasoning may not appear to be satisfactory to some Protestants, it is entirely in accord with the Orthodox theological framework. Any judgment on the validity of the position needs to be made in the context of the theological understanding of the Church that is maintained by the Orthodox.

Orthodox Missionary Societies

Having thus far sustained the argument that the Orthodox have not needed missionary societies because of their theological understanding, it is necessary at this point to examine efforts made by the Orthodox to encourage special interest in mission work. At the outset, the natural question presents itself: Are not mission societies a contradiction to the Orthodox ethos? Leaving the question unanswered for the present, the study now turns to an examination of two attempts made by the Orthodox to promote mission. This will aid in providing an adequate reply.

The Orthodox Missionary Society

One might actually wonder if indeed this project should be considered here for several reasons. The first is that the society was the handiwork of Bishop Innocent, the Alaska missionary, when he became metropolitan of Moscow. The plans for the society were approved by the Holy Synod, so the society was officially connected to the overall structure of the Russian Orthodox Church. Furthermore, according to the constitution the president of the society was the metropolitan of Moscow who, in terms of the church structure, was the primate of all Russia. It does not seem possible in light of these facts to consider this society any challenge to the established order but an attempt to be integrated fully into the ecclesiastical framework of the time.

At the first meeting of the society, Metropolitan Innocent announced that "the goal of our Society is to advance the conversion of those who do not yet believe in Christ our Saviour."[16] The society was established to support missions financially and by prayer. The reported text of Innocent's inaugural address stressed the aspect of prayer above all else.[17] The Orthodox Missionary Society had an enthusiastic base of support from its inception. The work quickly spread from Moscow to other centers, so that within a year it was represented in seventeen dioceses.[18] The society continued in existence until the Russian Revolution.[19]

From this brief sketch it is clear that the Orthodox Missionary Society functioned within the theological framework outlined above. The only possible criticism might be that it was exclusively Russian Orthodox. However, in the light of the political situation of the other Eastern Orthodox Churches, who had either just come out of or were still under the Turkish yoke, this criticism has no force. In any case, there was a great deal that could be done by the Russian Church in areas where there was a sphere of Russian political influence or previous mission work.

It can be said positively about the Orthodox Missionary Society that it was an attempt to broaden the base of support financially and spiritually throughout the entire Russian Church. Therefore in no sense can it be considered an exclusive or narrow society. The design of such a scheme of mobilizing the entire Church was also the dream of another Russian missionary, Macarius (or Macaire) Gloukharev, who was for the short span of his life Innocent's contemporary.[20]

The Inter-Orthodox Missionary Centre "Porefthendes"

In spite of a long history of missionary work, historical events had combined so "that the first part of the twentieth century was, throughout the world, the most sterile period of Orthodox mission."[21] Yet with the renewed missionary interest that commenced in the late fifties, one can say that the second half of the twentieth century has been one of the most creative periods for missionary theology in the history of the Orthodox Church. In September 1958, the Fourth General Assembly of Syndesmos, the International Organization of Orthodox Youth, was held in Thessaloniki. Out of this assembly came the first positive steps toward the revival of missionary awareness of the Orthodox Church. The establishment of a Pan-Orthodox Missionary Society was approved in principle. Far more important was the immediate establishment of an Executive Committee for External Mission.[22] This committee began to function immediately and issued its first bulletin in February 1959. With mimeograph format, published in Greek and English editions, it was entitled *Porefthendes* ("Go ye," from Mt. 28:19).

In addition to the periodical, various studies were published in other journals, which continued to develop Orthodox interest in missions. The committee also held a number of lectures, evening meetings, seminars, and other public activities designed to keep the need for missions at the forefront. At the Fifth General Assembly of Syndesmos, in 1961, the time was right for establishment of an Inter-Orthodox Missionary Centre.[23] This was established in Athens under the leadership of Anastasios Yannoulatos and carried on the name "Porefthendes," which also served as the name of the now-printed periodical of the center. There were four main areas in which the center was to labor: (1) study and research on the theoretical and practical problems of Orthodox foreign mission, (2) the fostering of a missionary and ecumenical awareness in the worldwide Orthodox Church, (3) the providing of assistance in the spiritual and scientific education of missionaries, (4) the establishment and maintenance of contact with the new missionary churches so as to be able to help with the solution of theoretical and organizational problems.[24]

There is no doubt that the Inter-Orthodox Missionary Centre succeeded in fulfilling its goals. The judgment of Elias Voulgarakis, professor of missiology at the University of Athens, is that "Porefthendes is the main lever for the renewal of mission in Greece."[25] The many publications of the center, in addition to the serious studies appearing in the journal itself, have contributed to the formation of an Orthodox missiology.[26] It is no exaggeration to state that the work of Porefthendes in its many facets has contributed to the renewal of mission interest not only in Greece, but throughout the entire Orthodox world. Furthermore, its work has brought Orthodox missiology to the attention of non-Orthodox missiologists, increasing the interest in Orthodox missions.

In assessing the work of Porefthendes, the question comes as to whether or not the center has usurped the role of the Church, and in particular that of the hierarchy. From the outset this was not the intention of the center.

The Inter-Orthodox Missionary Centre, "Porefthendes," studies, publishes, incites the missionary flame within Orthodox souls, trains, helps, guides, but does not itself carry out any missionary activity, in the strict sense of the word, as an autonomous authority. It simply places the fruits of its work (publications, studies, persons) at the disposal of the competent Ecclesiastical Authorities for subsequent canonical missionary action.[27]

The address given by the director of the center ten years later, when new premises were dedicated, indicates that the original purpose was still maintained.[28] It is seen as an auxiliary to the regular work of the Church, an organization whose purpose is to serve the whole Church, the hierarchy and the laity.[29]

The Church in Mission

From what has been shown above to be the motivation for the formation of Orthodox missionary interest groups, it is clear that the initiative for mission was never taken away from the Church. Instead, groups within the structure of the Church worked for the promotion of the task of mission, which they perceived to be the role of the whole Church. Efforts to mobilize support have always been perceived as primarily churchwide appeals. An example of this is the decisions taken by the Greek Orthodox Archdiocese of North and South America.[30]

Missionary awareness and activity is at different levels in the various national churches which make up the Eastern Orthodox Church. Generally speaking, the Orthodox Church of Greece and the Greek Orthodox Archdiocese of North and South America have had the most regular contact with and support of the mission work in Africa and in Korea, while the Russian Orthodox Diocese (now the Orthodox Church in America) has continued to support the former Russian missions in Japan and Alaska.

At this point the scope of the study has narrowed from worldwide Orthodoxy to the national churches.[31] It has been shown that mission belongs to the whole Church; however, in a real sense the fullness of the Church is represented in the national churches and their activity. This is not to undercut the call made for inter-Orthodox cooperation but to appraise realistically the opportunity for concerted action on so wide a front. But the process can and must be reduced even one step further, to the level of the local church and its involvement in mission. If the Church is to fulfill its mission, then mission must start in the local church. To the extent the local congregations are involved is the extent to which mission will belong to the whole Church.

THE MISSIONARY STRUCTURE OF THE CONGREGATION

When discussing the missionary involvement of the local congregation, two questions need to be considered. First, what differentiates the missionary involvement of the congregation from the liturgical witness of the congregation? Second, how realistic is it to speak of the mission of the congregation in contemporary Orthodox Church life?

In dealing with the first question, it needs to be acknowledged that, as was pointed out in chapter 11, the primary witness of the congregation is its liturgical witness. Furthermore, it is in the local congregation that all liturgical action takes place, save that performed at councils, synods, or other assemblies involving more than one congregation. Therefore, in this section the outworking of the total witness of the local congregation is the focal point. The theology presented above is placed in a concrete setting. The following discussion can be regarded as theory seen in practice.

This leads to the second question, whether the theory is really practiced. Does the theology of witness become actual witness? It is not the scope of this study to analyze the actual state of the Orthodox congregations. While many Orthodox writers lament the gap between theology and life, orthodoxy and orthopraxis, and therefore condemn the current stance of the Orthodox Churches,[32] nevertheless the theological analysis provided by these same writers of how things should be is of paramount concern to the study. While one must not ignore reality and dwell solely in the realm of pure theology, neither can one refuse to listen to the true prophets and pastors of the Orthodox Church, who maintain the vision and commission of missionary service entrusted to the Church by its Lord. It would indeed be a presumption for anyone to hold that the theology is not now in some places and could not become in others the standard of practice.

Therefore it is possible to explore the missionary theology of the local congregation without having to maintain that the theology is borne out in every individual case. In any event, there will be a critical evaluation of the theology and practice in the section following.

The Mission of the Congregation

In a most instructive paper M.A. Siotis presents a theology of the local congregation's involvement in mission. Siotis begins by reminding his readers of what the assembly of Christians is.

> The local Church constitutes the positive and fully concrete expression of the foundation on earth and the living reality of the Church of Christ. . . . Therefore, the local Church in its essence and nature is not simply a question of organization and structure. The essence and nature of the local Church are more than this. They are both divine and sacred: divine because every Church constitutes the continuation on earth of the redemptive grace of Christ, . . . sacred because every Church has as its mission, the sanctification of its members, and through them, the sanctification of the world.[33]

The cardinal fact of Orthodox ecclesiology is here highlighted. The Church, and hence the local manifestation, is a partaker in the life of Christ. To regard the Church merely as an organization is to miss the basic truth of its being, the fundamental mark of its character. One sees the theme repeatedly in Orthodox literature. Bulgakov can write: "The Church of Christ is not an institution; it is a new life with Christ and in Christ, guided by the Holy Spirit."[34] Even though Bulgakov goes on to describe the organizational structure of the Church, his point is clear. The Church does not exist primarily as an institution; it is a spiritual reality that expresses the life and mission of Christ on earth.

Siotis is therefore correct in calling attention to the essence and nature of the Church before discussing its mission, for its mission springs directly from them. The essence and nature are both divine and sacred because they carry on Christ's work of redemption and the Holy Spirit's work of sanctification. One notices two things about this definition. The first is that the understanding of the Church is predicated not by structures, but by activity. The second is that the activity that characterizes the Church is an extension of God's activity in the world. Therefore the Church's role is to carry out God's work in the world. One hesitates to use the word "mission" for what the Church does, not because the Church is not involved in mission, but because the word carries with it connotations and definitions that, in this case, may not be appropriate. Likewise, it would be all too easy to say that the Church conducts the *missio Dei;* however it would not be true. For the *missio Dei* is wider than the role Siotis sees for the local congregation.

What is this mission? To understand it, one must follow Siotis's argument concerning the local church. "That which constitutes in a sacramental manner the essence of the Church is the public confession of the common faith of two or more Christians in the name of Jesus Christ as Son of God and Saviour of the world."[35] What is meant here by the term, "in a sacramental manner," is the spiritual character of the Church's organization. Its commonality depends not on human-made criteria but on a God-given fellowship of faith. "The composition of the local Church therefore is the communion of the faithful."[36] The choice of words here is significant, for it is not only the communion of the faithful with each other, but primarily with the living Christ. Therefore the local congregation is the assembly of those who, by their common confession and shared sacrament, are the witnesses to the world of God's redeeming and sanctifying presence.

It would seem as though the study has not progressed beyond a summary of the preceding chapter. For what is the common confession and the shared sacrament, if not precisely the liturgical witness of the Church? Only when Siotis speaks of the sanctification of Christians as being part of the missionary work, does his argument go beyond what was already discussed. "Those of the faithful who are being spiritually perfected in the Church, through their life in it in Christ, are also fulfilling their divine mission in the world. . . . "[37] The argument, therefore, hinges on the advance of the Christians' spiritual perfection. If there is no progress in this area, then there is no mission.

One is faced here with an extremely interesting concept, namely, that the mission of the Church is dependent on the individual's contribution. What better way to see the missionary work of the Church than to see it in the development of the life of its members. Note two facts about this concept: first, that mission is seen as the role of each individual, not of some special person or group; second, that it again illustrates the corporate view of the Church. The sanctification of the individual is in the context of the local church, and the result of the individual's sanctification is the extension of the Church's mission in the world.

While there are serious limitations to this approach, there are certain benefits gained from viewing the missionary task of the Church from the perspective of the individuals in the congregation. Perhaps the most obvious is the possibility of the total mobilization of the congregation. Mission is not something "out there"; rather, it is something that the individual takes part in and contributes to. The believer should realize that one's own journey to sanctification affects more than one's own life. This insight is significant, since it is more common in both the Eastern and Western Churches to view the growth in holiness as a personal affair. One needs only to think of the monastic movement to verify this.[38] Therefore Siotis is correct in his emphasis that salvation is both an individual and a corporate experience.

Granting that this basic thesis of the individual's growth to spiritual perfection is a fulfilling of Christ's mission, then whatever facilitates this growth has the effect of promoting mission. Therefore Siotis lays out a scheme for enabling the growth of the congregation.

> The reorientation of the Church to carry out its evangelistic and missionary task appears from the Orthodox point of view primarily as a question of restoring to the Churches their true ecclesiastical character. The following appear to be the cardinal points of this reorientation:
>
> a) The strengthening of the sacramental and worshiping life of the faithful, so that thereby they will become more conscious of living in communion with Christ.
>
> b) The creation in the local Churches of cells and groups for the revival of spiritual aids to worship. . . .
>
> c) The deeper devotion of all members of the Church and their more active participation in the advancement and enrichment of all the activities and concerns of parochial church life, . . . especially its work of philanthropy and social service.
>
> d) The creation in its members of a conscience that is responsive to the Church's teaching, and the development in each member of a sense of personal responsibility for the spiritual poverty which exists within and outside the Church. . . .
>
> e) The awareness of each individual of his obligation to play a positive

part in picking out from among the faithful and putting forward those who are spiritually worthy and best qualified to take office in the Church. . . . [39]

In evaluating this list it is at once clear that if it were followed, there would be a worshiping and witnessing community that would have an impact on its surroundings. Furthermore, if the last two points were taken to their logical conclusion, there would be a missionary thrust coming from the congregation, since the spiritual poverty existing outside the church cannot be limited to the local congregation's area.

It can be clearly seen in an analysis such as that above, that it is feasible to regard the local congregation as a focal point for the mission of the Church. Indeed, this is obvious on another front as well, since it is the congregation that receives the financial gifts of the faithful so that all the Church's work, both local and in extension, can be carried out. Lest one regard this analysis as being superficial, it behooves one to remember that the basis of Siotis's argument is the relationship of the individuals in the congregation to the Lord and to each other. He is not merely suggesting an organizational structure that has proved its worth in other Christian confessions. Instead he is speaking primarily of a relationship that then yields organizational results.

There are, of course, limitations to this analysis. Siotis notes some of them himself. While acknowledging the role of the spiritual leadership of the congregation, he is aware that it is often missing. He can write that "the first priority for the evangelistic work of the Church is the recruitment, training and ordination of persons of high spiritual quality for the administration of their sacred tasks and affairs of the parish."[40] Yet he admits that these spiritual leaders are often lacking. However, his Orthodox ecclesiology causes him to maintain that the leadership is not ultimately decisive.

On the contrary, faith in the absolute value of the Church for the salvation of its members means recognition of the presence in it of Christ and of the Holy Spirit, operating even when the ministers of the grace of Christ are unworthy. . . . Still less should the devotion of the faithful depend on the personal worth and spirituality of the clergy.[41]

While this is indeed good Orthodox doctrine,[42] it is difficult to understand how the plan outlined by Siotis can be carried out in the absence of worthy pastoral leadership. The same question appears to be on Siotis's mind when he asks in his paper, "how far the laity of the Church are competent to accept the responsibility of taking office in the Church."[43] One suspects that there exists a cause-and-effect situation. Because the clergy have not given the proper spiritual leading, the laity are not in a position to take their role in the Church's mission. This has in fact been pointed out by several writers.[44]

A more serious limitation of Siotis's approach and one not dealt with by him is the dimension of what has been called by Yannoulatos "external mission."[45] There is no indication given as to how the work could be carried on at a distance from the congregation. No doubt, congregations having the characteristics described above would be missionaries in their own areas, yet the question of a wider witness is lacking. This is not to criticize the proposal for vibrant, living congregations. While such congregations might still need some further direction toward external mission, it is certain that spiritually inactive congregations would need first to come alive. But once alive, some thought would have to be given to the extension of the Church into new areas of the world.

The key then would seem to be the real spiritual awakening of the congregation, first to its life in Christ and the Holy Spirit, then to its obligation of service in carrying out the mission of Christ.

A Historical Illustration

In the historical survey presented above and in the theological analysis of the Orthodox position, reference was made to the problems caused by the Turkish oppression and the present domination of the Russian Church by a hostile regime. In light of the discussion of the missionary nature of the congregation, it is instructive to note that even under the Turkish domination of the Greek nation, there were converts to Orthodoxy. Without entering fully into the debate that surrounds the use of the words "mission" and "evangelism,"[46] it would seem reasonable to conclude that witness by Christians to Muslims, wherever they are found, is mission. That is to say that while there were no geographical barriers to witness, there were certainly cultural and linguistic barriers. However, for the purposes of this discussion, it makes little difference if one uses the term "mission" or "evangelism," since this concerns the witness of a local congregation.

Therefore the witness of the Orthodox Church in the Turkish period is relevant to the present discussion on the congregation and mission. An excellent treatment of this aspect of witness is found in an article by Demetrios Constantelos. He documents the pressure brought to bear on the Christians to convert to Islam and provides an analysis of the martyrdom of these Christians. While it is instructive to read of the Christian devotion of these believers, compared by some to the "martyrdoms in the early Church,"[47] two points must be especially noted.

The first is that among those who died for the Christian faith were some who had been born into Islam:

> For some reason, however, either on their own initiative or through the efforts of missionaries they became Christians. A Muslim was forbidden to deny his faith on pain of death. . . . The Roman Catholic missionary Francis Lucas of Smyrna recorded the extraordinary martyrdom of twenty-three Muslim Turks who were put to death in the year 1649 at Thyateira, Asia Minor.[48]

Considering the certainty of the penalty, it is surprising that anyone converted from Islam. As Constantelos points out, the pressure was entirely directed the other way, with riches and honor being given to converts to Islam. That some would give their lives for the Christian faith is not unique to this period. History is replete with such examples, from Stephen in the book of Acts to African Christians of the present day. But it is this consistent testimony with the other ages of Church history that leads to the second observation:

> A church which was able to produce men and women with a living faith and a commitment to spiritual values and principles could not have been a moribund church, or a church involved only in ritual and concerned with barren tradition, as the Orthodox Church has been portrayed by Western Christendom in the eighteenth and nineteenth centuries.[49]

Constantelos's point is well made. The existence of martyrs does demonstrate a certain vitality that is perhaps not present in the contemporary Orthodox Church.[50] Certainly the charge of spiritual deadness usually leveled at the Greek Church under Turkish rule does not appear to be accurate. Many authors have shown that the mere survival of the Church is a sign of spiritual power.[51] While the judgment that survival is a sign of spiritual power is debatable, the heroic witness of Orthodox Christians, many of them ordinary laity, cannot be dismissed so lightly.

Is it possible that what one sees there is the type of witness in which the congregation in mission should be engaged? One is not simply referring to martyrdom, since martyrdom is not a form of witness that can be pursued without suitable external pressures. Suicide is not martyrdom, but being put to death when one could recant is. Therefore martyrdom is not always an option for Christian witness. But the environment that bears and nourishes the type of spiritual awareness that regards a denial of Christ more serious that a denial of life is the type of environment that can produce other forms of congregational witness.

The purpose of this section has been to demonstrate the possibility of a type of witness as outlined by Siotis. While perhaps it could be illustrated in other ways, the graphic portrayal given by Constantelos speaks well of the theology. It must be freely admitted that to illustrate is not necessarily to prove conclusively, nor should it be thought that the Ottoman period was the height of Orthodox spirituality. However, what should be stressed are the basic themes that extend through the entire history of the Orthodox Church, and provide the researcher with a series of points against which to test theories and from which to draw theology.

Epilogue

Having completed our survey of Orthodox mission thinking, it is appropriate to make an evaluation of the success of the Orthodox in producing a missiology. Some who have read this study have questioned the use of the term "missiology." Their viewpoint is that the Orthodox have, at best, some thinking about mission, but not a fully developed missiology. My reply is that there is some truth in their claim. We have yet to see a thorough study of the subject from an Orthodox perspective. Anastasios Yannoulatos admits that what is needed is "to start from the general presuppositions and principles of Orthodox theology and to meditate upon Orthodox soteriology, ecclesiology and eschatology in the perspective of mission."[1]

More work needs to be done to draw out the richness of the Orthodox position. There are areas, in particular soteriology and eschatology, that are not adequately treated for purposes of mission. It is interesting to note that the neglect of these same areas also contributes to the internal crisis that Orthodoxy is facing. As cultural Orthodoxy breaks down when it meets secularism in traditionally Orthodox lands and religious pluralism (and therefore indifference) in the Diaspora, these same issues must be addressed. Failure to do so will result in increasing defections from the Orthodox Church. This can be seen in part in the history of the nonconformist movements in tsarist Russia.

Therefore "missiology" is an apt name for the task that faces the Orthodox Church. Mission work both at "home" and "abroad" is not optional but vital for the life and health of the Church. There is a real sense in which Orthodoxy must grow or die. This study has attempted to take the pulse of the patient and is able to report that there is life. However, what has been witnessed must continue and must be added to. The future demands more than a handful of mission specialists. The Orthodox Church needs to train a large number of theologians, priests, and laypeople who see the need to communicate the gospel of Christ. Anything less, and the critics will be right: there is mission thinking but no real study and work of mission, no missiology.

Thus it is possible to issue two challenges to the Orthodox. The first is on the level of the theoretical study. Are resources being channeled to the work of evangelism and mission? Is thought being given to the Orthodox witness to the world? How can the claims that the Orthodox Church makes be true, if more effort is not invested in carrying out the discipling envisioned by its Lord? The beginnings need to be encouraged. Orthodox theologians need to think along Orthodox lines and develop a missiology that can aid the rest of the Churches in

128

their task. Orthodox take pride in their witness to the truth, and rightly so. However, the focus is misplaced if it is on the pride and not the witness. What is needed is not to emphasize the triumphalism of a glorious heritage but to reveal humbly that heritage.

The second challenge concerns the Orthodox Church itself. The theologians write beautifully of the witness of the liturgy and the missionary structures of the congregation. But, if this is the case, why, especially in the Diaspora, are some of the churches centers of social activity that exclude outsiders? Can Orthodoxy break out of its cultural mentality so that it can witness? While there are positive trends opposing ethnocentrism, many problems still need to be resolved.

It is interesting to note Macarius Gloukharev's judgment "that the Russian masses were only superficially Christian, and therefore inadequate for the great apostolic task God had in store for them."[2] Is that judgment accurate today? It would seem that similar criticisms come from Orthodox writers even now. Is the present framework in which the theological treasures of Orthodoxy are preserved able to present those treasures to the world? These are real questions that need to be faced, and in some cases are being faced, by Orthodox theologians. Just as Gloukharev saw the need for educating the masses, so today the education of Orthodox congregations must be a priority for Orthodox mission.

What can be said then? Is the treasure so embedded in earthen vessels as to be unusable to the world? The answer comes from the gospel itself. "But we have this treasure in earthen vessels, to show that the transcendent power belongs to God and not to us" (2 Cor. 4:7). The transcendent power of God can be seen in greater glory against the background of earthen vessels. The vessels need only to let God's glory shine.

Notes

Note: When a work is cited both in the notes and in the suggested reading list for a chapter, full information about its publication is given only in the suggested reading section.

Preface

1. "From the Editor," *International Review of Mission* 54 (1965): 274.

Chapter 1

1. The title "Eastern Orthodox Church" signifies that branch of Christendom which historically had its main areas of strength in eastern Europe, in the old Byzantine empire, the Balkans, and Russia (hence the adjective "eastern") and who are in full communion with and recognize the honorary primacy of the ecumenical patriarch of Constantinople and who are themselves fully recognized by him. Other titles for this branch of Christendom include: the Greek Church, the Greco-Russian Church, the Orthodox Catholic Church, the Holy Orthodox Church, and simply the Orthodox Church. The last designation is the most convenient one to use in this presentation. (See Timothy Ware, *The Orthodox Church*, p. 16, for a brief discussion of these names.) On the basis of the above definition excluded are those commonly designated the "Lesser" and "Separated" Eastern Churches, which divided from the rest of Christendom in the fifth and sixth centuries. An excellent account of these Churches is found in Aziz S. Atiya, *History of Eastern Christianity* (Notre Dame, Ind.: University of Notre Dame Press, 1968). Also excluded are the Uniate Churches or Eastern Rite Roman Catholic Churches. An introductory work on these Churches is Adrian Fortescue, *The Uniate Eastern Churches* (London: Burns Oates and Washbourne, 1923).

2. See, e.g., W. C. Emhardt et al., *The Eastern Church in the Western World* (Milwaukee, 1928; reprinted., New York: AMS Press, 1970).

3. "From the Editor," *International Review of Mission* 54 (1965): 273. Even comprehensive texts take no notice of Orthodox missiology. E. g., Johannes Verkuyl, *Contemporary Missiology*, trans. Dale Cooper (Grand Rapids, Mich.: Wm. B. Eerdmans, 1978), does not mention the subject.

4. "About a third of the clergy serving the Syrian diocese—under the jurisdiction of the patriarch of Antioch—consists of converts which have come to Orthodoxy from other Christian confessions" (John Meyendorff, *The Orthodox Church*, p. 187). See also Chrysostomos H. Stratman, "To the Orthodox Christians of the United States of America," a pamphlet sponsored by the Eastern Orthodox Clergy Fellowship of Wisconsin (South Canaan, Pa.: St. Tikhon Press, 1969). Stratman is a convert to the Orthodox Church and describes his conversion in the pamphlet. The preface states:

"With the printing of this pamphlet, the Fellowship inaugurates a new phase of influence in its program: that of propagating our precious faith among Orthodox and non-Orthodox alike through the printed word" (p. 2). Timothy Ware, whose book was referred to above and who is now the Reverend Archimandrite Kallistos, is another prime example of a Western Christian converting to the Orthodox Church.

5. Cf. Zoe Brotherhood, ed., *A Sign of God,. Orthodoxy 1964: A Pan-Orthodox Symposium*.

6. A convenient summary of Orthodox involvement is found in Vasil T. Istavridis, "The Ecumenicity of Orthodoxy," pp. 182-95. See also Vasil T. Istavridis, "Orthodoxy in the Ecumenical Movement," pp. 71-80.

7. The Orthodox prelates who have served are Germanos of Thyatira (1948-51), Athenagoras of Thyatira (1951-54), Michael of America (1954-58), Archbishop Iakovos, Primate of North and South America (1961-68), German, Patriarch of the Serbian Orthodox Church (1968-75). See Vasil T. Istavridis, "The Orthodox Churches in the Ecumenical Movement 1948-1968," in *A History of the Ecumenical Movement*, vol. 2: *1948-1968*, ed. Harold E. Fey (Philadelphia: Westminster Press, 1970), p. 306.

8. *Ecumenical Press Service* no. 37/42, Dec. 9, 1975, p. 6.

9. See the various volumes on "Life and Work" and "Faith and Order" for a list of Orthodox contributions. On the encyclicals, see Robert George Stephanopoulos, "A Study in Recent Greek Orthodox Ecumenical Relations, 1902-1968," pp. 33-55.

10. Arthur Carl Peipkorn, *Profiles in Belief: The Religious Bodies of the United States and Canada*, vol. 1 (New York: Harper & Row, 1977), p. 52.

11. John E. Paraskevas and Frederick Reinstein, *The Eastern Orthodox Church: A Brief History* (Washington, D.C.: El Greco Press, 1969), pp. 3, 88.

12. Archbishop Iakovos, writing in the foreword of Demetrios J. Constantelos, *The Greek Orthodox Church: Faith, History and Practice* (New York: Seabury Press, 1967), states that the book "may be used as a primer for those previously unacquainted with Orthodoxy, and as an instructive source of information and food for thought by the practitioners of our faith" (p. 4). Mention should be made of St. Vladimir's Seminary Press, which has inaugurated a series entitled "The Orthodox Theological Library" containing some much needed Orthodox theological manuals in English. Other notable ventures include the reissue of Orthodox books by Eastern Orthodox Books (P.O. Box 302, Willits, Calif. 95490) and the Orthodox Christian Educational Society (1916 W. Warner Avenue, Chicago, Ill. 60613).

13. Ernst Benz, *The Eastern Orthodox Church: Its Thought and Life*, trans. Richard and Clara Winston (Garden City, N.Y.: Doubleday, Anchor Books, 1963), p. 1.

14. Ware, *Orthodox Church*, p. 10.

15. Alexis Khomiakov in a letter to an English friend, which was printed in W. J. Birkbeck, *Russia and the English Church*, p. 67, quoted in Ware, *Orthodox Church*, p. 9.

16. See the chapter entitled, "The Gulf Grows Wider between Christians of East and West," in Jean Daniélou and Henri Marrou, *The Christian Centuries*, vol. 1: *The First Six Hundred Years* (London: Darton, Longman & Todd, 1964), pp. 329-34.

17. Ware, *Orthodox Church*, p. 9. See also John Meyendorff, *Orthodoxy and Catholicity* (New York: Sheed and Ward, 1966), pp. 119-40, where he discusses "The Significance of the Reformation." His chapter originally appeared in *The Ecumenical Review*, 16 (1964): 164-79.

18. Alexander Schmemann, "Moment of Truth for Orthodoxy," in *Unity in Mid-*

Career: An Ecumenical Critique, ed. Keith R. Bridston and Walter D. Wagoner (New York: Macmillan, 1963), p. 47.

19. Ibid., p. 48.

20. Alexander Bogolepov, "Which Councils Are Recognized as Ecumenical?" *St. Vladimir's Seminary Quarterly* 7 (1963): 54-72.

21. John Meyendorff, *The Orthodox Church: Its Past and Its Role in the World Today*, p. 30. For a more detailed study of this question, see Charles J. Hefele, *A History of the Councils of the Church*, 5 vols. (Edinburgh: T. & T. Clark, 1894; reprinted New York: AMS Press, 1972).

22. Steven V. Roberts, "14 Orthodox Churches Prepare Council, as Halting Step to Unity," *New York Times*, Jan. 2, 1977, p. 12. Cf. John Meyendorff, "What Is an Ecumenical Council?" *St. Vladimir's Seminary Quarterly*, 17 (1973): 269-73, and Stanley S. Harakas, *Something Is Stirring in World Orthodoxy* (Minneapolis: Light and Life Publishing, Co., 1978). Harakas discusses the issues that could profitably be on the agenda for such a council.

23. Schmemann, "Moment of Truth," p. 49. Italics are in the original.

24. Ibid., pp. 50-51. Perhaps Schmemann overstates his case; surely the Orthodox Church remembers existentially the schisms of the fifth and sixth centuries when the "Lesser" Eastern Churches split off from the main body of Christendom. See Schmemann's own book, *The Historical Road of Eastern Orthodoxy*, pp. 118-57. "The foundation of the 'Jacobite' Church (named after Baradai) was laid, and it exists today. Copts and Syrians thus established their national Church, and the first permanent division between the churches was complete" (pp. 156-57). In recent years consultations have been held between the Eastern Orthodox (Chalcedonian) Churches and the Non-Chalcedonian Churches. See *The Greek Orthodox Theological Review*, vol. 13, for the papers of one of these consultations.

25. It is a moot point as to the degree of unanimity and uniformity that existed in the undivided Church. Certainly the two halves of the Church started to drift apart long before the usual date given for the schism of 1054. (See Steven Runciman, *The Eastern Schism* [Oxford: Clarendon Press, 1955], for a discussion of when the 1054 excommunication became irrevocable in the Eastern Church.) In terms of theological language, the drift can be detected much earlier. "There were differences and even violent conflicts between the East and West as early as the fourth century, but in spite of ever-recurring tension, there existed, until the eleventh century, a mutually recognized procedure for solving difficulties: the council" (John Meyendorff, *Byzantine Theology: Historical Trends and Doctrinal Themes* [London: Mowbrays, 1975], p. 101; cf. Jaroslav Pelikan, *The Christian Tradition*, vol. 2: *The Spirit of Eastern Christendom (600-1700)* [Chicago: University of Chicago Press, 1974], pp. 146-47).

26. Schmemann, "Moment of Truth," p. 52. Italics in the original.

27. Ibid.

28. A crisis erupted with regard to the Orthodox involvement with the National Council of Churches (United States). See "The Orthodox Revolt," *Newsweek*, Feb. 9, 1970, p. 78. The article deals with Orthodox criticisms of the NCC's policies and speaks of the possible withdrawal of the Orthodox Churches.

29. As to the possibility of presenting insights that could aid in the Protestant-Catholic discussions, see the suggestion of a Roman Catholic scholar: "It is perhaps not rash to suggest that solutions of the seemingly inextricable difficulties between us and the communion deriving from the Protestant Reformation may come from the East too" (C. J. Dumont, writing in the introduction to M. J. Le Guillou, *The Spirit of*

Eastern Orthodoxy, vol. 135: *The Twentieth Century Encyclopedia of Catholicism*, ed. Henri Daniel-Rops [New York: Hawthorn Books, 1962], p. 11).

Chapter 2

1. E. Every, "The Orthodox Church," *The Christian East* 1 (April 1951): 153. Useful for a comparison of the respective doctrines are Wilhelm Niesel, *Reformed Symbolics: A Comparison of Catholicism, Orthodoxy, and Protestantism*, and Einar Molland, *Christendom* (London: A.R. Mowbray, 1961). A convenient summary of Orthodox theology is John Karmiris, *A Synopsis of the Dogmatic Theology of the Orthodox Catholic Church*. Karmiris has also produced the standard work on Orthodox symbolics in his *Ta Dogmatika kai Symvolika Mnimeia tis Orthodoxou Katholikis Ekklisias*. Other notable works include Frank Gavin, *Some Aspects of Contemporary Greek Orthodox Thought*; Sergius Bulgakov, *The Orthodox Church* (London: Centenary Press, 1935); R. W. Blackmore, *The Doctrine of the Russian Church* (Aberdeen: A. Brown & Co., 1945; reprinted by Eastern Orthodox Books, Willits, Calif., 1973). A modern Orthodox systematic theology is that by Panagiotis N. Trempelas, *Dogmatiki tis Orthodoxou Katholikis Ekklisias*. A French translation by Pierre Dumont, *Dogmatique de L'Église Orthodoxe Catholique,* was published in 1966.

2. Quoted in Timothy Ware, *The Orthodox Church* (Baltimore, Md. Penguin Books, 1963), p. 9.

3. M. J. Le Guillou, *The Spirit of Eastern Orthodoxy* (New York: Hawthorn Books, 1962), pp. 20-21.

4. See Jaroslav Pelikan, *The Spirit of Eastern Christendom (600-1700)* (Chicago: University of Chicago Press, 1974), pp. 146-98.

5. Ernst Benz, *The Eastern Orthodox Church: Its Thought and Life*, pp. 43-47.

6. Ibid., p. 44.

7. This can be clearly illustrated from the service used to receive Roman Catholics as converts to the Orthodox Church. The converts are called upon specifically to renounce the Roman Catholic concept of the papacy. These questions are found in Isabel F. Hapgood, *Service Book of the Holy Orthodox-Catholic Apostolic Church*, 5th ed. (Englewood, N.J.: Antiochian Orthodox Christian Archdiocese, 1975), pp. 455-56. For a contemporary analysis of the issue of the papacy, see John Meyendorff et al., *The Primacy of Peter* (Leighton Buzzard, Bedfordshire: Faith Press, 1973), and Archbishop Methodios Fouyas, *Orthodoxy, Roman Catholicism, and Anglicanism*.

8. Benz, *Eastern Orthodox Church*, p. 45.

9. E.g., Justo L. González, *A History of Christian Thought*, 3 vols. (Nashville: Abingdon, 1970-75), 1:176-90. See also Jaroslav Pelikan, *The Christian Tradition*, vol. 1: *The Emergence of the Catholic Tradition (100-600)* (Chicago: University of Chicago Press, 1971), pp. 147f.

10. Paul Verghese, "A Sacramental Humanism," in *Theological Crossings*, ed. Alan Geyer and Dean Peerman (Grand Rapids, Mich.: Wm. B. Eerdmans, 1971), p. 139. His criticism of Augustine's position in general gives an Eastern perspective on this Western theological giant. Verghese is a bishop of the Syrian Orthodox Church, a Non-Chalcedonian Church (i.e., one not in full communion with the ecumenical patriarch). However, on this point the Orthodox Church and the Syrian Orthodox are in agreement. Bishop Verghese contributed an essay to a volume published in honor of Archbishop Iakovos, Greek Orthodox Primate of North and South America. See "The Role of Monasticism in Quickening the Churches in Our Time," in *Orthodoxy: Life and*

Freedom, ed. A.J. Philippou (Oxford: Studion Publications, 1973), pp. 73–79.

11. Meyendorff, *Byzantine Theology: Historical Trends and Doctrinal Themes*, p. 143.

12. González, *A History of Christian Thought*, 2:165–66.

13. Karmiris, *Synopsis*, p. 55.

14. L.A. Zander, *Vision and Action* (London: Gollancz, 1952), p. 59. It will be shown below to what degree the Orthodox Church was influenced by Scholasticism.

15. Vladimir Lossky, *The Mystical Theology of the Eastern Church*, p. 9.

16. See the citation from Maximus the Confessor, in Meyendorff, *Byzantine Theology*, p. 164.

17. Vladimir Lossky, *In the Image and Likeness of God*, p. 99.

18. Because of this combining of what the West regards as separate elements or stages, some accuse the Orthodox of having a poorly defined understanding of salvation. By that they mean that the Orthodox do not emphasize the same aspects of justification as is the custom of some Western Christians. Whether or not the Orthodox concept of salvation is clearly thought out is another question. "Fulfillment of man's being and his transfiguration by grace are all important to the Orthodox theologian. It is no wonder that the doctrine of justification has been given short shrift in Orthodox dogmatics. The most famous exposition of Orthodox dogmatics, that of John of Damascus (c. 700–50), does not even mention the idea of justification" (Benz, *Eastern Orthodox Church*, pp. 50–51). The Orthodox themselves admit there is no official Church pronouncement on the doctrine of salvation. See Savas Agourides, "Salvation according to the Orthodox Tradition," *The Ecumenical Review* 21 (1969):190–203. See also Vitaly Borovoy, "What Is Salvation? An Orthodox Statement," *International Review of Mission* 61 (1972):38–45.

19. Lossky, *In the Image and Likeness of God*, p. 97. Lossky gives references to several Church Fathers.

20. Benz, *Eastern Orthodox Church*, pp. 48–49.

21. Lossky, *Mystical Theology*, p. 7.

22. Ibid., p. 8.

23. Ibid.

24. "In the East the central way of approach is public worship, and doctrines are prayers rather than propositions" (Every, "The Orthodox Church," p. 153).

25. Demetrios J. Constantelos, "The Holy Scriptures in Greek Orthodox Worship," *The Greek Orthodox Theological Review* 12, no. 1 (1966):7–83.

26. See, e.g., Constantine N. Callinicos, *The Greek Orthodox Catechism* (New York: Greek Archdiocese of North and South America, 1960), and George Mastrantonis, *A New-style Catechism on the Eastern Orthodox Faith for Adults* (St. Louis, Mo.: Ologos Mission, 1969).

27. Demetrios J. Constantelos, "The Zoe Movement in Greece," *St. Vladimir's Theological Quarterly* 3, no. 2 (1959):11–25.

28. Alexander Schmemann, "Problems of Orthodoxy in America: III. The Spiritual Problem," *St. Vladimir's Theological Quarterly* 9 (1965): 171–93.

29. Timothy Ware, *Eustratios Argenti: A Study of the Greek Church under Turkish Rule*, p. 7.

30. Ibid.

31. Lucaris (also Lukaris or Lucar) was patriarch of Alexandria from 1601 to 1621 and patriarch of Constantinople on six different occasions between 1621 and his death at the hands of the sultan's Janissary Guards in 1631. For a Protestant interpretation of

his life and work, see George A. Hadjiantoniou, *Protestant Patriarch: The Life of Cyril Lucaris*. Correspondingly, for an Orthodox view, see Germanos Strenopoulos, *Kyrillos Loukaris, 1572-1638: A Struggle for Preponderance between Catholic and Protestant Powers in the Orthodox East*. Also useful is Charles Bradow, "The Career and Confession of Cyril Loukaris: The Greek Orthodox Church and Its Relations with Western Christians (1543-1638)."

32. For an English translation, see Hadjiantoniou, *Protestant Patriarch*, pp. 141-45. The Greek text appears in Karmiris, *Dogmatika*, 2:565-70.

33. Karmiris, *Dogmatika*, 2:564.

34. See Bradow, "Career and Confession," pp. 151-68.

35. This copy is dated 1631 and is preserved in the University of Geneva Library (Carnegie Samuel Calian, "Cyril Lucaris, The Patriarch Who Failed," p. 324).

36. Ibid., p. 332.

37. Quoted in Ware, *Eustratios Argenti*, p. 10, from J. H. Hottinger, *Analecta historico-theologica* (Zurich, 1952), p. 560.

38. "Most Mechanicks amongs us (are) more learned and knowing than the Doctors and Clergy of *Greece*" (Sir Paul Rycant, *The Present State of the Greek and Armenian Churches* [London, 1679], p. 107, quoted by Ware, *Eustratios Argenti*, p. 5).

39. Calian, "Cyril Lucaris," p. 322. Cf. Hadjiantoniou, *Protestant Patriarch*, pp. 27-35.

40. "Yet no one can deny that Loukaris, so sorely tried by Fortune, succeeded, by his long and patriotic exertions, in educating and reviving the national consciousness of the Greek People and in pointing the way towards new horizons in the life of the Nation." This is the conclusion of Germanos Strenopoulos, *Kyrillos Loukaris, 1572-1638*, p. 31.

41. Alexander Schmemann, "Russian Theology: 1920-1972, an Introductory Survey," p. 173. Cf. G. P. Fedotov, *The Russian Religious Mind, Kievan Christianity: the 10th to the 13th Centuries* (New York: Harper & Row, 1960).

42. Cf. Nicolas Zernov, *Moscow the Third Rome* (London: SPCK, 1937).

43. Schmemann, "Russian Theology: 1920-1972," p. 173.

44. Ibid., p. 174.

45. There are three main orthographic variations of the surname Moghila. The one given in the preceding sentence and used in the text is the rendering preferred by Russian scholars. "Mohila," favored by Ukrainians, and "Movila," transliterating the Romanian orthography, are frequently found in scholarly works. Ronald Popivchak, "Peter Mohila, Metropolitan of Kiev (1633-47): Translation and Evaluation of His 'Orthodox Confession of Faith' (1640)" (S.T.D. dissertation, Catholic University of America, 1975), p. 8.

46. James H. Billington, *The Icon and the Axe: An Interpretive History of Russian Culture* (New York: Random House, 1970), p. 128.

47. Ware, *Eustratios Argenti*, pp. 11-12. In his *Small Cathechism*, Moghila's Roman Catholic sacramentology is clearly evident. E.g., he uses the Roman formula *Ego te absolvo . . .* in the administration of the sacrament of penance. Moghila's "Confession" was toned down to make it more Orthodox before its acceptance as an Orthodox dogmatic statement; a competent authority, George Florovsky, thinks the *Small Catechism* expresses the real position of Moghila more than the altered confession does (see George A. Maloney, *A History of Orthodox Theology since 1453*) p. 36. Cf. Benz, *Eastern Orthodox Church*, p. 50. Benz points out that instead of the *Ego te absolvo*, the Orthodox priest confesses that he cannot forgive sins, only God can. Ware points out that there is a difference between the Greek formula of absolution and the Slavonic

formula. The Greek formula is as Benz reports, deprecative, "May God forgive you." Under the influence of Moghila, the Slavonic formula adds to the deprecative, "May Our Lord and God, Jesus Christ . . . forgive you," the indicative, "I, an unworthy priest, . . . forgive you." See *Orthodox Church*, pp. 296–97, where both formulae are given. This example is useful in noting that there are minor differences in the Orthodox Church.

48. The text of Syrigos's revision is found in Karmiris, *Dogmatika*, 2:593–686. There exists an English translation of the Latin text of A. Malvy and M. Viller, which, while not the original, follows the original 1640 version with some points that were changed in the 1642 revision of Syrigos. For this translation, see Popivchak, "Peter Mohila," pp. 54–261.

49. Ware, *Eustratios Argenti*, pp. 12–13.

50. Cf. Maloney, *Orthodox Theology*, p. 35, who lists a number of Orthodox theologians who have taught doctrines opposite to those found in Moghila's "Confession."

51. Popivchak claims Moghila's "Confession" is an authentic reflection of the Eastern Church ("Peter Mohila," p. 478).

52. Christos Yannaras, "Theology in Present Day Greece," p. 196.

53. Ibid.

54. Ibid., p. 214. Yannaras is not alone in his opinion. Maloney writes, "In the main, the theology of the new generation of Greek professors at Athens was academic with little relevance to the spiritual needs of their own faithful or to the patristic traditions of the past" (*Orthodox Theology*, p. 199). For more information on the subjects taught at these theological faculties, see Mario Rinvolucri, *Anatomy of a Church, Greek Orthodoxy Today* (New York: Fordham University Press, 1966), pp. 121–23. See also "The Church in Greece," *Pro Mundi Vita Dossiers*, November 1976, pp. 20–21.

55. See Stamoolis, "Scripture and Tradition as Sources of Authority in the Eastern Orthodox Church," pp. 12–26.

56. Schmemann, "Russian Theology: 1920–1972," p. 178.

57. Panagiotis Bratsiotis, *The Greek Orthodox Church*, p. 35. Bratsiotis refers to Zankow's *Orthodoxes Christentum des Ostens* (Berlin, 1928), pp. 37ff.

58. Schmemann, "Russian Theology," p. 178. Bulgakov centered his thought on the concept of divine wisdom, or Sophia. For an introduction in English to Sophiology, see Sergius Bulgakov, *The Wisdom of God: A Brief Summary of Sophiology* (New York: The Paisley Press, 1937).

59. Schmemann, "Russian Theology," p. 178. The quotation is from George Florovsky, from a discussion that appeared in *The Greek Orthodox Theological Review*, 10, no. 2 (1964–65) 132.

60. Florovsky, *Puti Russkogo Bogosloviya* (Ways of Russian Theology) (Paris, 1937), p. 509; cited by Schmemann, "Russian Theology," p. 179.

61. Bratsiotis, *The Greek Orthodox Church*, pp. 35–36.

62. Karmiris, *Synopsis of the Dogmatic Theology*, p. 1.

63. Bulgakov, *The Orthodox Church*, p. 9.

64. Karmiris, *Synopsis of the Dogmatic Theology*, p. 2.

65. Ibid., p. 8. Karmiris lists these secondary sources on p. 9.

66. Gavin, *Greek Orthodox Thought*, p. 259. See also pp. 260–63, where he explains why there can be no distinction between essential and secondary doctrines.

67. For a definition of what constitutes Tradition, see Gavin, *Greek Orthodox Thought*, pp. 27–30; Ware, *Orthodox Church*, pp. 203–15. My Th.M. thesis deals

extensively with the question of the content of Tradition, "Scripture and Tradition," pp. 12–43, 70–90.

68. See the excellent discussion of this problem by John Meyendorff entitled "Tradition and Traditions" in his volume of collected essays, *Orthodoxy and Catholicity*, pp. 91–106.

69. Ware, *Orthodox Church*, p. 319. For an example of how wide this divergence can be in the area of biblical studies, see Antony Gabriel, "Notes and Comments," *St. Vladimir's Theological Quarterly* 16 (1972):221. Gabriel comments on the debate between "the Biblical 'fundamentalists,' who accept every jot and tittle in the Scriptures as original and sacred, and the Biblical scholars who are concerned about the textual witness as well as the word of God."

70. Metropolitan James of Melita (later Archbishop Iakovos), "The Orthodox Concept of Mission and Missions," in *Basileia*, ed. Jan Hermelink and Hans Jochen Margull (Stuttgart: Evang. Missionsverlag GmbH, 1959), pp. 76–80.

71. Anastasios Yannoulatos (later bishop), "The Forgotten Commandment," *Porefthendes* 1 (1959):1–5.

72. Saints Cyril and Methodius who labored among the Slavs are considered "Equals of the Apostles" and are so remembered in the Slavonic version of the Divine Liturgy. See Isabel F. Hapgood, *Service Book of the Holy Orthodox-Catholic Apostolic Church*, p. 73.

73. Florovsky, "The Church: Her Nature and Task," in *The Universal Church in God's Design* (New York: Harper & Brothers, 1948), p. 43.

Chapter 3

1. This is admitted in a Roman Catholic history. See David Knowles and Dimitri Obolensky, *The Christian Centuries*, vol. 2: *The Middle Ages* (London: Darton, Longman & Todd, 1979), p. 16.

2. Stephen Neill expresses the problem well: "It used to be very difficult to get satisfactory information about the missions of the Orthodox Churches" (*A History of Christian Missions* [Baltimore, Md.: Penguin Books, 1977], p. 581).

3. See, e.g., the negative comments of George Smith, *Short History of Christian Missions* (Edinburgh: T. & T. Clark, n.d. [post-1910]), pp. 99, 220. Robert H. Glover, *The Progress of World-Wide Missions,* revised by J. Herbert Kane (New York: Harper & Row, 1960), completely ignores Orthodox missions, though it gives considerable coverage of Roman Catholic missions.

4. Walbert Bühlmann, *The Coming of the Third Church* (Maryknoll, N.Y.: Orbis Books, 1977), pp. 9f.

5. In seven volumes (New York: Harper & Row, 1937–45).

6. In five volumes (New York: Harper & Row, 1957–62).

7. Athens: Zoe, 1964. Some information on the history of the various national Churches can also be found in Ion Bria, ed. *Martyria/Mission, The Witness of the Orthodox Churches Today* (Geneva: WCC, 1980).

8. There is Orthodox mission work being done in East Africa, and material assistance is being given for Orthodox Churches in Korea and Japan. See the articles by Alexander Veronis in *The Orthodox Observer* (the official newspaper of the Greek Orthodox Archdiocese of North and South America) for a description of Orthodox involvement in these projects. Veronis has written for several years now a column on mission for *The Orthodox Observer*.

9. See Theodore H. Papadopoullos, *Studies and Documents Relative to the History*

of the Greek Church and People under Turkish Domination (Brussels, 1952; New York: AMS Press, 1973); C. H. Malik, "The Orthodox Church," in *Religion in the Middle East,* vol. 1, ed. A. J. Arberry (Cambridge, Eng.: Cambridge University Press, 1976), pp. 299-311; and Steven Runciman, *The Great Church in Captivity: A Study of the Patriarchate of Constantinople from the Eve of the Turkish Conquest to the Greek War of Independence* (London: Cambridge University Press, 1968).

10. John Perantonis, "The Concept of Mission and the Neomartyrs of Ottoman Stock," *Porefthendes* 8 (1966): 7-16, 40-42.

11. See Peter Hammond, *The Waters of Marah* (London: Rockliff, 1956), and Mario Rinvolucri, *Anatomy of a Church* (New York: Fordham University Press, 1966), especially pp. 135ff.

12. Francis Dvornik, *Byzantine Missions among the Slavs.* For an excellent survey (in Greek), see Anastasios Yannoulatos, "Byzantium, Evangelistic Works." See also the article by Yannoulatos, "Missions: Les missions des Églises d'Orient."

13. Demetrios J. Constantelos, *Byzantine Philanthropy and Social Welfare,* pp. 149-50.

14. Cyril was originally named Constantine and only assumed the name Cyril when he took monastic vows in 868. It is, however, by his monastic name that he is best known. For biographies of these brothers, see Michael Lacko, *Saints Cyril and Methodius.*

15. On whether this was the Cyrillic or Glagolitic alphabet, see Lacko, *Saints Cyril and Methodius,* pp. 83-87, where Lacko expresses the modern consensus that it was the Glagolitic.

16. This "heresy of the three languages" is called a "curious theory" by John Meyendorff ("Orthodox Missions in the Middle Ages," in *History's Lessons for Tomorrow's Mission* [Geneva: World's Student Christian Federation, 1960]), p. 102. Presumably it arose from a consideration and subsequent elaboration of the trilingual inscription on the cross of Christ (Jn. 19:19-20).

17. Meyendorff, "Orthodox Missions," p. 102.

18. Lacko, *Saints Cyril and Methodius,* pp. 56-60, 124ff. There is some question whether these were really the relics of St. Clement, bishop of Rome, or another Clement (cf. Dvornik, *Byzantine Missions,* pp. 66-67).

19. An interesting sidelight is that their appeal to Rome was addressed to Nicholas I, who was at the time quarreling with Photius, then patriarch of Constantinople. Cyril was a former student of Photius and his successor in the Imperial Academy. Ware comments that Cyril's action shows he did not take the quarrel between the two men very seriously, still regarding East and West as united in one Church (*The Orthodox Church* [Baltimore, Md.: Penguin Books, 1963], p. 84; cf. Steven Runciman, *The Eastern Schism* [Oxford: Clarendon Press, 1955], pp. 22-25). For an in-depth study of the quarrel, see Francis Dvornik, *The Photian Schism: History and Legend* (Cambridge, Eng.: University Press, 1948).

20. Lacko, *Saints Cyril and Methodius,* pp. 132-33.

21. The most important features of the dispensations for Uniate Churches are communion in both kinds, baptism by immersion, and the marriage of the lower clergy. These Uniate Churches are not properly regarded as missionary establishments of Roman Catholicism, as they were Churches of other communions that, for one reason or another, switched their allegiance to the pope. See Adrian Fortescue, *The Uniate Eastern Churches* (London: Burns Oates & Washbourne, 1923). For some of the concerns and problems facing these Churches today, see Maximos IV Sayegh, ed., *The Eastern Churches and Catholic Unity* (Edinburgh: Nelson, 1963).

22. The prohibition seems to have arisen because Pope John VIII was unwilling to risk a major clash with the Frankish Church over this issue of liturgy (see David Knowles and Dimitri Obolensky, *The Middle Ages,* p. 24).

23. Isabel F. Hapgood, trans. *Service Book of the Holy Orthodox-Catholic Apostolic Church,* 5th ed. (Englewood, N.J.: Antiochian Orthodox Christian Archdiocese, 1975), p. 73; cf. *The Priest's Service Book,* part 2 (New York: Orthodox Church in America, 1973), p. 236. For more information on Cyril and Methodius, see T. Hannick, "Notes et Documents: Cyrillo-Methodiana"; F. Grivec, "Cyrille et Methode"; Francis Dvornik, "Sts. Cyril and Methodius in Rome"; Dimitri Obolensky, "Sts. Cyril and Methodius: Apostles of the Slavs"; Eusebius Vittis, "Saints Cyril and Methodius, Enlighteners of the Slavs." The work by Vittis is a summary of two out-of-print commemorative publications, one a special issue of *Ecclesia* (nos. 16–17, 1966), the official journal of the Church of Greece, the other a book entitled, *To Cyril and Methodius: A Festive Volume on Their Eleven Hundredth Anniversary,* ed. J. E. Anastsiou (Thessaloniki: Holy Metropolitan See, 1966).

24. Ernst Benz, *The Eastern Orthodox Church* (Garden City, N.Y.: Doubleday, Anchor Books, 1963), pp. 105–7.

25. John Meyendorff, "Orthodox Missions in the Middle Ages," p. 102.

26. Bolshakoff, *Russian Nonconformity* (Philadelphia: Westminster Press, 1950).

27. Hammond, *The Waters of Marah,* pp. 154–56.

28. "Local church" is not always synonymous with "national church." "Some of these Churches are contained within the boundaries of one state and are, in effect, national Churches. Others, especially in the Near East, possess more traditional boundaries and include faithful belonging to several nationalities. Canonically speaking, the boundaries of all the local Churches are not national but territorial in nature, and correspond to former metropolitan provinces; that is, they form groups of dioceses whose bishops meet regularly in synod and elect their own primate, who bears the title of patriarch, archbishop, or metropolitan" (John Meyendorff, *The Orthodox Church* [London: Darton, Longman & Todd, 1962], p. 143; cf. Ware, *Orthodox Church,* pp. 13–15).

29. An autocephalous (from the Greek *auto* meaning "self" and *kephale* meaning "head") church is one that has the right to choose its own bishops (heads). For information on the establishment of the Orthodox Church in America, see *St. Vladimir's Theological Quarterly* 15 (1971), nos. 1–2; this issue was reprinted under the title, *Autocephaly: The Orthodox Church in America* (Crestwood, N.Y.: St. Vladimir's Seminary Press, 1971). See also Archimandrite Serafim, *The Quest for Orthodox Church Unity in America* (New York: Saints Boris and Gleb Press, 1973); Alexander A. Bogolepov, *Toward an American Orthodox Church: The Establishment of an Autocephalous Orthodox Church* (New York: Morehouse-Barlow, 1963). As in times past, so even today not all agree with the granting of autocephalous status. For the opposing point of view, see Panagiotes N. Trempelas, *The Autocephaly of the Metropolia in America,* trans. and ed. George S. Bebis et al. (Brookline, Mass.: Holy Cross Theological School Press, 1973).

30. An Orthodox theologian who consciously tries to avoid this tendency is Anastasios Yannoulatos. See his "The Purpose and Motive of Mission," *International Review of Mission* 54 (1965): 281–97. This article was reprinted in revised form in *Porefthendes* 10 (1967).

31. See Alexander Schmemann's criticisms, "Moment of Truth for Orthodoxy," in *Unity in Mid Career,* ed. Keith R. Bridston and Walter Wagoner (New York: Macmillan, 1963), pp. 54–55.

32. Benz, *Eastern Orthodox Church,* pp. 107-10.

33. Ibid., p. 110.

34. Kenneth Scott Latourette, *A History of the Expansion of Christianity,* vol. 1: *The First Five Centuries* (New York: Harper & Row, 1937), p. 214.

35. E.g., the Wycliffe Bible Translators, whose story is told in popular format by E. E. Wallis and M. A. Bennett, *Two Thousand Tongues to Go* (Chicago: Moody Press, 1959).

36. Ulfilas's Arianism keeps him from being claimed by the Orthodox Church although, as Benz and Latourette point out, he was consecrated in Constantinople as bishop of the Christians in Gothia. Stephen Neill makes an interesting observation in regard to Ulfilas's work. After calling his translation "one of the great monuments of courageous and vigorous Christian expansion," he goes on to say in a footnote that while Arianism is indeed unchristian in its reduction of the Son of God, yet "to simple people it may have presented itself as a rather attractive simplification, since it set them free from the knotty controversies about the nature and person of Christ, to follow him as a leader and to concentrate on the already sufficiently difficult task of learning how to live a sober, righteous, and godly life" (*A History of Christian Missions* [Baltimore, Md.: Penguin Books, 1964], p. 55).

37. Latourette, *The First Five Centuries,* p. 224.

Chapter 4

1. In his preface, Smirnoff chronicles the questions put to him concerning Russian missions. "I have noticed during the lengthy period of my life beyond the frontiers of Russia [at the time of his writing, Smirnoff had spent thirty-three years abroad, twenty-six of them as the superior of the Russian church in London] that the substance of these questions has gradually taken a different form. At first I used to be asked: 'Of course you have not yet any missions, any more than you had in former times?' Then: 'Is it true that you have established some sort of mission in Japan?' Further on: 'It seems that you have missions of some sort in Siberia?' Still further: 'Could you not give us some precise statistics as to the number of conversions in your missions?' And finally: 'What is your opinion—would it not be better for us to close our mission in Japan, in order not to hinder the regular growth of your mission, especially as our Church aims at reunion with yours?' " His book is an effort to answer these questions and to reply to critics of the Orthodox Church who claim that the Church is in a state of stagnation and backwardness. (*A Short Account of the Historical Development and Present Position of Russian Orthodox Missions,* pp. v-vi.)

2. Serge Bolshakoff, *The Foreign Missions of the Russian Orthodox Church,* p. 7.

3. Josef Glazik, *Die russisch-orthodoxe Heidenmission Seit Peter dem Grossen* and *Die Islammission der russisch-orthodoxen Kirche.*

4. This is demonstrated by the insistence of Russian theologians that they are heirs of Byzantine theology and their repeated calls for a return to the Byzantine roots. See John Meyendorff, *Byzantine Theology* (London: Mowbrays, 1974), pp. 1ff., 225ff. For a Greek theologian's evaluation of Russian mission work, see the articles by Anastasios Yannoulatos in *Porefthendes:* "Orthodoxy in China," 4 (1962) no. 14, pp. 26-30; no. 15, pp. 36-39; no. 16, pp. 52-55; "Orthodoxy in Alaska," 5 (1963) no. 17-18, pp. 14-22; no. 19-20, pp. 44-47.

5. Francis Dvornik, *Byzantine Missions among the Slavs* (New Brunswick, N.J.: Rutgers University Press, 1970), pp. 244-50.

6. Boris abdicated in 888 (after ruling for thirty-six years) and retired to a monas-

tery, coming out once to depose his son and install his younger son as king (see Dvornik, *Byzantine Missions*; also see Alexander Schmemann, *The Historical Road of Eastern Orthodoxy* (London: Harvill Press, 1963), pp. 260–63.

7. See Schmemann, *Historical Road,* pp. 262–67, for a historical summary.

8. Timothy Ware, *The Orthodox Church* (Baltimore, Md.: Penguin Books, 1963), p. 87.

9. Ibid. According to Ware, there was a church at Kiev in 945.

10. John Meyendorff, *The Orthodox Church* (London: Darton, Longman & Todd, 1962), p. 102. He points out that through this sequence of events, the Slavic dialect spoken around Thessalonica became Church Slavonic, the liturgical language of Slavs around the world.

11. Princess Olga, Vladimir's grandmother, became a Christian in 945 (Ware, *Orthodox Church*, p. 87).

12. Schmemann, *Historical Road*, p. 297.

13. Ware, *Orthodox Church*, p. 87. For more information on Vladimir, see Constantin de Grunwald, *Saints of Russia* (London: Hutchinson, 1960), pp. 17–30. For the account of Vladimir's examination of Judaism, Islam, Latin Christianity, and Eastern Christianity before finally choosing the last, see the following: Nicholas Zernov, *The Russians and Their Church* (London: SPCK, 1954), p. 7; Walter F. Adeney, *The Greek and Eastern Churches*, pp. 360–63; A. P. Stanley, *Lectures on the History of the Eastern Church,* pp. 292–303; Serge A. Zenkovsky, ed., *Medieval Russia's Epics, Chronicles, and Tales,* pp. 65–71.

14. Bolshakoff, *Foreign Missions*, p. 18.

15. Smirnoff, *Russian Missions*, p. 1.

16. Ibid., p. 2.

17. John Meyendorff, "Orthodox Missions in the Middle Ages," in *History's Lessons for Tomorrow's Missions* (Geneva: World's Student Christian Federation, 1960), pp. 103–4.

18. G. P. Fedotov, *The Russian Religious Mind, Kievan Christianity: The 10th to the 13th Centuries*, pp. 94–131. See also Pierre Kovalevsky, *Saint Sergius and Russian Spirituality*, trans. W. Elias Jones (Crestwood, N.Y.: St. Vladimir's Seminary Press, 1976).

19. John Meyendorff, *St. Gregory Palamas and Orthodox Spirituality*, trans. Adele Fiske (Crestwood, N.Y.: St. Vladimir's Seminary Press, 1974), pp. 162–66.

20. Meyendorff, *The Orthodox Church*, p. 182. Cf. Zoe Brotherhood, eds. *A Sign of God, Orthodoxy 1964* (Athens: Zoe, 1964), p. 63.

21. Meyendorff, "Orthodox Missions in the Middle Ages," p. 104.

22. Nikita Struve points out that Stephen used the local runes to compose his alphabet. ("The Orthodox Church and Mission," in *History's Lessons for Tomorrow's Mission*, p. 106).

23. The most accessible account of Stephen's life and work is found in G. P. Fedotov, *The Russian Religious Mind*, vol. 2: *The Middle Ages* (Cambridge, Mass.: Harvard University Press, 1966), pp. 230–45.

24. "From his time onward Russian missionaries always preached the gospel to the most uncivilized peoples in their native tongue. . . . One of the constants in Russian missions was to be the promotion as rapidly as possible of an indigenous clergy, the self-effacement of the teachers before their disciples" (Struve, "The Orthodox Church and Mission," p. 107).

25. Cf. Frank Gavin, *Some Aspects of Contemporary Greek Orthodox Thought*

(Milwaukee: Morehouse Publishing Co., 1923), p. 307. See the delightful summary of a twentieth-century Greek mission novel, where the hero, Philotheos, himself shipwrecked on a desert island, is saved from having to perform the baptism of his converts by the arrival (also by being shipwrecked) of an Orthodox bishop (Elias Voulgarakis, "The Greek Orthodox Missionary, Philotheos," *Porefthendes* 10 (1968): 2–4, 41–46, 55–62.

26. Struve, "The Orthodox Church and Mission" p. 108.

27. Bolshakoff, *Foreign Missions*, p. 54.

28. After all, were they not merely following Prince Vladimir's example in the use of the temporal sword? While it cannot be denied that the pattern of close state and Church cooperation was enshrined in history, yet the one significant difference is that Vladimir led his own people into the faith, a faith that was intelligible by virtue of its presentation in Slavonic. Later Russian missionaries, without making the real content of the faith intelligible, sought to coerce and bribe unbelievers into accepting baptism. The result was mass apostasy at the earliest opportunity (see Nadejda Gorodetzky, "The Missionary Expansion of the Russian Orthodox Church," pp. 402f.).

29. Struve, "The Orthodox Church and Mission," p. 109. Cf. Glazik, *Die russischorthodoxe Heidenmission*, p. 29.

30. For a fuller account of this dispute and others that divided the Russian Church, see Bolshakoff, *Russian Nonconformity* (Philadelphia: Westminster Press, 1950); cf. Ware, *Orthodox Church*, pp. 114–25. For current statistics, see Nikita Struve, *Christians in Contemporary Russia* (London: Harvill Press, 1967), pp. 218–25.

31. Cf. Schmemann, *Historical Road*, pp. 331f.

32. James Cracraft, *The Church Reforms of Peter the Great* (London: Macmillan, 1971), p. 65. Cracraft cites an edict concerned with trade in Siberia and with China in which Peter inserted a passage on missionary work. For the furtherance of the Christian faith, he proposed that a new metropolitan be appointed to the See of Tobol'sk and that two or three educated monks be sent with him to assist in the conversion of Chinese and Siberians. The monks were to engage in the study of language and culture so that they might refute their idolatry with solid arguments. As will be seen below, these studies could also serve political ends.

33. Struve, "The Orthodox Church and Mission," p. 110. Nevertheless, Struve rejoices in the founding of these missions, a bright spot in a dreary age.

34. Ware, *Orthodox Church*, p. 127.

35. Struve, "The Orthodox Church and Mission," p. 110.

36. For further details on the life and work of Macarius, see Glazik, *Die russischorthodoxe Heidenmission*, pp. 118–27. Also Nikita Struve, "Macaire Gloukharev, A Prophet of Orthodox Mission," pp. 308–14.

37. Velitchkovsky himself discovered hesychasm on Mount Athos and translated the *Philokalia*, a hesychist manual of devotion, into Slavonic. Velitchkovsky never returned to Russia, but the movement spread because of his translations and the work of his disciples. Two important studies on hesychasm are by John Meyendorff: *St. Gregory Palamas and Orthodox Spirituality*, trans. Adele Fiske (Crestwood, N.Y.: St. Vladimir's Seminary Press, 1974) and *A Study of Gregory Palamas*, trans. George Lawrence (London: Faith Press, 1964). Primary source material on hesychasm in English translation can be found in two volumes translated by E. Kadloubovsky and G. E. H. Palmer, *Writings from the Philokalia* (London: Faber and Faber, 1951) and *Early Fathers from the Philokalia* (London: Faber and Faber, 1954).

38. Struve, "Macaire Gloukharev," p. 310.

39. Ibid., p. 311.

40. Ibid.

41. Ibid., p. 312.

42. Meyendorff, "Orthodox Missions in the Middle Ages," p. 104.

43. Struve, "Macaire Gloukharev," p. 312.

44. "He [Macarius] constantly maintained that 'the work of conversion only begins with baptism' and therefore took even more care of a convert after his baptism than before" (Smirnoff, *Russian Missions*, p. 18).

45. Bolshakoff remarks that they remind the observer of the Jesuit Reductions of Paraguay (*Foreign Missions*, p. 59).

46. Struve, "Macaire Gloukharev," p. 313.

47. Ibid., p. 314.

48. Smirnoff, *Russian Missions*, pp. 20-21; Bolshakoff, *Foreign Missions*, p. 60.

49. Gorodetsky, "The Missionary Expansion of the Russian Orthodox Church," p. 407. Cf. Glazik, *Die russisch-orthodoxe Heidenmission*, p. 122.

50. Struve, "The Orthodox Church and Mission," p. 111.

51. For a general discussion of the effect of Western ideas on Russian culture, see James H. Billington, *The Icon and the Axe: An Interpretative History of Russian Culture*, pp. 163-306.

52. Struve, "Macaire Gloukharev," p. 310.

53. Bolshakoff, *Foreign Missions*, p. 39.

54. Smirnoff, *Russian Missions*, p. 33.

55. Ibid., pp. 41-42.

56. "Moreover, it is essential that the final touches should be put to the translations, with the assistance of natives by birth, because a Russian, as I know by my own experience, having occupied myself with Tartar translations for about thirty years, cannot possibly know all the subtleties, shades and psychological depths of a foreign tongue" (Ilminski, as quoted by Smirnoff, *Russian Missions*, p. 34).

57. Ilminski, as quoted by G. Florovsky, "Russian Missions: An Historical Sketch," *The Christian East* 14 (1933): 30-41.

58. See Smirnoff, *Russian Missions*, pp. 27-74, for a detailed account of Ilminski's labors and for the statistical tables showing the advance of the Orthodox Church among these tribes. See also Glazik, *Islammission*, pp. 133-43.

59. Bolshakoff, at least, thought so (cf. *Foreign Missions*, p. 71).

60. John's surname was originally Popov but he was renamed Veniaminov in honor of the bishop of Irkutsk. After his wife died, he became a monk, taking the name Innocent (Bolshakoff, *Foreign Missions*, p. 71). The most complete account of his life in English is Paul D. Garrett, *St. Innocent: Apostle to America*. See also Procius Yasuo Ushimaru, *Bishop Innocent: Founder of American Orthodoxy*.

61. Gorodetzky, "Missionary Expansion," p. 406.

62. Smirnoff, *Russian Missions*, p. 92.

63. As will be seen in the following chapter, one of the main objections to reinstituting Orthodox foreign missions today is the contention that the Church is too weak at home to undertake missionary work. The opponents of foreign missions feel that the priority is to strengthen the home Church by engaging in work among nominal Christians. This argument has been used in Greece because of the internal Church situation. Proponents of foreign missions point to this example and others like it to establish that foreign missions can bring great benefit and strength to the home Church. See Anastasios Yannoulatos, " 'Porefthendes,' An Inter-Orthodox Missionary Centre," *Porefthendes 3* (1961), no. 11, pp. 37-38.

64. The see was moved from Sitka in Alaska to Ayan on the coast of Siberia, to Yakutsk in the tundra, to a new town he helped to found in the new Russian province of Amur, Blagovyeshchensk ("Good News Town") (Struve, "The Orthodox Church and Mission," p. 112).

65. For more information on Bishop Innocent's life and work in addition to the works of Smirnoff, Bolshakoff, Garrett, and Struve, see Glazik, *Die russisch-orthodoxe Heidenmission*, pp. 145-57, 161-66; Michael Kovach, "The Russian Orthodox Church in Russian America," pp. 141-220; Constance J. Tarasar, ed., *Orthodox America, 1794-1976: Development of the Orthodox Church in America* (Syosset, N.Y.: Orthodox Church in America, 1975), pp. 15-23.

While by no means a mission strategist in the sense of those considered above, mention should be made of another missionary connected with the Alaskan mission, who is the first "American" saint of the Orthodox Church. Father Herman of Alaska (1756?-1837, canonized Aug. 9, 1970), was a simple monk, whose gentleness and purity of life attracted the indigenous peoples of Alaska. His defense of these people against the injustices of the Russian traders brought him into conflict with the local authorities and on at least one occasion caused an interruption of his work. However, the saint had a positive witness to both the indigenous peoples and the traders. For more information on St. Herman, see Tarasar, *Orthodox America*, pp. 24f., 294-30; Vsevolod Rochcau, "Saint Herman of Alaska and the Defense of Alaskan Native Peoples," *St. Vladimir's Theological Quarterly* 16 (1972): 17-39.

Chapter 5

1. Alaska and the Aleutian Islands were only sold to the United States in 1867.

2. See Zoe Brotherhood, eds., *A Sign of God, Orthodoxy 1964* (Athens: Zoe, 1964), pp. 301f., for Nicholas's early life.

3. Glazik, *Die russisch-orthodoxe Heidenmission seit Peter dem Grossen* (Münster: Aschendorffsche Verlagsbuchhandlung, 1954), p. 180.

4. Sawabe even began to take notes (Otis Cary, *A History of Christianity in Japan,* vol. 1: *Roman Catholic and Greek Orthodox Missions,* p. 379).

5. In the course of his instruction, Nicholas brought the discussion around to Christianity. The same method of evangelism is still being practiced today in Japan by English-speaking missionaries who conduct classes in English that are often centered around Christian themes.

6. Cary, *A History of Christianity in Japan,* 1: 383-84.

7. Ibid., 1: 390.

8. Meyendorff, *The Orthodox Church* (London: Darton, Longman & Todd, 1962), p. 184.

9. See Cary, *A History of Christianity in Japan,* vol. 1, pp. 394-404, for an account of the persecution undergone by the believers. At times it sounds like passages from the Acts of the Apostles, e.g., "The real inquirers had been bold, and considered it an honour to suffer persecution" (p. 398).

10. Ibid., 1: 406.

11. In the Orthodox Church, the entire church, laity and clergy, are the guardians of Orthodoxy. Thus it is not strange to see the laity represented on governing councils. See John Karmiris, *A Synopsis of the Dogmatic Theology of the Orthodox Catholic Church,* trans. from Greek by George Dimopoulos (Scranton, Pa.: Christian Orthodox Edition, 1973), pp. 88-89.

12. E.g., see I. F. Hapgood, *Service Book of the Holy Orthodox-Catholic Apostolic*

Church (Englewood, N.J.: Antiochian Orthodox Christian Archdiocese, 1975), p. 9.

13. Part of Nicholas's address to the church reads as follows: "I prayed as usual today in the Cathedral, but henceforth I will not take part in the public prayers. This is not for the reason that it might be dangerous for me to appear in the Cathedral, but for the reason that until now I prayed for the victory and the peace of the Japanese Emperor, but now in case of war I can not pray as a Russian subject that our native country should be conquered by an enemy. I have, as you also have, an obligation to my country, therefore I am glad to see that you realize your obligation to your country" (Cary, *A History of Christianity in Japan,* 1: 418). Cary cites the full text of Father Nicholas's statement.

14. An interesting sidelight on the literary labors of Nicholas is that, while for a considerable length of time the Orthodox had used the Protestant version of the Japanese New Testament, he prepared a new translation, since he considered the Protestant edition too colloquial and overly influenced by English. In order to preserve the dignity he thought appropriate for the Bible, he used more Chinese terms and archaic forms (Cary, *A History of Christianity in Japan,* 1: 421).

15. Henry St. George Tucker, *The History of the Episcopal Church in Japan* (New York: Charles Scribner's Sons, 1938), p. 103.

16. Richard Henry Drummond, *A History of Christianity in Japan,* p. 354.

17. "The Catholic and Protestant missions to Japan had at their disposal respectively twenty-six and fifteen times as much money as the Orthodox mission" (Drummond, *History of Christianity in Japan,* p. 115).

18. Drummond, *A History of Christianity in Japan,* pp. 356-59.

19. See Archimandrite Serafim, *The Quest for Orthodox Church Unity in America* (New York: Saints Boris and Gleb Press, 1973).

20. Constance J. Tarasar, ed., *Orthodox America 1794-1976* (Syosset, N.Y.: Orthodox Church in America, 1975), p. 336. An autocephalous church is self-governing in all respects including the selection of its primate. An autonomous church has its head selected by the patriarch under whose spiritual jurisdiction the church is. In most other respects, it is self-governing. (See George H. Demetrakopoulos, *Dictionary of Orthodox Theology: A Summary of the Beliefs, Practices and History of the Eastern Orthodox Church* [New York: Philosophical Library, 1964], pp. 21-22.) For a history of the Japanese Orthodox Church, see Procius Yasuo Ushimaru's *History of the Orthodox Church in Japan* (in Japanese; includes seven pages of illustrations) (Tokyo: Orthodox Church in Japan, 1978).

21. This study will not discuss the earlier entrance of Christianity into China as a result of the labor of Nestorian missionaries, since the Nestorian Church at the time was not in communion with the Eastern Orthodox Church. However, their valuable work should not be overlooked and an excellent summary of it may be found in Aziz S. Atiya, *History of Eastern Christianity* (Notre Dame, Ind.: University of Notre Dame Press, 1967), pp. 257-66. Walter F. Adeney also mentions the traditions of Christianity in China (*The Greek and Eastern Churches* [Clifton, N.J.: Reference Book Publishers, 1965; reprint of 1908 ed.], pp. 533-37). Greek Orthodox scholars also show an appreciation of the Nestorians' efforts; see Anastasios Yannoulatos, "The Missionary Activities of the Churches of the East in Central and Eastern Asia," *Porefthendes* 3 (1961): 26-31. For the text of the monument set up by the Nestorians outlining their faith and work, see James Legge, trans., *The Nestorian Monument of Hsi-An Fu in Shen-Hsi, China* (London, 1888).

22. Zoe Brotherhood, eds., *A Sign of God, Orthodoxy 1964,* p. 281.

23. Glazik, *Die russisch-orthodoxe Heidenmission*, p. 58.

24. James Cracraft points out that the presence of the Jesuits in Peking acted as a check on Peter's designs (*The Church Reforms of Peter the Great*, p. 67); see also Eric Widmer, *The Russian Ecclesiastical Mission in Peking during the Eighteenth Century*, pp. 29-30.

25. "Its [the mission's] situation until that year was very strange. The Archimandrite, head of the mission, was nothing less than the Russian Ambassador to China, and yet he was also a Chinese civil servant, receiving a salary from the court of Peking. All diplomatic relations between China and Russia were conducted through the Archimandrite of the Peking Monastery" (Bolshakoff, *The Foreign Missions of the Russian Orthodox Church* [London: SPCK, 1943], p. 65).

26. Zoe Brotherhood, eds., *A Sign of God, Orthodoxy 1964*, pp. 286-87. The history of the Orthodox work in China is well covered in the section "Orthodoxy in China," pp. 280-99. See also Kenneth Scott Latourette, *A History of Christian Missions in China*, pp. 200, 566, 742. An early account is found in Charles R. Hale, *Missions of the Russian Church in China and Japan*.

27. Zoe Brotherhood, eds., *A Sign of God, Orthodoxy 1964*, p. 289.

28. Kenneth Scott Latourette, *A History of the Expansion of Christianity*, vol. 6: *The Great Century in Northern Africa and Asia* (New York: Harper & Row, 1944), p. 294. Zoe Brotherhood, eds., *A Sign of God, Orthodoxy 1964*, p. 291, misquotes Latourette and makes the claim that the Orthodox suffered more martyrs in total number than either the Catholics or the Protestants.

29. Glazik, *Die russisch-orthodoxe Heidenmission*, p. 174.

30. Latourette, *Expansion of Christianity*, 6: 295. Others were more optimistic. ". . . Eastern Christianity may possibly be destined to be the religion of China and Japan, seeing that it is more suited to the genius of the Oriental than that form of Christ's religion which has clothed itself in Western dress" (F. G. Cole, *Mother of All Churches* [London: Skeffington & Son, 1908], p. 196.

31. No doubt this was because the Japanese were anti-Communist and looked with favor on those Russians who held the same outlook; see Latourette, *A History of the Expansion of Christianity*, vol. 7: *Advance through Storm* (New York: Harper & Row, 1945), p. 345.

32. Anastasios Yannoulatos, "Orthodoxy in China," *Porefthendes* 4 (1962-63): 54-55.

33. Nicolas Zernov, *Eastern Christendom* (London: Weidenfeld and Nicolson, 1961), p. 226.

34. See Donald E. MacInnis, *Religious Policy and Practices in Communist China* (London: Hodder and Stoughton, 1972), pp. 300-305, for the text of a 1969 denunciation of the Soviet leadership for their implicit approval of the Russian Orthodox Church. For the latest available information on the Orthodox Church in China, see Richard C. Bush, Jr., *Religion in Communist China* (Nashville: Abingdon 1970), pp. 239-41.

35. The man behind the evangelization of these Koreans was Bishop Innocent Veniaminov, whose life was reviewed above, pp. 33-34. The number of baptized Koreans at the close of the century was 10,000 (Bolshakoff, *Foreign Missions*, p. 73).

36. The best available history of the Korean mission is to be found in Igor A. Caruso, "Missions Orthodoxes en Corée." The facts presented here have been obtained mainly from that source.

37. Some authorities see the Russian mission as a part of the political intrigue that

Russia was working in the area. "It was to be anticipated that the Russian Orthodox Church would enter Korea. Russian territorial expansion and Russian political ambitions in the East of Asia could be expected to be accompanied by efforts to extend Russian influence through the Church which through Russian political absolutism had so long been employed as a tool by the state" (Latourette, *A History of the Expansion of Christianity,* vol. 6: *The Great Century* [New York: Harper & Row, 1944], p. 427; cf. Homer B. Halbert, *The Passing of Korea* [New York: Doubleday, Page & Co., 1906], p. 167). While Russia undoubtedly had ambitions in Asia, it is perhaps unfair to claim that the Church only advanced the imperial plans. Furthermore, it is a strange accusation to make only of the Orthodox when in the history of missions other powers employed the "civilizing" effects of missions to their own political ends. Nevertheless, the Koreans did refuse to grant visas to the Orthodox missionaries when at the time other Christian communions were active in Korea. This would indicate a certain amount of intrigue, perhaps on the part of the Japanese who sought to keep Russian influence out of Korea.

38. The head of the mission, Archimandrite Ambrosius Gudko (who had formerly been a Uniate) eventually was made a bishop and was martyred in 1918 (Bolshakoff, *Foreign Missions,* p. 74).

39. Caruso calls Archmandrite Chrysanthe, "le véritable createur de la mission coréenne" ("Missions Orthodoxes en Corée," p. 95).

40. Alexander Chang, "Orthodoxy in Korea," in Zoe Brotherhood, eds., *A Sign of God, Orthodoxy 1964,* p. 326.

41. I am grateful to Father Stanley Harakas, of Holy Cross School of Theology, Brookline, Mass., for providing this up-to-date information on Korea. More dated, but illustrative of the difficulties the Korean church has faced, is Borris Moon, in *A Sign of God, Orthodoxy 1964,* ed. Zoe Brotherhood, pp. 327–30.

Chapter 6

1. The documentation of a lack of missionary work is provided by the articles advocating the commencement of evangelistic work in the early volumes of *Porefthendes.* Cf. Anastasios Yannoulatos, "Discovering the Orthodox Missionary Ethos," in *Martyria/Mission,* ed. Ion Bria (Geneva: World Council of Churches, 1980), p. 25.

2. Cf. John S. Romanides, "The Orthodox: Arrival and Dialogue," *The Christian Century* 80 (1963): 1402.

3. Stanley S. Harakas, "Living the Orthodox Christian Faith in America," *Lutheran World* 23 (1976): 196–97. This article also appears in *Martyria/Mission,* pp. 153–58.

4. George Papaioannou, *From Mars Hill to Manhattan: The Greek Orthodox in America under Patriarch Athenagoras I* (Minneapolis: Light and Life Publishing Co., 1976), pp. 28f.

5. Stanley S. Harakas, "Living the Orthodox Christian Faith in America," p. 197. Cf. Ion Bria, "Concerns and Challenges in Orthodox Ecclesiology Today," *Lutheran World* 23 (1976): 188–91; and "Consultation on 'Orthodox Diaspora,' " *Porefthendes* 10 (1968): 29–31.

6. Take, e.g., the Greek Orthodox Church in South Africa. "In South African terms, the Greek Orthodox Church constitutes a middling-sized denomination. Its membership of 50,000 makes it a larger Church, in terms of White membership, than both the Presbyterian Church of Southern Africa, or the Baptist Union. However, little is ever heard of it, the reason being that it has never seen its task going beyond serving the local Greek community" (*Ecu News Bulletin* 12 [1975], p. 9).

7. "The majority of members of all the Orthodox jurisdictions are hardly missionary-minded. Most members of the Church today still consider Orthodoxy as their own faith, for themselves, as part of their cultural heritage, and it is presented to others in precisely this way, primarily for the sake of gaining recognition and respect in American society" (Thomas Hopko, "The Orthodox Church in America," in Bria, ed., *Martyria/Mission,* p. 146).

8. "Activity Report 1961–1966," *Porefthendes* 8 (1966): 52.

9. The best account of the beginnings of the African Orthodox Church is found in F. B. Welbourn, *East African Rebels: A Study of Some Independent Churches,* pp. 77–110. See also D. E. Wentink, "The Orthodox Church in East Africa," pp. 33–43; and Norman A. Horner, "An East African Orthodox Church," pp. 221–33. An extremely important contribution to the subject of why the church started is found in Nectarios Hatzimichalis, "L'Eglise Orthodoxe grecque et le messianisme en Afrique," pp. 85–95. There are also accounts of the African Orthodox Church in Zoe Brotherhood, eds., *A Sign of God: Orthodoxy 1964,* pp. 377–95, and in Bria, ed., *Martyria/Mission,* pp. 165–68. For the history of the American connection that was later repudiated, see Theodore Natsoulas, "Patriarch McGuire and the Spread of the African Orthodox Church to Africa," *Journal of Religion in Africa* 12, no. 2 (1981): 81–104.

10. Bühlmann, *The Coming of the Third Church* (Maryknoll, N.Y.: Orbis Books, 1977), p. 10. Bühlmann's sources are not the best and his information is not accurate.

11. See David Barrett, "Who's Who of African Independent Church Leaders," pp. 23–24. On the Independent Church movement, see Victor E. W. Hayward, ed., *African Independent Church Movements* (London: Edinburgh House Press, 1963), and D. B. Barrett, *Schism and Renewal in Africa: An Analysis of Six Thousand Contemporary Religious Movements* (London: Oxford University Press, 1968).

12. "The New Patriarch of Alexandria and All Africa," *Porefthendes* 10, nos. 38–39 (1968): 24.

13. N. Horner, "An East African Orthodox Church," p. 224.

14. D. E. Wentink, "The Orthodox Church in East Africa," p. 39.

15. Welbourn, *East African Rebels,* p. 93.

16. Barrett, "Who's Who of African Independent Church Leaders," p. 33. See also D. E. Wentink, "The Reaction of the Once Independent African Church to the Foreign Greek Orthodox Mission It Invited In," *Theory and Practice in Church Life and Growth,* ed. D. B. Barrett (Nairobi: Workshop in Religious Research, 1968).

17. D. E. Wentink, "The Orthodox Church in East Africa," p. 39. One should also add, "if they return." "Over the years since 1958, quite a number of young Ugandans have gone for study in Greece and other Orthodox countries, but few of them ever returned to their homeland. Those who came back were frequently in conflict with their colleagues who lacked a 'Greek' orientation" (Norman Horner, "An East African Orthodox Church," p. 226).

18. There are three national Orthodox Churches in East Africa: Kenya, Uganda, and Tanzania.

19. D. E. Wentink, "The Orthodox Church in East Africa," p. 40. At the present writing, Spartas is auxiliary bishop for Uganda. Cf. Anastasios Yannoulatos, "Father Spartas visits Greece," pp. 10–13.

20. This writer was at one of these meetings and witnessed firsthand the enthusiasm the Ugandan priest was able to arouse in the American Greeks (see Alexander Veronis, "Greek Orthodox Foreign Missions," *The Orthodox Observer,* September 1969, p. 11).

21. See the following reports in *Porefthendes* for details of these journeys: Theano Konstantopoulou, "From the Visit of the Faculty of Theology of the University of

Thessaloniki to Uganda"; Anastasios Yannoulatos, "A Brief Chronicle on the Founding of an Orthodox Community in West Tanzania"; "Among the Orthodox of West Kenya"; "Impressions from a Brief Contact with Orthodox Kikuyu."

22. The first missionary was Chrysostom Papasarantopoulos, a celibate priest and monk who went to Uganda in 1960. He served in Africa until his death in December 1972. One of the most remarkable missionaries was Stavritsa Zachariou, a Greek-American woman who has served in East Africa since 1971. She paints icons and teaches the Africans basic domestic-science skills. This information came from Alexander Veronis, a Greek Orthodox priest in the United States and vice-chairman of the Foreign Missions Committee of the Greek Orthodox Archdiocese (cf. Alexander Veronis, "Orthodox Concepts of Evangelism and Mission," *Greek Orthodox Theological Review* 27 [1982]: 44–45).

23. Bishop Theodoros, "The Orthodox Church in Uganda," *Martyria/Mission,* ed. Ion Bria, p. 168.

24. See Welbourn, *East African Rebels,* pp. 86–89.

25. Quoted in Norman Horner, "An East African Orthodox Church," p. 224.

26. Bishop Theodoros Nankyamas, "The Orthodox Church in Uganda," which was published in 1980.

27. Horner, "An East African Orthodox Church," p. 225. See also the relevant sections in David B. Barrett et al., *Kenya Churches Handbook: The Development of Kenyan Christianity, 1948–1973.*

28. Horner, "An East African Orthodox Church," p. 225.

29. Personal correspondence from Stanley Harakas, Oct. 14, 1983.

30. Horner, "An East African Orthodox Church," p. 225, gives the details of the consecration of the three African bishops of Uganda, Kenya, and Tanzania in 1973.

31. While this section has focused on the work in East Africa because both funds and personnel have been sent there, mention must be made of financial aid given to the Korean Orthodox Church and the Orthodox Church in Alaska. The Greek Church in the United States is also involved in establishing Orthodoxy in Mexico.

Chapter 7

1. J. H. Bavinck, *An Introduction to the Science of Missions,* trans. David H. Freeman (Philadelphia: The Presbyterian and Reformed Publishing Co., 1960), p. xi.

2. Ibid.

3. Ibid., pp. xii–xiii. See also Elias Voulgarakis, "Mission and Fathers, a Bibliography," *Porefthendes* 4 (1962): 31, which lists Western works on the subject.

4. See Chrysostom's epistle addressed "to the presbyters and monks in Phoenice who instruct the Greeks in the faith," Migne, *Greek Patrology,* vol. 52. The text is referred to by Nectarios Hatzimichalis, "Orthodox Monasticism and External Mission," *Porefthendes* 4 (1962): 12–15.

5. Alexander Schmemann, "Moment of Truth for Orthodoxy," in *Unity in Mid-Career,* ed. Keith R. Bridston and Walter D. Wagoner (New York: Macmillan, 1963), pp. 48, 54–56.

6. Anastasios Yannoulatos, "The Purpose and Motive of Mission from an Orthodox Theological Point of View," *Porefthendes* 9 (1967): 2. This is a revised and expanded version of an article that first appeared in the *International Review of Mission* 54 (1965): 281–97.

7. Anastasios Yannoulatos, "Purpose and Motive," p. 2. This and all subsequent references are to the article in *Porefthendes* 9 (1967).

8. Ibid., pp. 2–3.

9. The transfiguration features prominently in Orthodox theology and spirituality. See, e.g., Vladimir Lossky, *The Mystical Theology of the Eastern Church* (Cambridge, Eng.: James Clarke and Co., 1968), pp. 149, 215, 220–35.

10. Eastern saints have shared in this glory and "have very frequently been transfigured by the inward light of uncreated grace, and have appeared resplendent, like Christ on the Mount of Transfiguration" (Lossky, *Mystical Theology,* p. 243). An account of such a transfiguration is found in John Meyendorff, *St. Gregory Palamas and Orthodox Spirituality* (Crestwood, N.Y.: St. Vladimir's Seminary Press, 1974), pp. 165–66.

11. Anastasios Yannoulatos, "Purpose and Motive," p. 3. Italics in the original.

12. Ibid., p. 4.

13. E. Roels, *God's Mission: The Epistle to the Ephesians in Mission Perspective* (Franeker, Netherlands: Wever, 1962), p. 67, as cited in "Purpose and Motive," p. 4.

14. Anastasios Yannoulatos, "Purpose and Motive," p. 4.

15. Ibid. Byzantine theology makes a distinction between divine glory and divine essence. Human beings share in the glory of God's nature, but not in the divine nature itself. See John Meyendorff, *Byzantine Theology: Historical Trends and Doctrinal Themes* (New York: Fordham University Press, 1974), pp. 184–88.

16. Yannoulatos, "Purpose and Motive," p. 5.

17. See, e.g., the series of articles by Anastasios Yannoulatos, "Orthodoxy in China," *Porefthendes* 4 (1962): 26–30, 36–39, 52–55.

18. "The glory of God is repeatedly referred to in Scripture as the ultimate purpose" (Bavinck, *Science of Missions,* p. 156). The glory and manifestation of divine grace was stated as the ultimate goal of mission by Gisbertus Voetius (1589–1676). "How striking that in his theory of mission Voetius did not get all wrapped up in the theological dispute about hardening and reprobation in which some of the figures of the later Reformation became so exaggerated in their claims. Voetius rather put all his emphasis on the glory of God who was disclosing His liberating grace and on the praise which was due him for extending that grace" (J. Verkuyl, *Contemporary Missiology: An Introduction,* trans. and ed. Dale Cooper [Grand Rapids, Mich.: Wm. B. Eerdmans, 1978], p. 184).

19. Vsevolod Spiller, "Missionary Aims and the Russian Orthodox Church," p. 199.

20. A convenient example of this type of situation would be Greece where 98% of the population are members of the Greek Orthodox Church, which is recognized by the government as the established or state Church ("The Church in Greece," *Pro Mundi Vita Dossiers,* November 1976, p. 2). This is changed somewhat by the new Constitution of June 9, 1975; see Athanasios Basdekis, "Between Partnership and Separation," *The Ecumenical Review* 29 (1977): 52–61.

21. Anastasios Yannoulatos, "Purpose and Motive," p. 7.

22. John Meyendorff, *The Orthodox Church: Its Past and Its Role in the World Today* (London: Darton, Longman & Todd, 1962), p. 169. For a full history of the earlier period, see Matthew Spinka, *A History of Christianity in the Balkans* (Hamden, Conn.: Archon Books, 1968), pp. 1–72, 91–128. For a description of the nineteenth and twentieth centuries, see Totiu Koev, "The Bulgarian Patriarchate," in *Martyria/ Mission,* ed. Ion Bria, pp. 102–8. It should be noted that the theory of Byzantine ecclesiastical oppression is not universally accepted. "It is significant that, although the patriarchs of Constantinople and many bishops of the Bulgarians, Albanians, Armenians and Slavs were Greeks during the Ottoman period, they did not attempt to Hellenize their congregations; neither did they try to force them to abandon their liturgical traditions and cultures. Of course every rule has its exceptions. The fact is, however, that the tradition of the Greek Church has been one of religious toleration

rather than nationalism. If this had not been true, the Greek Church, in the Byzantine centuries and especially during the four hundred years under the Turks, could have Hellenized all the minorities under her aegis or at least a great majority of them. The Greek historian C. Paparrigopoulos, known for his patriotism, blamed the Church for not exploiting her numerous opportunities to Hellenize the various Balkan peoples in a period of four hundred years . . ." (Demetrios J. Constantelos, *Understanding the Greek Orthodox Church, Its Faith, History and Practice* [New York: Seabury Press, 1982], pp. 86–87).

23. Yannoulatos, "Purpose and Motive," p. 6.

24. Ibid.

25. N. A. Nissiotis, "The Ecclesiological Foundation of Mission from the Orthodox Point of View," *The Greek Orthodox Theological Review* 7 (1961–62): 31.

26. Ibid.

27. Ibid., p. 32.

28. Ibid., p. 31.

29. Yannoulatos, "Purpose and Motive," p. 7.

30. Florovsky, "The Church: Her Nature and Task," in *The Universal Church in God's Design* (New York: Harper and Brothers, 1948), p. 47.

31. Nissiotis, "Ecclesiological Foundation," p. 32.

32. Alexander Schmemann, "The Missionary Imperative in the Orthodox Tradition," p. 253.

33. Ibid., p. 254. Italics in the original.

34. "Reports from the Orthodox Consultation on Confessing Christ through the Liturgical Life of the Church Today," Etchmiadzine, Armenia, Sept. 16–21, 1975, *International Review of Mission* 64 (1975): 417.

35. See the article by Paul Feuter, "Confessing Christ through Liturgy: An Orthodox Challenge to Protestants," *International Review of Mission* 65 (1976): 123–28. Feuter outlines the challenges issued to Protestants by the Orthodox and in turn issues three challenges to the Orthodox on behalf of Protestants.

36. The Russian chronicler Nestor, as cited by Walter F. Adeney, *The Greek and Eastern Churches* (reprint of 1908 ed., Clifton, N.J.: Reference Book Publishers, 1965), p. 361. Adeney provides a readable account of the events surrounding Vladimir's conversion. In Adeney's words, "The traditional story . . . has the picturesque character of an early legend" (p. 360). Adeney also related another story of Vladimir's conversion, which he seemingly sets in opposition to the one just related. In this tale, Vladimir besieged the Tauric town of Cherson, part of the Byzantine empire. Aided by information from a traitorous priest within Cherson itself, Vladimir vows to be baptized if he takes the city, "For was not his friend the priest a Christian?" (p. 362). After taking the city, he demands and receives Anna, the sister of Emperor Basil, as his bride in return for the captured city. Arthur P. Stanley in his *Lectures on the History of the Eastern Church* (London: John Murray, 1908), pp. 283–91, treats the two stories as part of one whole. This latter course has much to commend it, for apart from the antiquity of the tales, the action at Cherson might have been the only way in which Vladimir would have been able to marry into the royal house of Byzantium. This alliance would no doubt be essential to the establishment of Orthodoxy in Russia as the state religion, as indeed it was likewise established in the empire itself. For an English translation of all the relevant texts, see *The Russian Primary Chronicle,* trans. S. H. Cross and O. P. Sherbowitz-Wetzor (Cambridge, Mass.: Harvard University Press, 1958), pp. 97–119. The translation also appears in *Medieval Russia's Epics, Chronicles and Tales,* ed. Serge A. Zenkovsky (New York: E. P. Dutton, 2nd ed., 1974).

37. Adeney, *Greek and Eastern Churches,* p. 361.

38. See Stanley, *Lectures,* p. 289, for a description of the pomp put on for the envoys and of their response.

39. On the subject of what is generally known as Caesaropapism, see A. A. Vasiliev, *History of the Byzantine Empire* (Madison: University of Wisconsin Press, 1952), pp. 148-50, 257-58, 283, 334, 469-70. Caesaropapism is defined (e.g., in the *Oxford Dictionary of the Christian Church*) as a system in which a monarch exercises complete civil and religious authority, including authority over church dogma. This definition is challenged by Deno J. Geanakoplos in a perceptive essay in his *Byzantine East and Latin West: Two Worlds of Christendom in the Middle Ages and Renaissance* (Oxford: Basil Blackwell, 1966), pp. 55-83. Geanakoplos freely admits the absolute control of the emperor over the administration of the Church, even to the extent of choosing and deposing patriarchs at will. However, he maintains that no emperor was ever able to enforce dogmatic decisions that were not in accord with the will of the people. The iconoclastic controversy is but one example where the emperor could enforce his view only while he lived, but could not change the Church's practice forever. Geanakoplos takes this as proof that the common definition of Caesaropapism is incorrect. The emperor never had supreme authority over matters of doctrine. This is in keeping with Orthodox theology, which sees the people of God as the guardian of doctrine.

40. See Franklin H. Littell, *The Macmillan Atlas History of Christianity* (New York: Macmillan, 1976), p. 26; cf. Arthur Koestler, *The Thirteenth Tribe: The Khazar Empire and Its Heritage* (London: Picador, 1976).

41. Francis Dvornik, *Byzantine Missions among the Slavs* (New Brunswick, N.J.: Rutgers University Press, 1970), p. 49.

42. Ibid., pp. 51-52.

43. Cf. Michael Lacko, *Saints Cyril and Methodius* (Rome: Slovak Editions, 1963), p. 50.

44. Dvornik, *Byzantine Missions,* p. 69. See also Lacko, *Saints Cyril and Methodius,* p. 50.

45. Dvornik, *Byzantine Missions,* p. 69.

46. Eric Widmer, *The Russian Ecclesiastical Mission in Peking during the Eighteenth Century* (Cambridge, Mass.: Harvard University Press, 1976), pp. 24f.

47. Widmer, *Ecclesiastical Mission,* p. 25, citing Gaston Cahen, *Histoire des relations de la Russie avec la Chine sous Pierre le Grand, 1689-1730* (Paris, 1911), pp. 247-48.

48. Widmer, *Ecclesiastical Mission,* p. 27.

49. Cf. James Cracraft, *The Church Reforms of Peter the Great* (London: Macmillan, 1971), p. 65.

50. See Widmer, *Ecclesiastical Mission,* pp. 35-39, for the details of these negotiations.

51. Ibid., p. 49.

52. Serge Bolshakoff, *The Foreign Missions of the Russian Orthodox Church* (London: SPCK, 1943), pp. 64-65.

53. Widmer, *Ecclesiastical Mission,* p. 151.

54. Ibid., p. 138.

55. In fairness to the missionaries, though not in any sense to excuse them, one should note the judgment of the noted Russian Orthodox theologian, George Florovsky: "In the eighteenth century the circumstances of missionary activities were not, in general, favorable: the State interfered too powerfully with the affairs of the mission, pursuing its own interests, that is to say, getting the maximum benefit for itself from the people"

("Russian Missions: An Historical Sketch," in *Aspects of Church History,* vol. 4 of *The Collected Works of George Florovsky* (Belmont, Mass.: Nordland Publishing Co., 1975), pp. 144–45. This problem is not limited to the eighteenth century. A strong case can be made for the political aims of the Communist party being manifested in some of the activities of the Russian Orthodox Church in the twentieth century. See John Shelton Curtiss, *The Russian Church and the Soviet State: 1917–1950* (Boston: Little, Brown and Co., 1953).

Chapter 8

1. As examples of this, see the material on St. Stephen of Perm and on Macarius Gloukharev in chap. 4, above.

2. While it might seem that the methodology remained the same and only the motivation changed, one need only consider the use of the sword as a method of mission. See Nikita Struve, "Orthodox Missions, Past and Present," *St. Vladimir's Seminary Quarterly* 7 (1963): 34.

3. The Orthodox Church in America, *Mission: The Fourth All-American Council, Working Papers and Documents* (Syosset, N.Y.: American Orthodox Church, 1975).

4. Vladimir Lossky, in *In the Image and Likeness of God,* ed. John H. Erickson and Thomas E. Bird (Crestwood, N.Y.: St. Vladimir's Seminary Press, 1974), p. 97.

5. Documentation on the Orthodox doctrine of *theosis* can be found in Vladimir Lossky, *The Mystical Theology of the Eastern Church* (Cambridge, Eng.: James Clarke, 1968), passim. John Karmiris, *A Synopsis of the Dogmatic Theology of the Orthodox Catholic Church* (Scranton, Pa.: Christian Orthodox Edition, 1973), pp. 55–74. John Meyendorff, *St. Gregory Palamas and Orthodox Spirituality* (Crestwood, N.Y.: St. Vladimir's Seminary Press, 1974), passim. Panagiotis I. Bratsiotis, "The Fundamental Principles and Main Characteristics of the Orthodox Church," in *The Orthodox Ethos,* ed. A. J. Philippou (Oxford: Holywell Press, 1964), pp. 23–31.

6. See the article by Efthimios Stylios, "The Missionary as an Imitator of Christ," pp. 8–10.

7. George Florovsky speaks of the need for the missionary to have "the faculty of sympathetic reincarnation" ("Russian Missions: An Historical Sketch," in *Aspects of Church History* [Belmont, Mass.: Nordland Publishing Co., 1975], p. 142).

8. Ware, *The Orthodox Church* (Baltimore, Md.: Penguin Books, 1963), pp. 273f.

9. Stylios, "The Missionary as an Imitator of Christ," p. 8.

10. This is not the same as a wholesale acceptance of the culture; obviously the pagan elements were discarded. In some cases the converts were settled in Christian villages, either to remove them from heathen influences or simply to provide them with a place to live in the face of rejection because of their conversion. But the emphasis of the missionaries was on understanding the culture. "As we have seen, religion dominates the whole life, especially among the primitive. Consequently, the missionaries should know in advance the full life and culture of the people among whom they are sent to work" (Leonidas J. Philippides, "The Duty and Possibilities of Evangelizing the Non-Christians," *Porefthendes* 8 [1966]: 45). Note the way this has been carried out by Anastasios Yannoulatos in his books on African religions: *The Spirits Mbandwa and the Framework of Their Cult: A Study of Some Aspects of African Religion in West Uganda* (in Greek), (Athens: Porefthendes, 1970); *"Lord of Brightness," The God of the Tribes Near Mount Kenya* (in Greek), (Athens: Porefthendes, 1973); *Forms of African Ritual: Initiation and Possession Rites East of Ruwenzori* (in Greek), (Athens:

n.p., 1973); *Ruhanga—The Creator: A Contribution to the Investigation of African Beliefs Concerning God and Man* (in Greek), (Athens: n.p., 1975).

11. In addition to the missionary examples, it is helpful to note here the labors of Ilminski, who used the vernacular of the Tartars coupled with the Russian alphabet to communicate the Christian message (see Smirnoff, *A Short Account of the Historical Development and Present Position of Russian Orthodox Missions* [London: Rivingtons, 1903], pp. 31ff.).

12. Indigenous peoples were often used in the translation process. Beyond that, suitable candidates for the ministry were ordained. The actual practice varied from field to field. In Japan the great strength of the Orthodox Church was in its use of indigenous evangelists: "In sharp contrast to the slow growth of Protestant missions was the rapid growth of the Orthodox Church. . . . Nicolai from the first intended that his Church should be independent of the Church in Russia, and truly Japanese. To this end, he placed great emphasis upon preparing Japanese leadership, evangelization of Japan by the Japanese, and the active participation of laymen in the administration of the Church" (Neil Braun, *Laity Mobilized: Reflections on Church Growth in Japan and Other Lands* [Grand Rapids, Mich.: Wm. B. Eerdmans, 1971], p. 117).

13. One skirts a difficult issue at this point over which some small difference of opinion can be noted. An autocephalous church is one that has the right to choose its own head(s) or bishop(s). However, Orthodox doctrine rejects the Roman Catholic view of the need of the Church to have an earthly head, i.e., a pope: "Our Lord spoke only of *Himself* as pastor of the sheep. . . . This means the Church, the body of Christ, has Christ as its head. . . . Christ left no vicar after Him" (Sergius Bulgakov, *The Orthodox Church* [London: Centenary Press, 1935], p. 72). There is a limit to what the head of an autocephalous church can do. Since in Orthodox doctrine the Church as a whole is the guardian of Orthodoxy and is indwelt by the Holy Spirit, the clergy and laity together are the fullness of the Church. (See Hamilcar Alivisatos, "The Holy Greek Orthodox Church," in *The Nature of the Church,* ed. R. Newton Flew [London: SCM Press, 1952], p. 53.) It is therefore technically not accurate to speak as though the bishop is the head of the church, even if in practice the result is that the bishop is the head. A mild protest against the abuses of the episcopacy can be found in Sergius Bulgakov, "The Episcopate," in *A Bulgakov Anthology,* ed. Nicolas Zernov and James Pain (Philadelphia: Westminster Press, 1976), pp. 15-21. The importance of the bishop in the Orthodox tradition can be seen more clearly in relationship to the sacraments. As the living link in the line of succession from the apostles, his place is one of assuring the continuity of the sacramental graces necessary to the life of the Church. (See the chap. "Sacraments and Hierarchy," in John Meyendorff, *Orthodoxy and Catholicity* [New York: Sheed and Ward, 1966], pp. 1-16.

14. Anastasios Yannoulatos, "Orthodoxy in China," *Porefthendes* 4 (1962): 55.

15. "Without language human culture would be almost nil" (Howard W. Law, *Winning a Hearing: An Introduction to Missionary Anthropology and Linguistics* [Grand Rapids, Mich.: Wm. B. Eerdmans, 1968], p. 89).

16. The expression "evangelical poverty" is found in many contemporary writers. See, e.g., George Khodre, "Church and Mission," *St. Vladimir's Seminary Quarterly* 6 (1962): 24; Chrysostomos Constantinides, "Lord's 'Go Ye . . .' and the Theology," *Porefthendes* 3 (April-June 1961): 20; and Nectarios Hatzimichalis, "Orthodox Monasticism and External Mission," pp. 14-15.

17. Steven Runciman, *The Greek Church in Captivity* (Cambridge, Eng.: Cambridge University Press, 1968), p. 410; cf. Demetrios J. Constantelos, "The 'Neomartyrs' as

Evidence for Methods and Motives Leading to Conversion and Martyrdom in the Ottoman Empire," *Greek Orthodox Theological Review* 23 (1978): 216–34.

18. "The Church in Greece," *Pro Mundi Vita Dossiers,* November 1976, pp. 4–5.

19. See Nikita Struve, "Dissent in the Russian Orthodox Church," in *Religion in the Soviet State,* ed. Max Hayward and William C. Fletcher (New York: Frederick A. Praeger, 1969), pp. 143–57, where Struve argues that the dissent seen in the recent era marks the beginning of the recovery of the Orthodox Church. See also his *Christians in Contemporary Russia* (London: Harvill Press, 1969), especially pp. 336–39. A journalist's impression of the deep resurgence of Orthodox spirituality, which is at issue here, is found in Hedrick Smith, *The Russians* (New York: Quadrangle, 1976), pp. 417–38 where he discusses "Solzhenitsyn and the Russianness of Russia."

20. As, e.g., the close identification between Church and state in Greece; cf. Athanasios Basdekis, "Between Partnership and Separation, Relations between Church and State in Greece under the Constitution of 9 June, 1975," *The Ecumenical Review* 29 (January 1977): 52–61.

21. Runciman, *The Greek Church,* p. ix.

22. This statement should not be interpreted as meaning that all subsequent attempts at indigenization followed the Orthodox pattern, as the Western Church did not choose to adopt the Orthodox methods. Instead its purpose is to call attention to the originality of the Orthodox contribution and to pose it as an alternate solution to the current missiological problems facing the Western Churches and their daughter churches.

23. See, e.g., John Meyendorff, *The Orthodox Church* (London: Darton, Longman & Todd, 1962), p. 169, where he discusses the attempts at the Hellenization of the Bulgarian Orthodox Church. This issue is keenly debated between Russian and Greek theologians. See Demetrios J. Constantelos, *Understanding the Greek Orthodox Church* (New York: Seabury Press, 1982), pp. 86–87, for the opposing view.

24. George Florovsky, "The Ways of Russian Theology," in *Aspects of Church History,* p. 195.

25. In the United States of America, it might be more correct to speak in terms of an emerging American Orthodoxy, which uses English as its language of worship and theology.

26. See Ware, *Orthodox Church,* pp. 190, 273f., for the minor exceptions to this rule.

27. Elias Voulgarakis, "Language and Mission," pp. 42–44.

28. Ibid., p. 42; cf. Josef Glazik, *Die russisch-orthodoxe Heidenmission seit Peter dem Grossen* (Münster: Aschendorffsche Verlagsbuchhandlung, 1959), pp. 44, 59, 73, 78, 116, 137, 140, 166, 207.

29. Cf. John Papavassiliou, "Necessity for and Problems of Foreign Missions," *Porefthendes* 3 (1961): 47.

30. Voulgarakis, "Language and Mission," p. 42.

31. Ibid.

32. Smirnoff, *Russian Orthodox Missions,* pp. 31f.

33. See, e.g., Alexander Veronis, "Report on the Foreign Missions Program of the Greek Orthodox Archdiocese of North and South America," *Porefthendes* 10 (1968): 25–28, and "Activity Report, 1961–1966," *Porefthendes* 8 (1966): 49–53. The latter covers the work done toward the furtherance of Orthodox missionary work by the Inter-Orthodox Missionary Centre, Porefthendes, based in Athens, Greece.

34. Voulgarakis, "Language and Mission," p. 42.

35. Ibid.

36. Ibid.

37. Ibid., p. 43.

38. Ibid.

39. Ibid.

40. Ibid.

41. Theano Konstantopoulou, "From the Visit of the Faculty of Theology of the University of Thessaloniki to Uganda," *Porefthendes* 8 (1966): 8.

42. Note, e.g., the elevation of Vassili Timoféieff, Ilminski's Tartar assistant, to the priesthood. Timoféieff rose from peasant to collaborator with Ilminski (Smirnoff, *Russian Orthodox Missions,* pp. 45-46).

43. See Konstantopoulou, "Visit to Uganda," p. 11. See also Alexander Veronis, "Report on Foreign Missions Program," p. 27, for the report of an American Greek Orthodox teacher serving in Uganda. Veronis describes the work of Chrysostomos Papasarantopoulos, who worked in Uganda, Kenya, Tanzania, and Zaire, in "Orthodox Concepts of Evangelism and Mission," *The Greek Orthodox Theological Review* 27 (1982): 44-45. *Porefthendes* 8 (1966): 53, under the title "Mission News from East Africa," reported on the arrival of two new members to the Nairobi mission, a Mr. Const. Vassilopoulos, an agricultural expert, and a Miss Thomais Tsatsou, a nurse.

44. Papavassiliou, "Necessity for and Problems of Foreign Mission," p. 47.

45. E. Stylios, "The Missionary as an Imitator of Christ," pp. 8-10.

46. Theodoros Nankyamas, "On the Orthodox Church in Uganda and Kenya," *Porefthendes* 3 (1961): 44.

47. Norman Horner "An East African Orthodox Church," *Journal of Ecumenical Studies* 2 (1975): 225.

48. Ibid., p. 226.

49. "Funds collected for the program are used primarily for scholarships awarded to Orthodox students from Africa, Latin America, the Middle East and Asia, who are trained and prepared for the priesthood of the Orthodox Church or serve in other capacities, such as teaching, in their local parishes and schools" ("Record Donation to Foreign Missions," *Orthodox Observer,* May 29, 1974, p. 22; see also Veronis, "Report on Foreign Mission Program," pp. 27-28).

50. Papavassiliou, "Necessity for and Problems of Foreign Missions," p. 47.

51. Ibid., p. 46.

52. Cf. C. K. Kibue's plea, "We are calling you to come today to Africa, for tomorrow never ends" ("The African Greek Orthodox Church in Kenya," *Porefthendes* 3 [1961]: 55).

53. Parthenios, Metropolitan of Carthage, "Christ in Africa," *Porefthendes* 3 (1961): 51.

54. Cf. Nikita Struve, "Orthodox Missions, Past and Present," *St. Vladimir's Seminary Quarterly* 7 (1963): 34-35.

55. Serge Bolshakoff, *The Foreign Missions of the Russian Orthodox Church* (London: SPCK, 1943), pp. 39f.

56. W. Jardine Grisbrooke, in his introduction to *The Spiritual Counsels of Father John of Kronstadt* (London: James Clarke & Co. 1966), pp. xix-xx.

57. "His influence in Russia extends far beyond the Orthodox population, and I noticed that not only several of the German Lutheran servants in the hotel were pressing round him, but even two of the Mohammedan Tartar waiters from the restaurant were seeking and receiving his blessing" (Athelstan Riley, ed., *Birkbeck and the Russian Church: Essays and Articles by the Late W. J. Birkbeck* [London: Anglican and Eastern Association, 1917], p. 124). For an illustration of Father John's influence outside of

Russia, see Alexander Whyte, *Father John of the Greek Church* (London: Oliphant Anderson & Ferrier, 1898), especially pp. 32f.

58. See the story by Nicolai Lyeskov, "On the Edge of the World," in *The Sentry and Other Stories,* trans. A. E. Chamot (New York: Alfred A. Knopf, 1923), p. 312. Leskov's hero in the story is Bishop Nil Isakovich, himself a notable missionary. (See Struve, "Orthodox Missions," p. 39.)

59. "It is impossible to wish well to the Russian missions anywhere. Undoubtedly one would rejoice to see heathen baptized and taught the faith of Christ, if only it were done by any one except by Russians. But Russian missions, enormously subsidized by the Government, are, always and everywhere, the thin end of the wedge for Russian conquest" (Adrian Fortescue, *The Orthodox Eastern Church* [London: Catholic Truth Society, 1916], p. 298).

60. This expression is found in the Divine Liturgy (*The Priest's Service Book, Part 2* [New York: Orthodox Church in America, 1973], p. 236).

61. Arthur Penrhyn Stanley, *Lectures on the History of the Eastern Church* (London: John Murray, 1908), p. 296. Italics in the original.

62. Reference has already been made to the Russian government's interference in the missionary work in Siberia. For the history of the sects in Russia, see Sergius Bolshakoff, *Russian Nonconformity* (Philadelphia: Westminster Press, 1950).

63. Chrysostomos Constantinides, "Lord's 'Go Ye . . .' and the Theology," *Porefthendes* 3 (1961): 20.

64. Leonidas Philippides, "The Duty and Possibilities of Evangelizing the Non-Christians," *Porefthendes* 8 (1966): 20-21.

65. Chrysostomos, "Lord's 'Go Ye . . .,' " p. 20.

66. John Papavassiliou, "Necessity for and Problems of Foreign Missions," pp. 46-47.

Chapter 9

1. Cf. Stanley S. Harakas, "Living the Orthodox Christian Faith in America," pp. 192-99.

2. See John E. Paraskevas and Frederick Reinstein, *The Eastern Orthodox Church: A Brief History* (Washington, D.C.: El Greco Press, 1969), pp. 113-24, for a listing of prominent Orthodox laity. The list was not designed to be exhaustive, but was meant to reflect the rise of Orthodox to the highest levels of responsibility and competence.

3. The plural "Churches" must be used to describe the situation in the United States where, as in other areas of the Diaspora, no one national Orthodox Church exists. The Churches are separated by language, many still employing the mother tongue of the immigrants, and episcopal jurisdiction. A list of the different Orthodox Churches in America can be found in Paraskevas, *The Eastern Orthodox Church,* pp. 103-11. More complete listings and information concerning location can be found in either *Parishes and Clergy of the Orthodox, and Other Eastern Churches in North and South America* (N.p.: Joint Commission on Co-operation with the Eastern and Old Catholic Churches of the General Convention of the Protestant Episcopal Church, 1963), or Anastasia Bespuda, *Guide to Orthodox America* (Crestwood, N.Y.: St. Vladimir's Seminary Press, 1965). The situation has changed somewhat with the formation of the Orthodox Church in America, a body comprising some of the Orthodox Churches united into one and which some envisage will one day encompass all Orthodox in America. The formation of the Orthodox Church in America occasioned

no small controversy about its status, with both sides claiming canonical support. See *St. Vladimir's Theological Quarterly* 15 (1971) and Panagiotes N. Trempelas, *The Autocephaly of the Metropolia in America* (Brookline, Mass.: Holy Cross Theological School Press, 1973) for opposing viewpoints. At the present time there are still a number of Orthodox Churches in America with no prospects for union in sight.

4. One need only examine the catalogues of the Holy Cross Orthodox Book Store (50 Goddard Avenue, Brookline, Mass. 02146) and St. Vladimir's Bookstore (575 Scarsdale Road, Crestwood, N.Y. 10707) to document this statement.

5. Forty percent of St. Vladimir's Theological Seminary student body is from non-Orthodox backgrounds. This figure is based on a private interview with John Meyendorff, professor at St. Vladimir's (Oct. 27, 1975). The figure is substantiated by an examination of the list of students for 1974-75 published in the Seminary Catalogue for 1975-76.

6. For the names of these American bishops and brief biographical sketches, see *Orthodox America 1974-1976* (Syosset, N.Y.: Orthodox Church in America, 1975), pp. 285-87.

7. Paraskevas and Reinstein, *The Eastern Orthodox Church*, p. 94.

8. "Consultation on 'Orthodox Diaspora,' " *Porefthendes* 10 (1968): 29.

9. Stanley S. Harakas, "Living the Orthodox Faith in America," pp. 198-99.

10. Yannoulatos, "The Forgotten Commandment," *Porefthendes* 1, no. 1 (1959): 5.

11. The Orthodox Church in America, *Mission: The Fourth All-American Council, Working Papers and Documents*, p. 3.

12. Envisioned here is the upward movement of the immigrants and their descendants, not the reverse. Therefore the penetration should be thought of in terms of lower middle class to the top of society, rather than elements of extreme poverty also comprising American Orthodoxy. Nicon Patrinacos points out that "few of the original business establishments of their immigrant fathers or grandfathers have survived to the present generation." Most of the members of Orthodox congregations are professionals who have an intellectual orientation (*The Individual and His Orthodox Church* [New York: Orthodox Observer Press, 1970], p. vii).

13. An unchurched Orthodox could be defined as a person who was baptized and confirmed (confirmation or chrismation is performed immediately after baptism) but who is not currently an active member of an Orthodox parish. To be a member in good standing, a person must abide by the faith and canons of the Church and the regulations laid down by the ecclesiastical authority that one is under. These regulations include the person's financial obligations to the parish of which one is a member. Nonpayment of these dues causes the forfeiture of certain privileges, such as participation in the Parish Assembly. (See *Uniform Parish Regulations of the Greek Orthodox Archdiocese of North and South America* [New York, 1973], pp. 17-19.) A clear case of a person not being in "good standing" would be in a mixed (Orthodox/non-Orthodox) marriage. "If a couple is not married in the Orthodox Church, then the Orthodox member is denied Holy Communion and participation in the Sacraments, such as a sponsor at a wedding or baptism" (Dean Timothy Andrews, *What Is the Orthodox Church?* [New York: Greek Archdiocese of North and South America, 1964], p. 41). These persons who are partners in a mixed marriage form the bulk of the unchurched Orthodox.

14. See Orthodox Church in America, *Mission, The Fourth All-American Council*, p. 3.

15. Numerous examples could be given here. Among the most notable are Nicon Patrinacos, *The Individual and His Orthodox Church;* Demetrios J. Constantelos, *The*

Greek Orthodox Church: Faith, History, and Practice (New York: Seabury Press, 1967); Chrysostomos H. Stratman, *To the Orthodox Christians of the United States of America* (South Canaan, Pa.: St. Tikhon Press, 1959). The Orthodox Church in America has published four volumes of elementary handbooks on Orthodoxy: Thomas Hopko, *The Orthodox Faith* (New York: Department of Religious Education, Orthodox Church in America, 1971-75).

16. For an example of the dialogue, see John Meyendorff and Joseph McLelland, eds., *The New Man: An Orthodox and Reformed Dialogue* (New Brunswick, N.J.: Standard Press for Agora Books, 1973). A survey of Orthodox-Protestant dialogues is published as Faith and Order Paper no. 76, *The Orthodox Church and the Churches of the Reformation* (Geneva: World Council of Churches, 1975). The papers of the consultation with the Southern Baptists have been published in *The Greek Orthodox Theological Review* 22 (1977): 357-463, and 27 (1982): 2-82.

17. Harakas, "Living the Orthodox Faith in America," p. 198.

18. See, e.g., George Florovsky, "Patriarch Jeremiah II and the Lutheran Divines," in *Christianity and Culture,* vol. 2 of *The Collected Works of George Florovsky* (Belmont, Mass.: Nordland Publishing Co., 1974), pp. 143-55. This essay originally appeared as "An Early Ecumenical Correspondence," in *World Lutheranism of Today* (Stockholm: AB Verbum, 1950), pp. 98-111.

19. *Orthodox America, 1974-1976,* pp. 317f.

20. "Kansas City Episcopal Group Joins Orthodox," *The Orthodox Church* vol. 2, no. 9 (November 1975): 1.

21. The question of the validity of Anglican orders has been a topic of discussion in Orthodox circles. The question has been answered in the affirmative on the basis of "economy" by some Orthodox bodies; however, no consensus on the question exists in the whole Orthodox Communion, nor can any exist until such a time as a Pan-Orthodox Synod decides the issue. A negative decision on the validity of Anglican orders was reached by the Moscow Conference in 1948. The reordination of the Episcopal priest should no doubt be interpreted in the light of the decision. On the question of Anglican orders, see especially Methodios Fouyas, *Orthodoxy, Roman Catholicism and Anglicanism* (London: Oxford University Press, 1972), pp. 99-109; cf. Chrysostom Papadopoulos, *The Validity of Anglican Ordinations,* trans. J. A. Douglas (London: Faith Press, 1920).

22. The vexing question of proselytism is dealt with below. While historically the Orthodox have been opposed to proselytism, there does not seem to be a reluctance in receiving converts from other Christian confessions. The apparent contradiction is resolved, from the Orthodox view, by defining "proselytism" as the drawing away of Orthodox adherents by promises of material gain or reward, while conversion to Orthodoxy is seen as a coming to the truth. (See Fouyas, *Orthodoxy, Roman Catholicism, and Anglicanism,* pp. 20-22.)

Chapter 10

1. Johannes van den Berg, *Constrained by Jesus' Love* (Kampen, Netherlands: J. H. Kok, 1956), pp. 211f.

2. Anastasios Yannoulatos, "The Purpose and Motive of Mission," *Porefthendes* 9 (1967): 2.

3. See the key work in this area, Demetrios J. Constantelos, *Byzantine Philanthropy and Social Welfare* (New Brunswick, N.J.: Rutgers University Press, 1968), pp. 25-27.

4. E. Stylios, "The Missionary as an Imitator of Christ," *Porefthendes,* 5 (1963): 8.

5. See Nectarios Hatzimichalis, "Orthodox Monasticism and External Mission," *Porefthendes* 4 (1962): 12-15. Hatzimichalis not only reviews the role of monks in the past but makes a strong case for the use of monks in contemporary Orthodox missions.

6. *Porefthendes* 1, no. 1 (1959): 2.

7. The journal and the center both carry the same name. For a discussion of the activities of the center, see the two articles in *Porefthendes:* " 'Porefthendes,' an Inter-Orthodox Missionary Centre," 3 (1961): 35-38; and "Activity Report 1961-1966," 8 (1966): 49-53. *Porefthendes* ceased publication in 1969. In 1981, *Panta Ta Ethne* ("All Nations") commenced publication. This new quarterly missionary periodical is edited by Anastasios Yannoulatos. Subscriptions are available from Apostoliki Diakonia, 14 lo. Gennadiou St., Athens, Greece.

8. Nectarios Hadzimichalis, "Some Thoughts on Orthodox Mission," *Porefthendes* 2, no. 7 (1960): 4.

9. The phrase "evangelical poverty" appears frequently in Orthodox articles on mission. See, e.g., George Khodre as interviewed by Paul Löffler, "An Eastern Orthodox Viewpoint," *International Review of Mission* 60 (1971): 65, and George Khodre, "Church and Mission," *St. Vladimir's Seminary Quarterly,* 6 (1962): 24.

10. Anastasios Yannoulatos, "The Purpose and Motive of Mission," p. 34 of the *Porefthendes* article; in the *International Review of Mission's* version of this article, 54 (1965): 293. Italics in the original.

11. *Porefthendes* 3 (1961): 48.

12. Cf. Efthimios Stylios, "Missionary Echoes of the Triodion," *Porefthendes* 4 (1962): 10-12; Aimilianos Timiadis, "The Missionary Nature of the Church," *Porefthendes* 11 (1969): 8-11, 31; Leonidas J. Philippides, "The Duty and Possibilities of Evangelizing the Non-Christians," *Porefthendes* 8 (1966): 18-21, 45.

13. Anastasios Yannoulatos, "Orthodox Spirituality and External Mission," p. 301. Italics in the original.

14. Yannoulatos, "The Purpose and Motive of Mission," *Porefthendes* article, p. 36; also in *International Review of Mission* 54 (1965): 297.

Chapter 11

1. George Florovsky, "The Elements of Liturgy in the Orthodox Catholic Church," *One Church* 13, nos. 1-2 (1959): 24, as cited by Timothy Ware, *The Orthodox Church* (Baltimore, Md.: Penguin Books, 1963), p. 271.

2. Ware, *Orthodox Church,* p. 271. The same conviction is expressed by other Orthodox writers, e.g., Demetrios J. Constantelos, *The Greek Orthodox Church* (New York: Seabury Press, 1967), pp. 23f.

3. Peter Hammond, "The Liturgical Movement and Eastern Christendom," *The Christian East* n.s. 2 (1952): 51.

4. E.g., Ware, *Orthodox Church,* p. 272.

5. E.g., Isobel F. Hapgood, *Service Book of the Holy Orthodox-Catholic Apostolic Church,* p. 64.

6. The most convenient treatment is to be found in the section entitled "Our Liturgy," by Nicon D. Patrinacos, in the book edited by him, *The Orthodox Liturgy* (Garwood, N.J.: Graphic Arts Press, 1976). The first part of this book contains the Greek text of the Ecumenical Patriarchate with the English text of the Liturgical Commission of the Greek Orthodox Archdiocese of North and South America on the

opposite pages. This is the official version to be used in the Greek Orthodox Church of the Americas. A more detailed treatment of the development of the liturgy is found in Alexander Schmemann, *Introduction to Liturgical Theology*. See also the work of the Roman Catholic scholar, Casimir Kucharek, *The Byzantine-Slav Liturgy of St. John Chrysostom* (Allendale, N.J.: Alleluia Press, 1971).

7. An example of an allegorical treatment respected by Orthodox is Nicholas Cabasilas, *A Commentary on the Divine Liturgy* (Crestwood, N.Y.: St. Vladimir's Seminary Press, 1977).

8. Patrinacos, *The Orthodox Liturgy* is one example. See George Mastrantonis, ed., *The Divine Liturgy of St. John Chrysostom.* Mastrantonis reprints the English text of the liturgy from the Faith Press edition (n.d.) approved by Archbishop Germanos, Metropolitan of Thyatira, and matches it on the opposite pages with well-taken photographs of the priest's liturgical movements. The Greek text is printed in a separate section. The book is designed for use in the church by the worshipers, that they may both see and understand what is being enacted before them. Cf. also S. M. Sophocles, *The Liturgy of the Orthodox Church* (Athens: n.p., n.d.).

9. Carnegie Samuel Calian, *Icon and Pulpit* (Philadelphia: Westminster Press, 1968).

10. See, e.g., Timothy Ware, *Eustratios Argenti: A Study of the Greek Church under Turkish Rule* (Oxford: Clarendon Press, 1964), pp. 5–16.

11. Herbert Stroup, "The Zoe Brotherhood," *The Christian Century* 72 (1955): 331–32. See also P. I. Bratsiotis, "The Evangelistic Work of the Contemporary Greek Orthodox Church," *The Christian East*, n.s. 1 (1950): 28–29; Demetrios J. Constantelos, "The Zoe Movement in Greece," *St. Vladimir's Seminary Quarterly* 3 (1959): 11–25.

12. A fair indication of the importance and use of the sermon can be gained from an examination of the following collections of sermons. One distinct difference can be noted from this collection, which highlights the difference between Greece and America. Whereas in Greece the preacher is often a layperson, in America the sermon is almost the sole prerogative of the clergy. See Dean Timothy Andrews, ed. *Contemporary Sermons by Greek Orthodox Preachers* (New York: Greek Orthodox Archdiocese of North and South America, 1966); Anthony Coniaris, *Eastern Orthodoxy: A Way of Life* (Minneapolis: Light and Life Publishing Co., 1966); George Dimopoulos, *Orthodox Sermons for All Sundays of the Year* (Scranton, Pa.: Christian Orthodox Editions, 1971); Leonidas Condos, *In Season and Out of Season* (New York: Orthodox Observer Press, 1972).

13. The most striking example of the use of the pulpit can be found in the pulpit discussions of Dmitrii Dudko, an Orthodox priest in Russia. Dudko's story appears under the title, "The Trials of a True Believer" in the Religion section of *Time,* May 1, 1978, p. 54. His sermons are available in English: Dmitrii Dudko, *Our Hope,* trans. Paul D. Garrett.

14. Alexander Schmemann, *Liturgy and Life: Christian Development Through Liturgical Experience,* p. 47. Italics in the original.

15. E.g., Mastrantonis, *Divine Liturgy,* pp. 144–48; Hapgood, *Service Book,* pp. xxiii–xxvii. Of particular usefulness is *The Divine Liturgy: The Sunday Epistles and Gospels,* which has the complete text of the liturgy in Greek and English along with a phonetic Greek text and the complete texts of the standard readings.

16. See also Georges Barrois, "Scripture Readings for Mid-Pentecost and Pentecost," which provides an update on his book.

17. Barrois, *Scripture Readings,* pp. 14f., 70; Hapgood, *Service Book,* p. xxii.

18. Barrois, *Scripture Readings,* p. 20.

19. Demetrios J. Constantelos, "The Holy Scriptures in Greek Orthodox Worship," p. 9.

20. The Divine Liturgy of the Presanctified Gifts, the Divine Liturgy of St. Basil the Great, the Divine Liturgy of St. John Chrysostom, Baptism, Chrismation, Holy Unction, and Matrimony.

·21. Demetrios J. Constantelos, "The Holy Scriptures in Greek Orthodox Worship," p. 7. Cf. Timothy Ware, *The Orthodox Church,* pp. 207-10.

22. Constantelos, "The Holy Scriptures in Greek Orthodox Worship," p. 78.

23. Ibid.

24. They are Numbers, Joshua, Ruth, Ecclesiastes, 4 Kings, Obadiah, Nahum, Haggai, Zechariah, and 3 John.

25. Only the Epistle of Jeremiah, and Bel and the Dragon are not referred to.

26. Constantelos, "The Holy Scriptures in Greek Orthodox Worship," p. 83.

27. Ibid.

28. Ibid., p. 82. For an Orthodox interpretation of the role of the Bible, see Thomas Hopko, "The Bible in the Orthodox Church," *St. Vladimir's Theological Quarterly* 14 (1970): 66-99.

29. See Paul Fueter, "Confessing Christ through Liturgy: An Orthodox Challenge to Protestants," pp. 123-28.

30. "During the period of the missionary expansion of Christianity adult baptism remained the prevailing custom, . . ." (Alexander Schmemann, *Liturgy and Life,* p. 7).

31. The prayers for the catechumens can be found in complete form in Mastrantonis, *The Divine Liturgy,* pp. 42-43; *The Priest's Service Book,* part 2 (New York: Orthodox Church in America, 1973), pp. 258-59 (312-13 for the Liturgy of St. Basil). Hapgood conveniently prints both prayers on the same page (*Service Book,* p. 92). A diglot Greek-English text is found in *The Divine Liturgy of St. John Chrysostom* (London: Faith Press, n.d.), pp. 21-22. Other copies of the liturgy omit part or all of the prayers, since, if they are used at all, they are inaudible.

32. "But as the catechumens became fewer and fewer as a result of the introduction of infant baptism, all the prayers offered for the sake of the catechumens were not read and the so-called Liturgy of the Catechumens lost in length, . . ." (Patrinacos, *The Orthodox Liturgy,* p. 250).

33. Schmemann, *Liturgy and Life,* pp. 47-48. Italics are in the original.

34. Anastasios Yannoulatos, "Orthodox Spirituality and External Mission," *Porefthendes* 4 (1962): 4. This article was reprinted under the same title in the *International Review of Mission* 52 (1963): 300-302.

35. Ibid., p. 5.

36. The Triodian is the "liturgical book containing the variable portions of the services from the fourth Sunday before Lent till the Saturday before Easter" (F. L. Cross and E. A. Livingstone, eds., *The Oxford Dictionary of the Christian Church,* 2nd ed. [London: Oxford University Press, 1974], p. 1395). See also R. L. Langford-James, *A Dictionary of the Eastern Orthodox Church* (London: Faith Press, 1923), p. 131, where in addition to the definition above, he gives two others, the time period covered by the book and a canon (or kanon) containing three odes sung during this period.

37. See Langford-James, *Dictionary,* "Troparion," p. 132.

38. Stylios, "Missionary Echoes of the Triodion," *Porefthendes* 4 (1962): 10.

39. Alexander Schmemann, "The Missionary Imperative in the Orthodox Tradi-

tion," in *The Theology of the Christian Mission,* ed. Gerald H. Anderson (London: SCM Press, 1961), p. 255.

40. The separation from the world is symbolized by the deacon's proclamation, "The doors, the doors." In the early Church, the deacons and subdeacons were entrusted to keep heathen out during the eucharistic service. Schmemann sees this as the total separation of the church from the world during the communion service. The church is, for these moments, ascended on high with Christ ("Missionary Imperative," p. 255).

41. Ibid., pp. 255–56.

42. This is not to imply that there is not a place in Orthodoxy for private devotion, for there most certainly is but, rather, that the church services are corporate expressions of devotion. See, e.g., Nicholas Zernov, "Worship in the Orthodox Church," in *Christian Orthodox Devotion* (Westfield, N.J.: Ecumenical Publications, n.d.), pp. 1–14.

43. "It is most significant that all eucharistic prayers are composed in the plural, including the prayer of consecration *(anaphora),* which is recited by the celebrant alone, but obviously in the name and on behalf of the faithful. For indeed the whole congregation is supposed 'to con-celebrate' with its pastor . . ." (George Florovsky, "Orthodox," p. 60).

44. The writer recalls a visit in 1969 to a small monastery high on a mountain on the island of Chios, where only one priest-monk still lived. In order that the Eucharist might be celebrated, a reader made the difficult trip up the mountainside every Sunday. Canonically, the priest could not celebrate alone.

45. That some, or perhaps even the majority, of the congregation do not truly participate in the liturgy because they do not understand what they are witnessing is a fact lamented by Orthodox theologians; cf. Patrinacos, *The Orthodox Liturgy,* p. 291.

46. Alexy Stepanovich Khomiakov, *The Church Is One* (London: Fellowship of St. Alban and St. Sergius, 1968), pp. 38–39.

47. Anastasios Yannoulatos, "Orthodox Mission and Holy Communion," p. 58. Italics in the original.

48. "Reports from the Orthodox Consultation on Confessing Christ through the Liturgical Life of the Church Today, Etchmiadzine, Armenia, Sept. 16–21, 1975," p. 417.

49. See the report by Ion Bria, "Confessing Christ Today: An Orthodox Consultation," pp. 67–94. The reports also appear in *St. Vladimir's Theological Quarterly* 18 (1974): 193–212. Included in the St. Vladimir's article is a complete list of the participants. John Meyendorff's address to the consultation, "Confessing Christ Today and the Unity of the Church" is printed in the same number of *St. Vladimir's,* pp. 155–65.

50. "Reports from the Orthodox Consultation on Confessing Christ through the Liturgical Life of the Church Today, Etchmiadzine, Armenia, Sept. 16–21, 1975," pp. 417–21. The reports also appear, with a brief introduction giving the participants, in *St. Vladimir's Theological Quarterly* 20 (1976): 31–37. A follow-up article, which gives some suggestions as to the continuation of the liturgy in life, a theme at Etchmiadzine, is Ion Bria, "The Liturgy after the Liturgy," pp. 86–90.

51. M. V. George, in Ion Bria, "Confessing Christ Today: An Orthodox Consultation," p. 69.

52. One need only to think of the part of the liturgy, still used today, where the priest cries out, "The doors, the doors!" "Guarding the doors of the Church against the intrusion of the uninitiated was a matter of strict obligation" (Kucharek, *Byzantine-Slav Liturgy,* pp. 536–37).

53. In Ion Bria, "Confessing Christ Today: Reports of Groups at a Consultation of Orthodox Theologians," *International Review of Mission* 64 (1975): 75.

54. Ibid., p. 85.

55. Ibid., p. 84.

56. Alexander Schmemann, "The Missionary Imperative in the Orthodox Tradition," p. 254.

57. Ibid.

58. Alexander Schmemann, *The World as Sacrament*, p. 23. Italics in the original.

59. Reports from the Orthodox Consultation on "Confessing Christ through the Liturgical Life of the Church Today," p. 417.

60. Ibid., p. 418.

61. Ibid.

62. Ibid.

63. In Ion Bria, "Confessing Christ Today," p. 85.

64. On the doctrine of the Holy Spirit, see Vladimir Lossky, *The Mystical Theology of the Eastern Church* (Cambridge, Eng.: James Clarke & Co. 1968), pp. 156–73.

65. The prayer of consecration reads in part: ". . . send Your Holy Spirit upon us and upon these Gifts before us and make this bread . . ." (Patrinacos, ed., *The Orthodox Liturgy*, p. 55).

66. This concept of the Holy Spirit as the interpreter of the Eucharist is in line with the Holy Spirit's function as the revealer of Christ (Jn. 14:26; 15:12). See Angelos J. Philippou, "The Mystery of Pentecost," in the book edited by him, *The Orthodox Ethos* (Oxford: Holywell Press, 1964), pp. 70–97.

67. Sergius Bulgakov, *The Orthodox Church* (London: Centenary Press, 1935), p. 149.

68. Schmemann, "Missionary Imperative," p. 255.

69. This by no means implies that the Orthodox feel the liturgy is a perfect representation of heaven on earth. Many voices are raised in the plea for the reform and adaptation of the liturgy. However, in spite of the imperfections that have crept into the liturgy, the form still conveys the reality and presence of the spiritual world. For suggestions as to reforms, see Nicon Patrinacos, ed., *The Orthodox Liturgy*, pp. 197–248, and Alexander Schmemann, "Problems of Orthodoxy in America: The Liturgical Problem," *St. Vladimir's Theological Quarterly* 8 (1964): 164–85.

70. On the theme of the Eucharist as a manifestation of the kingdom of God, see Alexander Schmemann, *The World as Sacrament*, pp. 32–55.

71. It is to be freely admitted that the liturgy has changed over the years; however, the basic structure has remained unaltered. See Schmemann, *Introduction to Liturgical Theology*, pp. 72–167.

72. Anastasios Yannoulatos, "Initial Thoughts toward an Orthodox Foreign Mission," *Porefthendes* 10 (1968): 23.

73. An African theologian from the Cameroons, in discussion with the author on this topic, admitted that had his church had a choice between Orthodoxy and Protestantism, they would have chosen Orthodoxy. Perhaps an argument can be made for the Orthodox mode of worship being more suited to Africa.

74. D. E. Wentink, "The Orthodox Church in East Africa," *The Ecumenical Review* 20 (1968): 42–43. Italics added.

75. "It is of paramount interest too from a missionary viewpoint, that during the first centuries of the One Church differing liturgies were in use, with considerable variants and in dozens of various languages" (Yannoulatos, "Initial Thoughts," p. 23).

76. See Meyendorff, *The Orthodox Church*, pp. 188–89, for a discussion of Western rite Orthodoxy.

77. Yannoulatos, "Initial Thoughts," p. 23.

78. Chrysostomos Constantinides, "Lord's 'Go Ye . . .' and the Theology," *Porefthendes* 3 (1961): 20.

79. Anastasios Yannoulatos, "The Purpose and Motive of Mission," *Porefthendes* 9 (1967): 7.

80. Ibid., p. 9.

81. The connection between the Church's worship and the eschatological hope of the Church has been well documented by a Methodist theologian: Geoffrey Wainwright, *Eucharist and Eschatology* (London: Epworth Press, 1971). Wainwright notes in several places the eschatological understanding of the Orthodox liturgy. However, in terms of the present study, Wainwright's most important section is the one on the relationship between eschatology and mission. "To put the matter in one sentence: the Eucharist has an inescapable missionary significance in so far as it is the sign of the great feast which God will offer in the final kingdom to express forever the universal triumph of His saving will and purpose" (p. 128).

Chapter 12

1. An indication of how central a concept the Church is can be gained by examining standard Orthodox dogmatic works. See, e.g., Paul Evdokimov, *L'Orthodoxie* (Neuchatel: Delachaux et Niestlé, 1959), pp. 123–66. See also Chrestos Androutsos, *Dogmatika tes Orthodoxos Anatolikes Ekklesias* (Dogmas of the Eastern Orthodox Church) (Athens: Papademetrios, 1956), pp. 259–92.

2. George Florovsky, "The Church: Her Nature and Task," p. 43.

3. Sergius Bulgakov, *The Orthodox Church* (London: Centenary Press, 1935), p. 12.

4. Florovsky, "The Church: Her Nature and Task," p. 43.

5. The term "Nicene Creed" here means the creed commonly known as such, and not the first Nicene Creed issued by the Council of Nicaea in 325. It is referred to in the form that is in use in the East, i.e., without the Filioque clause. For further discussion on the two creeds, see "Nicene Creed," *The Oxford Dictionary of the Christian Church,* 2nd ed.

6. The centrality of this act of confession is noted by many authors. In the Orthodox liturgy the creed immediately precedes the anaphora (the central eucharistic prayer) and the epiclesis (the calling down of the Holy Spirit on the elements). See, e.g., Stanley Harakas, *Living the Liturgy* (Minneapolis: Light and Life Publishing Co., 1974), pp. 99–101.

7. Vladimir Lossky, "Concerning the Third Mark of the Church: Catholicity," in *In the Image and Likeness of God,* ed. John H. Erickson and Thomas E. Bird (Crestwood, N.Y.: St. Vladimir's Seminary Press, 1974), pp. 169–70.

8. N. M. Zernov, "The Church and the Confessions," in *The Church of God: An Anglo-Russian Symposium,* ed. E. L. Mascall (London: SPCK, 1934), p. 211.

9. This statement is not rendered false by recent Roman Catholic opinion. For while Vatican II affirmed that salvation is available for all, "not just to schismatics, heretics and Jews, but to non-Christians too and even to atheists if they are in good faith" (Hans Küng, *The Church* [Garden City, N.Y.: Doubleday, Image Books, 1976], p. 406), yet it is only in the church that the fullness of this salvation is found. See Küng, p. 407, for the quotation from the Vatican Council document, and pp. 403–11 for an extended discussion of the implications of that statement.

10. Zernov, "The Church and the Confessions," p. 212.

11. Ibid.

12. Ibid., pp. 216–17.

13. Ibid., p. 213.

14. Alexy Stepanovich Khomiakov, *The Church Is One* (London: Fellowship of St. Alban and St. Sergius, 1968), p. 38. The Russian original was written around 1850.

15. Zernov, "The Church and the Confessions," p. 214.

16. Ibid., p. 221.

17. Ibid., p. 219.

18. Ibid., p. 225.

19. Ibid., p. 219.

20. John Meyendorff, "The Orthodox Concept of the Church," *St. Vladimir's Seminary Quarterly* 6 (1962): 60.

21. Ibid. Italics in the original.

22. As cited by Meyendorff, "The Orthodox Concept of the Church."

23. Lossky, "Concerning the Third Mark of the Church," p. 175.

24. See Panagiotis E. Bratsiotis, "The Fundamental Principles and Main Characteristics of the Orthodox Church," in *The Orthodox Ethos,* ed. A. J. Philippou (Oxford: Holywell Press, 1964), pp. 28–29.

25. A useful study on this subject is Ieronumou Kotsone, *The Place of the Laity* (in Greek), (Athens, n.p., 1956). For an interesting critique on the Orthodox position, see Hendrik Kraemer, *A Theology of the Laity* (London: Lutterworth Press, 1958), pp. 96–98.

26. An example of such opposition to no less a personage than the Greek Orthodox archbishop of North and South America appears in the epilogue to a pamphlet entitled, *The Reply of the Orthodox Churches to Roman Catholic Overtures on Reunion: Being the Answer of the Great Church of Constantinople to a Papal Encyclical on Reunion* (first issued in 1895; reprinted with epilogue by Chrysostomos Stratman in 1973).

27. Lossky, "Concerning the Third Mark of the Church," p. 176.

28. Meyendorff, "The Orthodox Concept of the Church," p. 61.

29. Ibid.

30. For a brief discussion of apostolicity, see Meyendorff, "The Orthodox Concept of the Church," pp. 62–68. To understand the difference between the Roman Catholic and the Orthodox positions, see John Meyendorff et al., *The Primacy of Peter* (London: Faith Press, 1963). On the question of apostolicity as viewed by the Eastern Church, consult Francis Dvornik, *The Idea of Apostolicity in Byzantium and the Legend of the Apostle Andrew* (Cambridge, Mass.: Harvard University Press, 1958).

31. Further study on the Orthodox view of the Church can be found in Hamilcar Alivisatos, "The Holy Greek Orthodox Church," pp. 41–53; Alexander Schmemann, "Freedom in the Church," in his volume of collected essays, *Church, World, Mission* (Crestwood, N.Y.: St. Vladimir's Seminary Press, 1979), pp. 179–91. See also several essays in the excellent volume, edited by Angelos J. Philippou, *The Orthodox Ethos* (Oxford: Holywell Press, 1964). Of particular value are the essays by Philippou, Nissiotis, and Ware.

32. Constantin G. Patelos, ed., *The Orthodox Church in the Ecumenical Movement* (Geneva: World Council of Churches, 1978).

33. Articles by Orthodox theologians that have appeared in *The Ecumenical Review* include: Savas Agourides, "The Goal of the Ecumenical Movement," 25 (1973): 266–69; Ion Bria, "Living in the One Tradition: An Orthodox Contribution to the Question

of Unity," 26 (1974): 224–33; Olivier Clément, "Athenagoras I, Orthodoxy in the Service of Unity," 25 (1973): 310–28; George Khodre, "Christianity in a Pluralistic World—The Economy of the Holy Spirit," 23 (1971): 118–28; John Meyendorff, "Unity of the Church—Unity of Mankind," 24 (1972): 30–46 (two responses appear with Meyendorff's article, one by José Míguez Bonino, the other by John Gatu); Metropolitan Nikodim, "The Russian Orthodox Church and the Ecumenical Movement," 21 (1969): 116–29; Dumitru Staniloae, "Jesus Christ: Incarnate Logos of God, Source of Freedom and Unity," 26 (1974): 403–12; Emilianos Timiadis, "Disregarded Causes of Disunity," 21 (1969): 299–309; Anastasios Yannoulatos, "Towards World Community," 26 (1974): 619–36.

34. Michel Evdokimov, "Réflexions Actuelles sur L'Orthodoxie et L'Oecuménisme," *Contacts* 26 (1974): 74–84.

35. Nectarios Hatzimichalis, "Orthodox Ecumenism and External Mission," *Porefthendes* 4, no. 16 (1962): 60–63; 5 (1963): 28–31, 52–55; 6 (1964): 42–46. The entire series was later published as a book.

36. Elias Voulgarakis, "Mission and Unity from the Theological Point of View," pp. 298–307.

37. In *The Greek Orthodox Theological Review* the following have appeared: Archbishop Michael, "The Tensions of the World and Our Unity in Christ, An Address to the Evanston Assembly of the W.C.C.," 1, no. 1 (1954): 10–15; John S. Romanides, "An Orthodox Look at the Ecumenical Movement," 10, no. 1 (1964): 7–14. Three articles by Vasil T. Istavridis are of particular interest: "The Orthodox Youth and the Ecumenical Movement," 2, no. 2 (1956): 81–88; "The Ecumenical Patriarchate and the World Council of Churches," 9, no. 1 (1963): 9–28; "Orthodoxy in the Ecumenical Movement," 20, nos. 1–2 (1975): 71–80.

38. A review of two books, one expressing horror at the thought of any ecumenical compromise and the other embracing ecumenicity under the rubric of love, at once highlights the three views of Orthodoxy, or representatives of Orthodoxy, toward Christian unity: rejection, acceptance, cautious and serious discussion. William Schneirla, "Notes and Comments: Orthodoxy and Ecumenism," *St. Vladimir's Seminary Quarterly* 12 (1968): 86–88. Also in the same journal (later renamed *St. Vladimir's Theological Quarterly*), see John Meyendorff, "Confessing Christ Today and the Unity of the Church," 18 (1974): 155–65. The proceedings of the Second International Conference of Orthodox Theology on the theme "The Catholicity of the Church" contains three papers on ecumenism. These with the other papers of the conference appear in *St. Vladimir's Theological Quarterly* 17 (1973). Also of interest on this subject is the article in the journal by W. A. Visser 't Hooft, "Fr. Georges Florovsky's Role in the Formation of the W.C.C.," 23 (1979): 135–38.

39. In the *Journal of Ecumenical Studies:* Helene Iswolsky, "Uppsala and Orthodox Involvement," (1968): 661–68; Robert G. Stephanopoulos, "Reflections on Orthodox Ecumenical Directions after Uppsala," 9 (1972): 301–15.

40. Noteworthy articles appearing in *The Christian East* include: Metropolitan Panteleimon, "On the Ecumenical Christian Movement," 1, no. 3 (1950): 67–77 (this is a translation from the official periodical of the Church of Greece, *Ekklesia*); and George Florovsky, "The Eastern Orthodox Church and the Ecumenical Movement," 1, no. 3 (1950): 89–96, and 1, no. 4 (1951): 127–28.

41. To mention only two: Carnegie Samuel Calian, *Icon and Pulpit: The Protestant-Orthodox Encounter* (Philadelphia: Westminster Press, 1968), and Nicolas Zernov, *Orthodox Encounter* (London: James Clarke & Co., 1961).

42. Robert G. Stephanopoulos, "A Study in Recent Greek Orthodox Ecumenical Relations, 1902-1968" (Ph.D. dissertation, Boston University Graduate School, 1970).

43. In the seventeenth century, there were many Orthodox-Anglican contacts. Cyril Lukaris corresponded with the archbishop of Canterbury. Lukaris also presented King James I with the Codex Alexandrinus. In the early eighteenth century, the Non-Jurors attempted to receive recognition from the Eastern patriarchs. For a brief history, see Timothy Ware, *The Orthodox Church* (Baltimore, Md.: Penguin Books, 1964), pp. 108ff, 324-29. See also Vasil T. Istavridis, *Orthodoxy and Anglicanism,* trans. Colin Davey (London: SPCK, 1966).

44. Metropolitan James of Melita, "The Orthodox Concept of Mission and Missions," in *Basileia,* ed. Jan Hermelink and Hans J. Margull (Stuttgart: Evang. Missionsverlag GMBH, 1959), p. 77.

45. It has seemed prudent to use the clumsy term "non-Roman Catholic" to refer to such diverse bodies as Lutherans, Calvinists, Non-Jurors, Old Catholics, and Anglicans.

46. Metropolitan James of Melita, "The Orthodox Concept of Mission," p. 78.

47. Ibid., p. 79.

48. Ibid.

49. Ibid.

50. Ibid.

51. Ibid., p. 77.

52. Elias Voulgarakis, "Mission and Unity from the Theological Point of View," *Porefthendes* 7 (1965): 46. In the text, Voulgarakis has a footnote after "among the Orthodox," and in the footnote refers to the article by Metropolitan James in *Basileia.* Nearly the identical quotation is in the version of Voulgarakis's article of the same title, which appears in *International Review of Mission* 54 (1965): 305; however, the *IRM* article suffers from a lack of footnotes.

53. Elias Voulgarakis, "Mission and Unity," p. 6.

54. Ibid., p. 7.

55. Ibid.

56. Ibid., p. 31.

57. Ibid.

58. Ibid., p. 32.

59. Ibid.

60. Ibid., p. 46.

61. Nectarios Hatzimichalis, "Orthodox Ecumenism and External Mission," *Porefthendes.* The series was also published as a book under the same title (Athens, 1966). Quotations for this section are from the book.

62. See Hatzimichalis's argument in his introduction to *Orthodox Ecumenism and External Mission,* p. 9.

63. Ibid., p. 34.

64. Ibid., p. 39.

65. Ibid., p. 51.

66. Ibid., p. 57.

67. "Tradition" is spelled here with a capital T because it refers to the scriptural witness and the patristic witness, which form the basis of Orthodox theological reflection. "Tradition is the sacramental continuity in history of the communion of saints; in a way, it is the Church itself" (John Meyendorff, *Living Tradition* [Crestwood, N.Y.: St. Vladimir's Seminary Press, 1978], p. 16).

68. Anastasios Yannoulatos, "Orthodox Spirituality and External Mission," *Porefthendes* 4 (1962): 4-5.

Chapter 13

1. This is not to ignore the Reformed Churches' emphasis on the local church being the mission sending center. As will be shown below, there is some correspondence between the Reformed concept and the Orthodox concept. However, even in the Reformed Churches one finds the use of an agency overseeing the work. Johannes Hoornbeeck (1617-66) went so far as to suggest a Protestant counterpart to the Roman Catholic Congregatio de Propaganda Fide (see Johannes Verkuyl, *Contemporary Missiology: An Introduction,* trans. and ed. Dale Cooper [Grand Rapids, Mich.: Wm. B. Eerdmans, 1978], p. 22). For a discussion of the comparative strategies of the Western Churches, see Norman A. Horner, *Cross and Crucifix in Mission* (Nashville: Abingdon, 1965).

2. Vsevolod Spiller, "Missionary Aims and the Russian Orthodox Church," *International Review of Mission* 52 (1963): 197-98. Italics in the original.

3. "The bishop was, first of all, the image of Christ in the Eucharistic mystery" (John Meyendorff, *Byzantine Theology* [New York: Fordham University Press, 1974], p. 209).

4. "And there can be no liturgy without the laos, the people, the congregation: for it is the prayers and oblations of the people that the priest offers to God, and it is in order to transform the congregation into the Body of Christ that he has received the grace of Christ's priesthood" (Alexander Schmemann, *Liturgy and Life* [New York: Orthodox Church in America, 1974], p. 38).

5. See Stanley S. Harakas, *Living the Liturgy* (Minneapolis: Light and Life Publishing Co., 1974) for a coherent and complete guide to the layperson's participation in Orthodox worship.

6. P. Demetropoulos, "The Kingdom of God: Starting Point for the Mission Abroad," *Porefthendes* 7 (1965): 21.

7. Cf. Dimitri Obolensky, "Sts. Cyril and Methodius: Apostles of the Slavs," *St. Vladimir's Seminary Quarterly* 7 (1963): 3f.

8. Francis Dvornik, *Byzantine Missions among the Slavs* (New Brunswick, N.J.: Rutgers University Press, 1970), p. 106.

9. See Serge Bolshakoff, *The Foreign Missions of the Russian Orthodox Church* (London: SPCK 1943), passim, for references to the work of the Holy Synod in missions.

10. See, e.g., Nectarios Hatzimichalis, "Orthodox Ecumenism and External Mission," *Porefthendes* 6 (1964): 44-45.

11. A description of Innocent's missionary activities as a bishop is found in Paul D. Garrett, *St. Innocent: Apostle to America* (Crestwood, N.Y.: St. Vladimir's Seminary Press, 1979), pp. 125-280.

12. Anastasios Yannoulatos was one of the main supporters of the renewal of Orthodox missionary activity and the establishment of a missionary center. He has been the director of the Orthodox Missionary Centre in Athens since its inception in 1961.

13. Panayotis Nellas, "The Ministry of the Laity," in *Martyria/Mission,* ed. Ion Bria (Geneva: World Council of Churches, 1980), p. 61.

14. See Athenagoras Kokkinakis, *The Liturgy of the Orthodox Church* (London: Mowbrays, 1970), pp. 58, 129, 130, 138, 140, for the prayers that are prayed by the

celebrant in the first-person singular. The prayers are the ones offered before the service, during the time the celebrant receives the elements, and during the post-Communion prayers.

15. Sergius Bulgakov, *The Orthodox Church* (London: Centenary Press, 1935), p. 68-69.

16. Paul D. Garrett, *St. Innocent: Apostle to America,* p. 309.

17. Procius Yasuo Ushimaru, *Bishop Innocent: Founder of American Orthodoxy* (Bridgeport, Conn.: Metropolitan Council Publications Committee, 1964), p. 40.

18. At the time, the Russian Orthodox Church consisted of sixty-three dioceses (Nicolas Zernov, *The Russian Religious Renaissance of the Twentieth Century* [London: Darton, Longman & Todd, 1963], p. 41.

19. Paul D. Garrett, *St. Innocent: Apostle to America,* p. 311. For more details on the early years of the society, see Charles R. Hale, *The Orthodox Missionary Society* (England: privately printed, 1878).

20. "Macaire cherished the idea of creating a missionary society which would be the work of the whole Russian people" (Nikita Struve, "Macaire Gloukharev, A Prophet of Orthodox Mission," *International Review of Mission* 54 [1965]: 313).

21. Elias Voulgarakis, "The Church of Greece," in *Martyria/Mission,* p. 116.

22. Sophia Mourourouka, "A Beginning," *Porefthendes* 1, no. 1 (1959): 6.

23. *The First Five Years of Porefthendes* (Athens: Porefthendes, 1966), p. 7.

24. Anastasios Yannoulatos, " 'Porefthendes,' An Inter-Orthodox Missionary Centre," *Porefthendes* 3 (1961): 36.

25. Voulgarakis, "The Church of Greece," *Martyria/Mission,* ed. Bria, p. 117.

26. The output of the director Anastasios Yannoulatos has been truly remarkable. In addition to numerous smaller studies, he has published several major works, which are of great importance in the field of missiology. At this writing he is a professor of comparative religions at the University of Athens and also the bishop in charge of the Apostoliki Diakonia (the home missions department) of the Church of Greece. Among his publications are the following: *Various Approaches to the Other Religions* (Athens: Porefthendes, 1971); *Ruhanga, the Creator: A Contribution to the Investigation of African Beliefs concerning God and Man* (in Greek), (Athens: n.p., 1975); *Lord of Brightness: The God of the Tribes near Mount Kenya* (in Greek), (Athens: Porefthendes, 1973); *Forms of African Ritual: Initiation and Possession Rites East of Ruwenzori* (in Greek), (Athens: n.p., 1973); *Islam: A General Survey* (in Greek), (Athens: Ethne and Laoi, 1975). The last-named volume, on Islam, is the first objective informative study to appear on the religion in Greek. Byzantine works and those produced under Turkish rule were polemical and defensive.

27. Yannoulatos, " 'Porefthendes,' An Inter-Orthodox Missionary Centre," p. 37.

28. Anastasios Yannoulatos, *The Inter-Orthodox Centre of Athens: Perspectives and Presuppositions,* passim.

29. Ibid., p. 6.

30. Alexander Veronis, "Report on the Foreign Missions Programme of the Greek Orthodox Archdiocese of North and South America," *Porefthendes* 10 (1968): 25-28.

31. The best survey of the mission awareness of the national Churches today appears in the reports in "Section II: The Witnessing Churches," in *Martyria/Mission,* ed. Ion Bria.

32. See, e.g., Alexander Schmemann, "Problems of Orthodoxy in America: The Spiritual Problem," *St. Vladimir's Seminary Quarterly* 9 (1965): 171-93. Nicon Patrinacos, in his book, *The Individual and His Orthodox Church* (New York: Orthodox

Observer Press, 1970), states as one of his purposes in writing: to meet the needs of a "class of men and women who are Orthodox by baptism and outward conformity but scarcely so by inward choice" (p. vii).

33. M. A. Siotis, "Thoughts of an Orthodox Theologian on 'The Missionary Structure of the Congregation,' " *Concept* 3 (1963): 1.

34. Sergius Bulgakov, *The Orthodox Church*, p. 9.

35. Siotis, "Missionary Structure of the Congregation," p. 1.

36. Ibid.

37. Ibid., p. 3.

38. It must be noted that certain monks freely shared with others their progress to spiritual maturity. See, e.g., Theodore Stylianopoulos, "Staretz Silouan: A Modern Orthodox Saint," in *God and Charity: Images of Eastern Orthodox Theology, Spirituality, and Practice*, ed. Francis D. Costa (Brookline, Mass.: Holy Cross Orthodox Press, 1979), pp. 33-54. (*Staretz* is Russian for an elder who is a spiritual guide.)

39. Siotis, "Missionary Structure of the Congregation," p. 8.

40. Ibid., p. 3.

41. Ibid., p. 5.

42. "La vie privée et l'indignité des ministres n'influencent pas et ne peuvent nullement amoindrir ou neutraliser la sainteté et la valeur du sacrement" (Panagiotis N. Trempelas, *Dogmatique de L'Église Orthodoxe Catholique* [Paris: Éditions de Chevetogne et Desclée de Brouwer, 1968], pp. 43-44).

43. Siotis, "Missionary Structure of the Congregation," p. 8.

44. The situation in rural Greece in the 1960s is described by Mario Rinvolucri: "After an examination of Greek village parishes, one is left with an impression of fine leaven but poor bakers, of a religious people, but of educationally and, above all, spiritually inadequate pastors" (*Anatomy of a Church: Greek Orthodoxy Today* [London: Burns & Oates, 1966], p. 30). Rinvolucri's comment testifies to the depth of spiritual penetration of the Orthodox faith in the people. While this is a generally recognized universal characteristic of the Orthodox, secularization has made increasing inroads. In Greece, organizations like Zoe and Sotir have been founded to meet the need for Christian instruction. There is also a home missions department of the Orthodox Church in Greece, headed at the present by Bishop Anastasios Yannoulatos, who was and is one of the chief advocates of foreign mission in the Orthodox Church. While the situation that Rinvolucri describes is perhaps the worst example of the lack of an adequate clergy, both numerically and spiritually, the situation could be documented in other areas as well, though to a lesser degree. In the Diaspora, the majority of priests have been adequately trained, and have both undergraduate and graduate theological degrees. This is a key factor in providing adequate spiritual leadership. "Not only has there been a significant improvement in the training of Church leaders in recent years, but there has emerged in our time a more homogeneous clergy, a clergy more united and more willing and able to communicate not only with the members of the Church, but with each other as well. There is little doubt that one of the major achievements of the second half of this century in American Orthodox history will be the improvement of spiritual, liturgical and theological unanimity and harmony among the bishops and priests of the Church, as well as the Church membership as a whole" (Thomas Hopko, "The Orthodox Church in America," in *Martyria/Mission*, ed. Bria, p. 149). While the entire volume is of value, in particular "Section II: Witnessing Churches" provides a valuable survey of the present state of world Orthodoxy.

45. Anastasios Yannoulatos, "Initial Thoughts toward an Orthodox Foreign Mission," *Porefthendes* 10 (1968): 19.

46. For an excellent survey of the controversy regarding the concepts of mission and evangelism, see David J. Bosch, *Witness to the World: The Christian Mission in Theological Perspective* (London: Marshall, Morgan & Scott, 1980), pp. 11–20.

47. Demetrios J. Constantelos, "The 'Neomartyrs' as Evidence for Methods and Motives Leading to Conversion and Martyrdom in the Ottoman Empire," p. 230.

48. Ibid., p. 224.

49. Ibid., pp. 230–31.

50. This is in no way meant to be a slight against Orthodoxy. It is the recognition of the acknowledgment made by the Orthodox themselves on the need to combat the present-day enemy, secularism. While numerical comparisons cannot be made accurately, nevertheless the threat of apostasy today is as great, if not greater, than it was then. If Constantelos is correct that political, economic, and social motives "contributed to apostasy from Christianity to Islam" ("The 'Neomartyrs,' " p. 219), then it is the selfsame motives that tempt people away from the faith in these days. The need to combat secularism has been responsible for numerous publications—books, pamphlets, and articles—by Orthodox around the world. Many have been referred to above. It is worthwhile to mention again the work of Apostoliki Diakonia of the Church of Greece, which publishes a wide range of material from Sunday school manuals to leaflets that are handed out on the streets on Sundays to passersby.

51. See, e.g., the comment by Paul Ricaut, that the continued existence of the Greek Church is a sign "no less convincing than the miracles and power which attended the beginnings of the early Church" (*The Present State of the Greek and Armenian Churches, Anno Christi 1678* [London, 1679; reprinted New York, 1970], pp. 1–30, as cited by Constantelos, "The 'Neomartyrs,' " p. 217). See also John Meyendorff's judgment: "These various episodes in the life of the Church under Turkish rule add nothing of great importance to our understanding of the history of Orthodox theology, but they may serve as a sort of proof of the vitality of Greek Orthodoxy and the determination of the Orthodox to retain their identity under very trying circumstances" (*The Orthodox Church* [London: Darton, Longman & Todd, 1962], p. 98).

Epilogue

1. Yannoulatos, "The Purpose and Motive of Mission from an Orthodox Theological Point of View," *Porefthendes* 9 (1967): 2.

2. Nikita Struve, "Macaire Gloukharev, A Prophet of Orthodox Mission," *International Review of Mission* 54 (1965): 314.

Suggested Readings

Chapter 1

Bulgakov, Sergius. *The Orthodox Church.* London: Centenary Press, 1935.

Constantelos, Demetrios J. *Understanding the Greek Orthodox Church: Its Faith, History, and Practice.* New York: Seabury Press, 1982.

Evdokimov, Michel. "Réflexions Actuelles sur l'Orthodoxie et l'Oecuménisme." *Contacts* 26 (1974): 74–84.

Florovsky, George. "The Eastern Orthodox Church and the Ecumenical Movement." *The Christian East* n.s. 1 (1950): 89–96, 127–128.

Hammond, Peter. *The Waters of Marah.* London: Rockliff Publishing Co., 1956.

Istavridis, Vasil T. "The Ecumenical Patriarchate and the World Council of Churches." *The Greek Orthodox Theological Review* 9 (1963): 9–28.

———. "The Ecumenicity of Orthodoxy." *The Ecumenical Review* 29 (1977): 182–195.

———. "Orthodox Youth and the Ecumenical Movement." *The Greek Orthodox Theological Review* 2 (1956): 81–88.

———. "Orthodoxy in the Ecumenical Movement." *The Greek Orthodox Theological Review* 20 (1975): 71–80.

Iswolsky, Helen. "Uppsala and Orthodox Involvement." *Journal of Ecumenical Studies* 5 (1968): 661–68.

Langford-James, R.L. *A Dictionary of the Eastern Orthodox Church.* London: Faith Press, 1923.

Meyendorff, John. *The Orthodox Church: Its Past and Its Role in the World Today.* Translated by John Chapin. London: Darton, Longman & Todd, 1962.

Michael, Archbishop. "The Tensions of the World and Our Unity in Christ: An Address to the Evanston Assembly of the W.C.C." *The Greek Orthodox Theological Review* 1 (1954): 10–15.

Nikodim, Metropolitan. "The Russian Orthodox Church and the Ecumenical Movement." *The Ecumenical Review* 21 (1969): 116–29.

Panteleimon, Metropolitan of Edessa and Pella. "On the Ecumenical Christian Movement." *The Christian East* n.s. 1 (1950): 67–77.

Papastephanou, E.A. "The Eastern Church in the Western World." *The Christian East* n.s. 1 (1951): 107–11.

Patelos, Constantin G. *The Orthodox Church in the Ecumenical Movement: Documents and Statements, 1902–1975.* Geneva: World Council of Churches, 1978.

Philippou, Angelos James, ed. *The Orthodox Ethos: Essays in Honour of the Centenary of the Greek Orthodox Archdiocese of North and South America.* Oxford: Holywell Press, 1964.

———, ed. *Orthodoxy: Life and Freedom.* Oxford: Studion Publications, 1973.

Rinvolucri, Mario. *The Anatomy of a Church: Greek Orthodoxy Today.* New York: Fordham University Press, 1966.

Romanides, John S. "An Orthodox Look at the Ecumenical Movement." *The Greek Orthodox Theological Review* 10 (1964): 7–14.

Schmemann, Alexander. *Church, World, Mission.* Crestwood, N.Y.: St. Vladimir's Seminary Press, 1979.

———. *The Historical Road of Eastern Orthodoxy.* Translated by Lydia Kesich. London: Harvill Press, 1963.

Stephanoupolos, Robert G. "Reflections on Orthodox Ecumenical Directions after Uppsala." *Journal of Ecumenical Studies* 9 (1972): 301–15.

———. "A Study in Recent Greek Orthodox Ecumenical Relations, 1902–1968." Unpublished Ph.D. dissertation, Boston University, 1970.

Ware, Timothy. *The Orthodox Church.* Baltimore, Md.: Penguin Books, 1963.

Zernov, Nicholas. *Orthodox Encounter: The Christian East and the Ecumenical Movement.* London: James Clarke and Co., 1961.

Zoe Brotherhood, eds. *A Sign of God, Orthodoxy 1964: A Pan-Orthodox Symposium.* Athens: Zoe, 1964.

Chapter 2

Androutsos, Chrestos. *Dogmatika tes Orthodoxos Anatolikes Ekklesias* (Dogmas of the Eastern Orthodox Church). Athens: Al. & E. Papademetrios, 1956.

Benz, Ernst. *The Eastern Orthodox Church: Its Thought and Life.* Translated by Richard and Clara Winston. Garden City, N.Y.: Doubleday, Anchor Books, 1963.

Bradow, Charles. "The Career and Confession of Cyril Loukaris: The Greek Orthodox Church and Its Relations with Western Christians (1543–1638)." Unpublished Ph.D. dissertation, Ohio State University, 1960.

Bratsiotis, Panagiotis. *The Greek Orthodox Church.* Translated by Joseph Blenkinsopp. Notre Dame, Ind.: University of Notre Dame Press, 1968.

Calian, Carnegie Samuel. "Cyril Lucaris: The Patriarch Who Failed." *Journal of Ecumenical Studies* 10 (1973): 319–35.

———. *Icon and Pulpit: The Protestant-Orthodox Encounter.* Philadelphia: Westminster Press, 1968.

Constantelos, Demetrios J. "The Evangelical Character of the Orthodox Church." *Journal of Ecumenical Studies* 9 (1972): 544–55

Emhardt, Wm. C.; T. Burgess; R.T. Lau, *The Eastern Church in the Western World.* Milwaukee, 1928; reprint ed., New York: AMS Press, 1970.

Evdokimov, Paul. *L'Orthodoxie.* Neuchatel: Delachaux et Niestlé, 1959.

Florovsky, George. *Bible, Church, Tradition: An Eastern Orthodox View.* Vol. 1 of *The Collected Works of George Florovksy.* Belmont, Mass.: Nordland Publishing Co., 1974.

———. *Christianity and Culture.* Vol. 2 of *The Collected Works of George Florovsky.* Belmont, Mass.: Nordland Publishing Co., 1974.

———. *Creation and Redemption.* Vol. 3 of *The Collected Works of George Florovsky.* Belmont, Mass.: Nordland Publishing Co., 1976.

———. *Ways of Russian Theology, Part One.* Vol. 5 of *The Collected Works of George Florovsky.* Belmont, Mass.: Nordland Publishing Co., 1979.

Fouyas, Methodius. *Orthodoxy, Roman Catholicism, and Anglicanism.* London: Oxford University Press, 1972.

Gavin, Frank. *Some Aspects of Contemporary Greek Orthodox Thought.* Milwaukee, Wis.: Morehouse Publishing Co., 1923.

Geanakoplos, Deno J. *Byzantine East and Latin West.* Oxford: Basil Blackwell, 1966.

Hadjiantoniou, George A. *Protestant Patriarch: The Life of Cyril Lucaris (1572-1638).* Richmond, Va.: John Knox Press, 1961.

Hopko, Thomas. *The Orthodox Faith.* 4 vols. New York: Department of Religious Education, Orthodox Church in America, 1971-75.

Istavridis, V.T. *Orthodoxy and Anglicanism.* Translated by Colin Davey. London: SPCK, 1966.

Karmiris, John. *A Synopsis of the Dogmatic Theology of the Orthodox Catholic Church.* Translated by George Dimopoulos. Scranton, Pa.: Christian Orthodox Edition, 1973.

——. *Ta Dogmatika kai Symvolika Mnimeia tis Orthodoxou Katholikis Ekklisias* (Dogmatic and symbolic monuments of the Orthodox Catholic Church). 2 vols. Athens: Apostoliki Diakonia, 1952-53.

Kovalevsky, Pierre. *Saint Sergius and Russian Spirituality.* Translated by W. Elias Jones. Crestwood, N.Y.: St. Vladimir's Seminary Press, 1974.

Lossky, Vladimir. *In the Image and Likeness of God.* Edited by John H. Erickson and Thomas E. Bird. Crestwood, N.Y.: St. Vladimir's Seminary Press, 1974.

——. *The Mystical Theology of the Eastern Church.* Cambridge, Eng.: James Clarke & Co., 1968.

——. *Orthodox Theology: An Introduction.* Translated by Ian and Ihita Kesarcodi-Watson. Crestwood, N.Y.: St. Vladimir's Seminary Press, 1978.

Maloney, George A. *A History of Orthodox Theology since 1453.* Belmont, Mass.: Nordland Publising Co., 1976.

Meyendorff, John. *Byzantine Theology: Historical Trends and Doctrinal Themes.* London: Mowbrays, 1975.

——. *Christ in Eastern Christian Thought.* Crestwood, N.Y.: St. Vladimir's Seminary Press, 1975.

——. *Living Tradition.* Crestwood, N.Y.: St. Vladimir's Seminary Press, 1978.

——. *Orthodoxy and Catholicity.* New York: Sheed and Ward, 1966.

——. *St. Gregory Palamas and Orthodox Spirituality.* Translated by Adele Fiske. Crestwood, N.Y.: St. Vladimir's Seminary Press, 1974.

——. *A Study of Gregory Palamas.* Translated by George Lawrence. London: Faith Press, 1964.

——. "What is an Ecumenical Council?" *St. Vladimir's Theological Quarterly* 17 (1973): 269-73.

Meyendorff, John, and Joseph McLelland, eds. *The New Man: An Orthodox and Reformed Dialogue.* New Brunswick, N.J.: Agora Books, 1973.

Meyendorff, John; A. Schmemann; N. Afanassieff; and N. Koulomzine. *The Primacy of Peter.* London: Faith Press, 1963.

Niesel, Wilhelm. *Reformed Symbolics: A Comparison of Catholicism, Orthodoxy, and Protestantism.* Translated by David Lewis. Edinburgh: Oliver and Boyd, 1962.

The Orthodox Church and the Churches of the Reformation: A Survey of Orthodox-Protestant Dialogues. Geneva: World Council of Churches, 1975.

Palachovsky, V., and C. Vogel. *Sin in the Orthodox Church and in the Protestant Churches.* New York: Desclee Co., 1960.

Popivchak, Ronald. "Peter Mohila, Metropolitan of Kiev (1633-47): Translation and

Evaluation of His 'Orthodox Confession of Faith' (1640)." Unpublished S.T.D. dissertation, Catholic University of America, 1975.

Ricaut, Paul. *The Present State of the Greek and Armenian Churches, Anno Christi: 1678.* London, 1679; reprinted., New York: AMS, 1970.

Schmemann, Alexander. "Russian Theology: 1920–1972, An Introductory Survey." *St. Vladimir's Theological Quarterly* 16 (1972): 172–94.

Stamoolis, James. "Scripture and Tradition as Sources of Authority in the Eastern Orthodox Church." Unpublished Th.M. thesis, Trinity Evangelical Divinity School, 1971.

Strenopoulos, Germanos. *Kyrillos Loukaris, 1572–1638: A Struggle for Preponderance between Catholic and Protestant Powers in the Orthodox East.* London: SPCK, 1951.

Trempelas, Panagiotes N. *Dogmatiki tis Orthodoxou Katholikis Ekklisias* (Dogmas of the Orthodox Catholic Church). 3 vols. Athens: Zoe, 1959. Translated into French by Pierre Dumont: *Dogmatique de L'Église Orthodoxe Catholique.* Paris: Éditions de Chevetogne/Desclée de Brouwer, 1968.

Ware, Timothy. *Eustratios Argenti: A Study of the Greek Church under Turkish Rule.* Oxford: Clarendon Press, 1964.

———. *The Orthodox Way.* London: Mowbrays, 1979.

Yannaras, Christos. "Theology in Present Day Greece." *St. Vladimir's Theological Quarterly* 16 (1972): 195–214.

Chapter 3

Constantelos, Demetrios J. *Byzantine Philanthropy and Social Welfare.* New Brunswick, N.J.: Rutgers University Press, 1968.

Dvornik, Francis. *Byzantine Missions among the Slavs.* New Brunswick, N.J.: Rutgers University Press, 1970.

———. "Sts. Cyril and Methodius in Rome." *St. Vladimir's Seminary Quarterly* 7 (1963): 20–30.

Grivec, F. "Cyrille et Méthode." *Irénikon* 3 (1927): 67–78.

Hannick, T. "Notes et Documents: Cyrillo-Methodiana." *Irénikon* 41 (1968): 97–105.

Lacko, Michael. *Saints Cyril and Methodius.* Rome: Slovak Editions, 1963.

Obolensky, Dimitri. "Sts. Cyril and Methodius: Apostles of the Slavs." *St. Vladimir's Seminary Quarterly* 7 (1963): 3–13.

Spinka, Matthew. *A History of Christianity in the Balkans.* Hamden, Conn.: Archon Books, 1968.

Theophylactos, Archbishop of Achris. "Life and Activity of St. Clemens, Apostle of Bulgaria." *Porefthendes* 9 (1967): 20–31, 48–63; 10 (1968): 5–7, 11.

Vittis, Eusebius. "Saints Cyril and Methodius, Enlighteners of the Slavs." *Porefthendes* 9 (1967): 10–19, 39–46; 10 (1968): 12–16.

Vlasto, A. P. "The Mission of SS. Cyril and Methodius and Its Aftermath in Central Europe." In *The Mission of the Church and the Propagation of the Faith*, pp. 1–16. Edited by G. J. Cuming. Cambridge, Eng.: University Press, 1970.

Voulgarakis, Elias. "Mission and Fathers: A Bibliography." *Porefthendes* 4 (1962): 31.

Yannoulatos, Anastasios. "Byzantium, Evangelistic Works." In *The Encyclopedia of Religion and Ethics* (in Greek). Vol. 4, pp. 19–59. Athens: n.p., 1964.

———. "Mission aus der Sicht eines Orthodoxen." *Neue Zeitschrift für Missionswissenschaft* 26 (1970): 241–52.

————. "The Missionary Activities of the Churches of the East in Central and Eastern Asia." *Porefthendes* 3 (1961): 26–31.

————. "Mission: Les missions de Églises d'Orient." In *Encyclopaedia Universalis*. Vol. II, pp. 99–102. Paris: n.p., 1968.

————. "Monks and Mission in the Eastern Church during the 4th Century." *International Review of Mission* 58 (1969): 208–226. The same article with fuller documentation appears in *Porefthendes* 8 (1966): 34–39, 46, 54–58.

Chapter 4

Adeney, Walter F. *The Greek and Eastern Churches*. Clifton, N.J.: Reference Book Publishers, 1965, reprint of 1908 ed.

Billington, James H. *The Icon and the Axe: An Interpretive History of Russian Culture*. New York: Random House, 1970.

Bolshakoff, Serge. *The Foreign Missions of the Russian Orthodox Church*. London: SPCK, 1943.

————. "Les Missions étrangeres dans l'Eglise orthodox russe." *Irénikon* 28 (1955): 159–75.

Fedotov, G. P. *The Russian Religious Mind, Kievan Christianity: The 10th to the 13th Centuries*. New York: Harper & Row, 1960.

Florovsky, George. *Aspects of Church History*. Vol. 4 of *The Collected Works of George Florovsky*. Belmont, Mass.: Nordland Publishing Co., 1975.

Garrett, Paul D. *St. Innocent: Apostle to America*. Crestwood, N.Y.: St. Vladimir's Seminary Press, 1979.

Glazik, Josef. *Die Islammission der russisch-orthodoxen Kirche*. Münster: Aschendorffsche Verlagsbuchhandlung, 1959.

————. *Die russisch-orthodoxe Heidenmission seit Peter dem Grossen*. Münster: Aschendorffsche Verlagsbuchhandlung, 1954.

Gorodetzky, Nadejda. "The Missionary Expansion of the Russian Orthodox Church." *International Review of Mission* 21 (1942): 400–411.

Kovach, Michael George. "The Russian Orthodox Church in Russian America." Unpublished Ph.D. dissertation, University of Pittsburgh, 1957.

Petrov, Alexis. "Etienne de Perm." *Eglise Vivante* 12 (1960): 418–21.

The Russian Primary Chronicle. Translated by S. H. Cross and G. P. Sherbowitz-Wetzor. Cambridge, Mass.: Harvard University Press, 1958.

Smirnoff, Eugene. *A Short Account of the Historical Development and Present Position of Russian Orthodox Missions*. London: Rivingtons, 1903; reprint ed., Willits, Calif.: Eastern Orthodox Books, n.d.

Spiridon, Archimandrite. *Mes Missions en Sibérie*. Translated by Pierre Pascal. Paris: Editions du Cerf, 1950.

Stanley, Arthur Penrhyn. *Lectures on the History of the Eastern Church*. London: John Murray, 1862.

Struve, Nikita. "Macaire Gloukharev: A Prophet of Orthodox Mission." *International Review of Mission* 54 (1965): 308–14.

————. "The Orthodox Church and Mission." In *History's Lessons for Tomorrow's Mission*, pp. 105–18. Geneva: World's Student Christian Federation, n.d. A slightly longer revision with fuller documentation appears as "Orthodox Missions, Past and Present." *St. Vladimir's Seminary Quarterly* 7 (1963): 31–42.

Ushimaru, Procius Yasuo. *Bishop Innocent: Founder of American Orthodoxy*. Bridgeport, Conn.: Metropolitan Council Publications Committee, 1964.
Yannoulatos, Anastasios. "Orthodoxy in Alaska." In *The Encyclopedia of Religion and Ethics* (in Greek). Vol. 5, pp. 14–22. Athens, 1963.
———. "Orthodoxy in Alaska." *Porefthendes* 5 (1963): 14–22, 44–47.
Zenkovsky, Serge A., ed. *Medieval Russia's Epics, Chronicles, and Tales*. New York: E. P. Dutton, 1974.

Chapter 5

The general works listed in the suggested reading for chap. 4 should also be consulted for this chapter. Particular attention is called to the works by Bolshakoff, Smirnoff, and Struve, and to Glazik's Heidenmission.

Caruso, Igor A. "Missions Orthodoxes en Corée." *Irénikon* 11 (1934): 93–101.
Cary, Otis. *Roman Catholic and Greek Orthodox Missions*. Vol. 1 of *A History of Christianity in Japan*. New York: Fleming H. Revell Co., 1909.
Cracraft, James. *The Church Reforms of Peter the Great*. London: Macmillan, 1971.
Drummond, Richard H. *A History of Christianity in Japan*. Grand Rapids, Mich.: Wm. B. Eerdmans, 1971.
Hale, Charles R. *Missions of the Russian Church in China and Japan*. N.p.: privately printed, 1878; reprint ed., Willits, Calif.: Eastern Orthodox Books, 1975.
Latourette, Kenneth Scott. *A History of Christian Missions in China*. London: SPCK, 1929.
Meyendorff, John. "L'Église Orthodoxe du Japon," *Le Messager Orthodox* 3 (1958): 20–23.
Piovesana, G. K. "La mission russe au Japon." *Église Vivante* 12 (1960): 422–27.
Vital, Archimandrite. "Missions orthodoxes du Japon et de Perse." *Irénikon* 8 (1938): 17–26.
Widmer, Eric. *The Russian Ecclesiastical Mission in Peking during the Eighteenth Century*. Cambridge, Mass.: Harvard University Press, 1976.
Yannoulatos, Anastasios. *The Dawn of Orthodoxy in Japan* (in Greek). Athens: n.p., 1971.
———. "Orthodoxy in China." In *The Encyclopedia of Religion and Ethics* (in Greek). Vol. 5, pp. 566–81. Athens, 1963.
———. "Orthodoxy in China." *Porefthendes* 4 (1962): 26–30, 52–55.

Chapter 6

Autocephaly: The Orthodox Church in America. Crestwood, N.Y.: St. Vladimir's Seminary Press, 1971.
Barrett, David, ed. "Who's Who of African Independent Church Leaders." *RISK* 7 (1971): 23–24.
Barrett, David; George K. Mambo; Janice McLaughlin; and Malcolm J. McVeigh. *Kenya Churches Handbook: The Development of Kenyan Christianity, 1948–1973*. Nairobi: Evangel, 1973.
Bogolepov, Alexander A. *Toward an American Orthodox Church*. New York: Morehouse-Barlow, 1963.
Bolshakoff, Serge. "Orthodox Missions Today." *International Review of Mission* 42 (1953): 275–84.

Bruls, Jean. "Une génération spontanée l'Orthodoxie en Uganda." *Église Vivante* 12 (1960): 428–33.

Hatzimichalis, Nectarios. "L'Église Orthodoxe grecque et le messianisme en Afrique." *Social Compass* 22 (1975): 85–95.

Horner, Norman A. "An East African Orthodox Church." *Journal of Ecumenical Studies* 12 (1975): 221–33.

Kibue, C. K. "The African Greek Orthodox Church in Kenya." *Porefthendes* 3 (1961): 54–55.

Konstantopoulou, Theano. "From the Visit of the Faculty of Theology of the University of Thessaloniki to Uganda." *Porefthendes* 8 (1966): 8–11.

Nankyamas, Theodoros. "On the Orthodox Church in Uganda and Kenya." *Porefthendes* 3 (1961): 43–45.

"The New Patriarch of Alexandria and All Africa." *Porefthendes* 10 (1968): 24.

"The Orthodox Church: A New Dynamic in Australian Church Life." *International Review of Mission* 68 (1979): 22–25.

"Orthodoxy's Window to the West: A New Center in Geneva." *Lutheran World* 23 (1976): 186–87.

Read, James J. "Orthodoxy in New Zealand." *Eastern Churches Review* 8 (1976): 81–84.

Tarasar, Constance J., ed. *Orthodox America 1794–1976: Development of the Orthodox Church in America.* Syosset, N.Y.: Orthodox Church in America, 1975.

Welbourn, F. B. *East African Rebels: A Study of Some Independent Churches.* London: SCM Press, 1961.

Wentink, D. E. "The Orthodox Church in East Africa." *The Ecumenical Review* 20 (1968): 33–43.

White, Gavin. "Eastern African Orthodoxy." *Sobornost* series 5, no. 5 (1967): 357–64.

Yannoulatos, Anastasios. "Among the Orthodox of West Kenya." *Porefthendes* 7 (1965): 24–28, 48–51.

———. "A Brief Chronicle on the Founding of an Orthodox Community in West Tanzania." *Porefthendes* 7 (1965): 8–11.

———. "Father Spartas Visits Greece." *Porefthendes* 2 (1960): 10–13.

———. "Impressions from a Brief Contact with Orthodox Kikuyu." *Porefthendes* 10 (1968): 8–11.

Chapter 7

Note for Chapters 7–10: *The literature relating to Orthodox missiology often discusses several topics in one book or article. For that reason it is difficult to divide the suggested reading into separate topics. This is particularly true for chapters 7 through 10. Listed below under the chapter headings are the most important, but not the only, items on the subject. The reader may find it useful to begin his or her study with an examination of my annotated bibliography: Stamoolis, James. "A Selected Bibliography of Eastern Orthodox Mission Theology." Occasional Bulletin of Missionary Research 1 (1977): 24–27.*

Bria, Ion, ed. *Martyria/Mission: The Witness of the Orthodox Churches Today.* Geneva: World Council of Churches, 1980.

Demetropoulos, P. "The Kingdom of God: Starting Point for the Mission Abroad." *Porefthendes* 7 (1965): 18–23.

Evdokimov, Paul. "L'action missionnaire de l'Église orthodoxe." *Église Vivante* 12 (1960): 413–17.

Hatzimichalis, Nectarios. "Some Thoughts on Orthodox Mission." *Porefthendes* 2 (1960), no. 7:3–6, no. 8:6–8.

Meyendorff, John. "The Orthodox Church and Mission: Past and Present Perspectives." In *Mission Trends No. 1*, pp. 59–71. Edited by Gerald H. Anderson and Thomas F. Stransky. New York: Paulist Press, and Grand Rapids, Mich.: Wm. B. Eerdmans, 1974.

Philippose, K. "Orthodoxy and Mission." *The Student World* 50 (1957): 361–69.

Ramaios, Antonios. "The Cross and Mission." *Porefthendes* 10 (1968): 53–54.

Schmemann, Alexander. "The Missionary Imperative in the Orthodox Tradition." In *The Theology of the Christian Mission*, pp. 250–57. Edited by Gerald H. Anderson, New York: McGraw-Hill, 1961.

Spiller, Vsevolod. "Missionary Aims and the Russian Orthodox Church." *International Review of Mission* 52 (1963): 195–205.

Tsami-Dratsella, Maria. "The Founding of External Mission in the Book of Acts." *Porefthendes* 10 (1968): 38–40.

Yannoulatos, Anastasios. "Orthodoxy and Mission." *St. Vladimir's Seminary Quarterly* 8 (1964): 139–48.

———. "A Prayer Campaign." *Porefthendes* 1 (1959): 1–3.

———. "The Purpose and Motive of Mission." *International Review of Mission* 54 (1965): 281–97. The same article appears in expanded form with fuller documentation in *Porefthendes* 9 (1967): 2–10, 34–36.

———. "Theology-Mission and Pastoral Care." *The Greek Orthodox Theological Review* 22 (1977): 157–80.

Chapter 8

Bratsiotis, P. I. "The Evangelistic Work of the Contemporary Greek Orthodox Church." *The Christian East* n.s. 1 (1950): 21–32, 38–41.

Bria, Ion. "The Church's Role in Evangelism: Icon or Platform?" *International Review of Mission* 64 (1975): 243–50.

Hatzimichalis, Nectarios. "Orthodox Monasticism and External Mission." *Porefthendes* 4 (1962): 12–15.

Hopko, Thomas. "The Bible in the Orthodox Church." *St. Vladimir's Theological Quarterly* 14 (1970): 66–69.

Istavridis, Vasil T. "Theological Education for Mission." *The Greek Orthodox Theological Review* 13 (1968): 7–14.

Khodre, George. "An Eastern Orthodox Viewpoint, an Interview by Paul Löffler." *International Review of Mission* 60 (1971): 65–69.

———. "Mission et Développement dans la théologie Orthodoxe." *Contacts* 26 (1974): 66–73.

Meyendorff, John. "Orthodox Missions in the Middle Ages." In *History's Lessons for Tomorrow's Mission*, pp. 99–104. Geneva: World's Student Christian Federation, n.d.

Nissiotis, N. A. "An Orthodox View of Modern Trends in Evangelism." In *The Ecumenical World of Orthodox Civilization, Russia and Orthodoxy*. Vol. 3 of *Essays in Honour of Georges Florovsky*, pp. 181–192. Edited by Andrew Blane. The Hague: Mouton & Co., 1974.

Rochcau, Vsevolod. "Saint Herman of Alaska and the Defense of Alaskan Native Peoples." *St. Vladimir's Theological Quarterly* 16 (1972): 17–39.

Schneirla, W. "Conversion in the Orthodox Church." *St. Vladimir's Seminary Quarterly* 11 (1967): 87–95.

Stylios, Efthimios. "The Missionary as an Imitator of Christ." *Porefthendes* 5 (1963): 8–10.

Voulgarakis, Elias. "The Greek Orthodox Missionary, Philotheos." *Porefthendes* 10 (1968): 2–4, 41–46, 55–56, 59–62.

————. "Language and Mission." *Porefthendes* 4 (1962): 42–44.

Yannoulatos, Anastasios. "Initial Thoughts toward an Orthodox Foreign Mission." *Porefthendes* 10 (1968): 19–23, 50–52.

————. "A Letter from the Other Hemisphere." *Porefthendes* 6 (1964): 40–41.

————. *Various Christian Approaches to the Other Religions.* Athens: Porefthendes, 1971.

Chapter 9

Bedis, George. "The Valamo Consultation." *The Greek Orthodox Theological Review* 23 (1978): 167–68.

"Confessing Christ Today: Reports of Groups at a Consultation of Orthodox Theologians." *International Review of Mission* 64 (1975): 74–94. Also in *St. Vladimir's Theological Quarterly* 18 (1974): 193–212.

"Consultation on 'Orthodox Diaspora.' " *Porefthendes* 10 (1968): 29–31.

"The Ecumenical Nature of Orthodox Witness: Report of the Consultation of Orthodox Theologians, New Valamo, Finland." *Eastern Churches Review* 10 (1978): 141–44.

Harakas, Stanley. "Living the Orthodox Christian Faith in America." *Lutheran World* 23 (1976): 192–99.

Mastrantonis, George. *A New-Style Catechism on the Eastern Orthodox Faith for Adults.* St. Louis, Mo.: Ologos Mission, 1969.

Mourouka, Sophia. "A Beginning." *Porefthendes* 1 (1959), no. 1: 6–7.

The Orthodox Church in America. *Mission: The Fourth All-American Council, Working Papers and Documents.* Syosset, N.Y.: American Orthodox Church, 1975.

"Report of the Valamo Consultation: The Ecumenical Nature of the Orthodox Witness." *The Greek Orthodox Theological Review* 23 (1978): 169–74.

Rodzianko, Vladimir. "The International Conference of Orthodox Youth, April 7th–12th, 1953." *The Christian East* n.s. 2 (1953): 139–48.

Romanides, John S. "The Orthodox: Arrival and Dialogue." *The Christian Century* 80 (1963): 1399–1403.

Sahas, Daniel. "Catholicity and Mission to the World." *St. Vladimir's Seminary Quarterly* 17 (1973): 117–34.

Schmemann, Alexander. "Problems of Orthodoxy in America." *St. Vladimir's Seminary Quarterly.* "I. The Canonical Problem." 8 (1964): 67–86; "II. The Liturgical Problem." 8 (1964): 164–85; "III. The Spiritual Problem." 9 (1965): 171–93.

————. "The Task of Orthodox Theology in America Today." *St. Vladimir's Seminary Quarterly* 10 (1966): 180–88.

Veronis, Alexander. "Report on the Foreign Missions Program of the Greek Orthodox Archdiocese of North and South America." *Porefthendes* 10 (1968): 25–28.

"Your Kingdom Come: An Orthodox Contribution to the World Missionary Conference in Melbourne, 1980." *International Review of Mission* 68 (1979): 139–47.

Zernov, Nicholas. *The Russian Religious Renaissance of the Twentieth Century*. London: Darton, Longman & Todd, 1963.

———. "The Significance of the Russian Orthodox Diaspora and Its Effect on the Christian West." In *The Orthodox Churches and the West*, pp. 307–27. Edited by Derek Baker. Oxford: Basil Blackwell, 1976.

Chapter 10

Constantelos, Demetrios J. "The Zoe Movement in Greece." *St. Vladimir's Seminary Quarterly* 3 (1959): 11–25.

Constantinides, Chrysostomos. "The Lord's 'Go Ye. . .' and the Theology." *Porefthendes* 3 (1961): 19–20.

Papavassiliou, J. "Necessity for and Problems of Foreign Mission." *Porefthendes* 2 (1961): 46–47.

Parthenios, Metropolitan of Carthage. "Christ in Africa." *Porefthendes* 3 (1961): 51.

Philippides, Leonidas. "The Duty and Possibilities of Evangelizing the Non-Christians." *Porefthendes* 8 (1966): 18–21, 45.

Yannoulatos, Anastasios. "The Forgotten Commandment." *Porefthendes* 1 (1959), no. 1:1–5, no. 2:3–5.

———. *Indifference to Mission Signifies a Denial of Orthodoxy* (in Greek). Athens: Apostolike Diakonia, 1972.

———. *Initial Thoughts toward an Orthodox Foreign Mission*. Athens: n.p., 1969.

———. "Orthodox Spirituality and External Mission." *Porefthendes* 4 (1962): 4–5. The same article appears in the *International Review of Mission* 52 (1963): 300–302.

———. *The Purpose and Motive of Mission* (in Greek). Athens: n.p., 1971.

Chapter 11

Agourides, Savas. "The Biblical Content and Vision of Orthodox Worship and Spirituality." *The Greek Orthodox Theological Review* 23 (1978): 1–14.

Ajamian, Shahe. "Confessor le Christ par la vie liturgique d'aujourd'hui." *Contacts* 28 (1976): 13–19.

Andrews, Dean Timothy, ed. *Contemporary Sermons by Greek Orthodox Preachers*. New York: Greek Orthodox Archdiocese of North and South America, 1966.

Anthony, Metropolitan of Leningrad and Novgorod. "Christian Witness Today in a Socialist Society." *International Review of Mission* 68 (1979): 294–300.

Barrois, Georges. "Scripture Readings for Mid-Pentecost and Pentecost." *St. Vladimir's Theological Quarterly*, 21 (1977): 148–59.

———. *Scripture Readings in Orthodox Worship*. Crestwood, N.Y.: St. Vladimir's Seminary Press, 1977.

Bria, Ion. "Confessing Christ Today: An Orthodox Consultation." *International Review of Mission* 64 (1975): 67–94.

———. "The Liturgy after the Liturgy." *International Review of Mission* 67 (1978): 86–90.

———. "Living in the One Tradition." *The Ecumenical Review* 26 (1974): 224–33.

———. "Renewal of the Tradition through Pastoral Witness." *International Review of Mission* 55 (1976): 182–85.

Condos, Leonidas. *In Season and Out of Season*. New York: Orthodox Observer Press, 1972.

Coniaris, Anthony. *Eastern Orthodoxy: A Way of Life*. Minneapolis: Light and Life Publishing Co., 1966.

Constantelos, Demetrios J. "The Holy Scriptures in Greek Orthodox Worship: A Comparative and Statistical Study." *The Greek Orthodox Theological Review* 12 (1966): 7–83.

Dimopoulos, George. *Orthodox Sermons for All Sundays of the Year*. Scranton, Pa.: Christian Orthodox Editions, 1971.

The Divine Liturgy of St. John Chrysostom. London: Faith Press, n.d.

The Divine Liturgy: The Sunday Epistles and Gospels. Westfield, N.J.: Ecumenical Publications, 1975.

Dudko, Dmitrii. *Our Hope*. Translated by Paul D. Garrett. Crestwood, N.Y.: St. Vladimir's Seminary Press, 1977.

"European Seminar on the Role and the Place of the Bible in the Liturgical and Spiritual Life of the Orthodox Church—Prague, September 12–18, 1977." *International Review of Mission* 66 (1977): 385–88.

Florovsky, George. "Orthodox." In *Ways of Worship: The Report of a Theological Commission of Faith and Order*, pp. 53–65. London: SCM Press, 1951.

Fueter, Paul. "Confessing Christ through Liturgy, an Orthodox Challenge to Protestants." *International Review of Mission* 65 (1976): 123–28.

Hapgood, Isabel F., comp. and trans. *Service Book of the Holy Orthodox-Catholic Apostolic Church*. Englewood, N.J.: Antiochian Orthodox Christian Archdiocese, 1975.

Harakas, Stanley S. *Living the Liturgy*. Minneapolis: Light and Life Publishing Co., 1974.

Jordan, Martin. "Liturgy as the Confession of the Church." *The Christian East* n.s. 2 (1952): 81–90.

Khodre, George. "La spiritualité liturgique." *Contacts* 28 (1976): 4–12.

Kokkinakis, Athenagoras. *The Liturgy of the Orthodox Church*. London: Mowbrays, 1979.

Mastrantonis, George. *The Divine Liturgy of St. John Chrysostom*. St. Louis, Mo.: Ologos Mission, 1966.

The Priest's Service Book. 2 vols. New York: Orthodox Church in America, 1973.

"Reports from the Orthodox Consulation on Confessing Christ through the Liturgical Life of the Church Today: Etchmiadzine, Armenia, Sept. 16–21, 1975." *International Review of Mission* 64 (1975): 417–21. Also in *St. Vladimir's Theological Quarterly* 20 (1976): 31–37.

Schmemann, Alexander. *Introduction to Liturgical Theology*. Translated by A. E. Moorhouse. London: Faith Press, 1966.

―――. *Liturgy and Life: Christian Development through Liturgical Experience*. New York: Orthodox Church in America, 1974.

―――. *Of Water and the Spirit: A Liturgical Study of Baptism*. Crestwood, N.Y.: St. Vladimir's Seminary Press, 1974.

―――. *The World as Sacrament*. London: Darton, Longman & Todd, 1966.

Stylios, Efthimios. "Missionary Echoes of the Triodion." *Porefthendes* 4 (1962): 10–11.

Yannoulatos, Anastasios. "Orthodox Mission and Holy Communion." *Porefthendes* 6 (1964): 58–59.

Chapter 12

Alivisatos, Hamilcar. "The Holy Greek Orthodox Church." In *The Nature of the Church*, pp. 41–53. Edited by R. Newton Flew. London: SCM Press, 1952.

Bria, Ion. "Concerns and Challenges in Orthodox Ecclesiology Today." *Lutheran World* 23 (1977): 188–91.

Evdokimov, Paul. "The Principal Currents of Orthodox Ecclesiology in the Nineteenth Century." *Eastern Churches Review* 10 (1978): 26–42.

Florovsky, George. "The Church: Her Nature and Task." In *The Universal Church in God's Design*, pp. 43–58. New York: Harper & Brothers, 1948.

Hatzimichalis, Nectarios. *Orthodox Ecumenism and External Mission*. Athens: n.p., 1966. This first appeared as a series: "Orthodox Ecumenism and External Mission." *Porefthendes* 4 (1962): 60–63; 5 (1963): 28–31, 52–55; 6 (1964): 42–46.

James, Metropolitan of Melita. "The Orthodox Concept of Mission and Missions." In *Basileia*, pp. 76–80. Edited by Jan Hermelink and Hans Jochen Margull. Stuttgart: Evang. Missionsverlag GMBH, 1959.

Mantzarides, George. "The Witness of Orthodoxy to the Contemporary World." *St. Vladimir's Theological Quarterly* 17 (1973): 170–80.

Meyendorff, John. "Confessing Christ Today and the Unity of the Church." *St. Vladimir's Theological Quarterly* 18 (1974): 155–165.

———. "The Orthodox Church and Mission: Past and Present Perspectives." *St. Vladimir's Theological Quarterly* 16 (1972): 59–71.

———. "The Orthodox Concept of the Church." *St. Vladimir's Seminary Quarterly* 6 (1962): 59–72.

———. "The Orthodox in the Ecumenical Movement: Problems of a Dialogue." *One World*. No. 24 (March 1977): 20–21.

———. "Unity and Mission." *Worldmission* 26 (1975), no. 3: 39–42.

———. "Unity of the Church—Unity of Mankind." *The Ecumenical Review* 24 (1972): 30–46.

Nissiotis, Nikos. "The Ecclesiological Foundation of Mission from the Orthodox Point of View." *The Greek Orthodox Theological Review* 7 (1961): 22–52.

———. "The Theology of the Church and Its Accomplishment." *The Ecumenical Review* 29 (1977): 62–76.

Timiadis, Emilianos. "Disregarded Causes of Disunity." *The Ecumenical Review* 21 (1969): 299–309.

Voulgarakis, Elias. "Mission and Unity from the Theological Point of View." *International Review of Mission* 54 (1965): 298–307. A much expanded version of this article appears under the same title in *Porefthendes* 7 (1965): 4–7, 13–32, 45–47.

Chapter 13

"Activity Report [of the Inter-Orthodox Missionary Centre (Porefthendes)], 1961–1966." *Porefthendes* 8 (1966): 49–53.

Ailmilianos, Metropolitan of Calabria. "The Missionary Nature of the Church." *Porefthendes* 11 (1969): 8–31.

Constantelos, Demetrios J. "The 'Neomartyrs' as Evidence for Methods and Motives Leading to Conversion and Martyrdom in the Ottoman Empire." *The Greek Orthodox Theological Review* 23 (1978): 216–34.

———. "Theological Considerations for the Social Ethos of the Orthodox Church." *Journal of Ecumenical Studies* 11 (1974): 25–43.

The First Five Years of Porefthendes. Athens: Porefthendes, 1966.

Hale, Charles R. *The Orthodox Missionary Society*. England: privately printed, 1878.

Harakas, Stanley. "The Local Church: An Eastern Orthodox Perspective." *The Ecumenical Review* 29 (1977): 141–53.

Khodre, George. "Christianity in a Pluralistic World—The Economy of the Holy Spirit." *The Ecumenical Review* 23 (1971): 118–28.

———. "Church and Mission." *St. Vladimir's Seminary Quarterly* 6 (1962): 16–25. Also in *Porefthendes* 3 (1961): 40–42, 56–58.

———. "La paradoxe de l'Église." *Contacts* 27 (1975): 45–66.

Kotsone, Ieronumou. *The Place of the Laity* (in Greek). Athens: n.p., 1956.

Perantonis, John. "The Concept of Mission and the Neomartyrs of Ottoman Stock." *Porefthendes* 8 (1966): 7–16, 40–42.

Popescu, Dumitru. "The Local Church and Conciliar Fellowship." *The Ecumenical Review* 29 (1977): 265–72.

Siotis, M.A. "Thoughts of an Orthodox Theologian on 'The Missionary Structure of the Congregation.' " *Concept 3* (January 1963): 2–11.

Stroup, Herbert. "The Zoe Brotherhood." *The Christian Century* 72 (1955): 331–32.

Voulgarakis, Elias. "Russian Missionary Societies." *Porefthendes* 3 (1961): 52–53.

Yannoulatos, Anastasios. *The Inter-Orthodox Centre of Athens: Perspectives and Presuppositions*. Athens: n.p., 1973.

———. " 'Porefthendes,' An Inter-Orthodox Missionary Centre." *Porefthendes* 3 (1961): 35–38.

Index

Hatzimichalis, Nectarios, 113-15
Hellenism, 16, 64-65
Hellenistic framework in theology, 15
Heresy, 5
Herman of Alaska, St., 145 n.65
Hesychasm, 29, 143 n.37
Holy Cross Greek Orthodox School of
Theology, 76
Holy Spirit, 99; as interpreter of Eucha-
rist, 165 n.66; replaced by formulae,
106
Home mission, 76; in Greece, 172 n.44;
in relationship to foreign mission, 77,
144 n.63
Horner, Norman, 46
Iakovos, Archbishop, 132 n.12. *See also*
James, Metropolitan of Melita
Iglesia Ortodoxa Católica, 79
Ignatius of Antioch, St., 107
Illuminated, 92
Ilminski, Nicholas, 31-33, 66, 144 n.56,
155 n.11
Incarnation, 62, 100; purpose of, 10
Indigenization, 64
Indigenous clergy, 22, 36-38, 142 n.24,
155 n.12
Indigenous people, defense of, 145 n.65
Individualism, contrasted with corporate
nature, 93
Indulgences, 7
Inner Asian Policy, 59
Inner mission, 76
Innocent, Bishop (Veniaminov), 34, 35,
62, 118-19, 144 n.60, 147 n.35
Inter-church dialogues, 78-79
Inter-Orthodox Centre, 44
Inter-Orthodox Missionary Centre, 83,
120-21
Islam, 126, 171 n.26
Ivanovsky, Paul (Archimandrite), 43
James, Metropolitan of Melita, 109-11,
113
Japan, 35-40, 146 n.13; imprisonment of
evangelists in, 39; Orthodox Church
Synod in, 39
Japanese New Testament, 146 n.14
Japanese Orthodox Church, 39-40, 155
n.12
John, St. (Evangelist), 81
John Chrysostom, St., 6, 48, 115, 118

John of Damascus, 135 n.18
John of Kronstadt, 71
John VIII, Pope, 21
Joseph of Volokalamsk, St., 27, 28
Josephites, 27
Judaism, 57
Julian of Eclanum, 8
Juristic terminology in theology, 7-8
Justice promoted by missionaries, 145
n.65
Justification, 8, 135 n.18; as a legal con-
cept, 7
Karmiris, John, 12, 16
Kassatkin, Nicholas, 35-40, 62, 63, 146
n.13, 146 n.14; as appraised by non-
Orthodox, 40
Kenosis, 50, 111-13
Kenoticism, Russian, 26
Kenya, 46, 69
Khazars, 57-58
Khomiakov, Alexis, 2, 6, 93, 105
Kiakhta, Treaty of, 60
Kiev, Theological Academy of, 13-14
Korea, 42-43; Orthodox mission to, 43
Korean War, 43
Laity, 117, 170 n.4; and the Eucharist,
164 n.43; as guardian of doctrine, 153
n.39; in Japan, 155 n.12; mobilization
of, 124-25; role of, 107, 145 n.11, 155
n.13
Language: in Moravia, 20; use of second,
66; use of trade, 65; use of tribal, 65;
use of vernacular, 63, 65; in worship,
53
Language instruction, as a method of
evangelism, 36, 145 n.5
Lapps, 27
Latourette, Kenneth Scott, 19, 23
Le Guillou, M.J., 6
Lectionary, NT, 89
Legal form of church government, 106
Legalism, 7, 106
Léger, Antoine, 12
Leibniz, 58
Leontiev, Maxim, 58, 59
Liberal theology, definition according to
Orthodox terms, 16
Liturgical year, 89
Liturgy: and African culture, 100; cele-
brated for the world, 55, 97; defini-

DATE DUE